Table of Content

Appendices

Introduction

Getting Started: Welcome students at the door as they enter your classroom. Welcome them warmly to class and use this opportunity to find out if there is anything happening with the child that could negatively impact their behavior throughout the day. For example: skipped breakfast, disruption in their usual routine, etc. Take appropriate action to rectify if needed, and/or offer positive support to get them back on track and not let it negatively impact their day.

Transitions: Use activities whenever moving from one activity or location throughout the center and grounds. This maintains the children attention and helps to keep them on track, while minimizing errant behaviors that occur when they are not constructively occupied. Use the Time to Sign Ready, Set, Sign: Songs for Everyday Transitions book songs between activities. Teach these during the Music/Creative Expression time throughout the first month of school. Choose different songs to use throughout the year to get from one activity to another. This helps to establish routines, so children know when to end, to get ready, to transition, and lets them know what activity will follow.

Classroom Management - Issues

Classroom management college and professional development training is of the utmost importance. *Research confirms this is the number one issue for new teachers.* Studies reveal that poor classroom management skills and disruptive students are the two most significant barriers to their professional success

Classroom Management - Definition

Classroom management is the actions teachers take to create an environment conducive to social, emotional, and academic learning. Effective classroom management is essential to successful teaching. Prevention is the key to classroom management. It sets the stage for learning.

Classroom Management for Teachers:

1. Teacher Attitude/Beliefs
    a. Be aware of own biases.
    b. Acknowledge negative thoughts.
    c. Believe all children can succeed.
    d. Be self-aware of one's own cultural experiences.
2. Interactions
    a. Greet all students at the door everyday as they enter the classroom.
    b. Create a climate of tolerance.
    c. Treat all members of the class with dignity, fairness, and respect.
    d. Provide students with opportunities to work with many people.
    e. Give feedback that is direct, immediate, authentic, and tactful.
3. Home/School Collaboration
    a. Learn about students' lives beyond the classroom.
    b. Understand that family structures vary.

    c. Maintain contact with the families based on students' needs.
4. Instruction
    a. Use direct and explicit instruction.
    b. Use active student responding and performance feedback.
    c. Use cooperative learning groups.
5. Management System
    a. Emphasize prevention strategies.
    b. Develop rules and explicitly teach them.
    c. Emphasize the use of reinforcement-based strategies.
    d. Provide individualized corrective consequences.

Improving Your Practice

Following are strategies that teachers can easily implement as they begin to establish an effective classroom management plan and move away from an over-reliance on extrinsic rewards.

1. **Organizing the Physical Layout of the Classroom**
   a. Clutter. Purge your classroom of all unwanted clutter.
   b. Personalize your room. Personalize the classroom so that it communicates information about you and your students.
   c. Materials storage. Make it clear where materials belong.
   d. Match the physical layout of the classroom to your teaching style.

2. **Developing Rules and Routines**
   a. Rules. Create four to six classroom rules that clearly specify appropriate behavior. Students should help in the creation of these rules. Write the rules using positive language. Post and refer to classroom rules as necessary.
   b. Routines. Develop routines to provide direction about how different classroom tasks are accomplished. A classroom's practiced and rehearsed daily procedures are essential to effective classroom management. Common routines and procedures include: arrival/entering the classroom, attendance, transitions between classroom activities, bathroom breaks, participating in class discussions, and cooperative learning groups. Teachers who frequently and consistently employ these types of routines are teaching and reinforcing their behavioral expectations.
   c. Rules & Routines. Teach and demonstrate classroom rules and routines as specifically as you do academic content.
   d. Expectations. Teachers establish expectations through classroom rules and procedures, but also by communicating explicit learning goals. Students should know what is expected of them and how they will be assessed. Take time to teach students about your expectations and what you mean by those expectations. Often, students don't necessarily know what we mean when we provide our rules and our expectations. Take time to teach students the behaviors they expect students to use. Teachers must reinforce the behaviors and support students who use them.

3. **Establishing Caring Relationships**
   a. Student Familiarity. Get to know something personal about each student. Greet each one at the door to see how their day is going. If they are off to a rough start, you can correct things right then and there with a hug.
   b. Knowing your children. Make it a point of knowing every student's name as quickly as possible, well enough to greet them outside of your normal classroom location. If students are going to trust and respect you, they need to know that I recognize them.
   c. Student's needs. Students need love, acceptance, and consistency.
   d. Believe in your students. Teachers should never 'give up' on any of their students.
   e. Accomplishments. Be aware of students' accomplishments and comment on them.
   f. Family Communication. Send positive notes, phone calls, or emails home.
   g. Sensitivity. Be sensitive to students' moods and concerns.
   h. Praise. Praise more, criticize less.
   i. Humor. Maintain a sense of humor.
   j. Mutual Respect. Establish mutual respect between students, parents, and teachers.
   k. Caring. Life has many difficult challenges for your students. You may be one of the few people that child believes cares about him or her. This could make a difference in his or her life choices, or at least in his or her decision not to disrupt your class. (If you think about your favorite teacher as a child, they were not your favorite because they were the best instructors, they were your favorite because they cared about you.)
   l. Learn students' names and greet them at the door. A student who is having a bad day can be disarmed by the genuine concern of a teacher.

4. **Social-Emotional Academic Learning (SEAL):** Often, young children displaying a lack of social emotional development are ill prepared to begin elementary school. This problem is important because success in school is impacted by children's social emotional readiness to positively engage in classroom activities. The National Academy of Sciences, in 2008, reported that 60% of children are entering school with the cognitive skills necessary to be successful, but only 40% have the social-emotional skills needed to succeed in kindergarten. Indeed, kindergarten teachers report their single greatest challenge is that a majority of the children lack some or all of the needed social and emotional skills needed for success in school and life. According to CASEL (Collaborative for Academic, Social, and Emotional Learning), there are five social and emotional learning core competencies. They are:
   1. Self-management. Managing emotions and behaviors to achieve one's goals.

2. Self-awareness. Recognizing one's emotions and values as well as one's strengths and challenges.
3. Social awareness. Showing understanding and empathy for others.
4. Responsible decision-making. Making ethical, constructive choices about personal and social behavior.
5. Relationship skills. Forming positive relationships, working in teams, dealing effectively with conflict.

It is through play that children develop friendships and seek to find the acceptance of their peers, which is how social skills are learned. Children who are socially and emotionally healthy have mastered the necessary social and emotional skills. As a result, they develop positive relationships with peers and teachers. Further, these skills have a lasting impact on academic achievement, because they contribute to more positive feelings about school, and eagerness to engage in classroom activities. According to Child Care and Early Education Research Connections (2013), development in social and emotional learning, communication, and understanding are important to kindergarten readiness. Researchers found that 8 of the top 11 skills required for kindergarten readiness involved social-emotional influences. The top 2 skills are self-regulation and problem-solving skills. Self-regulation levels predict school success better than cognitive skills and family background.

Lower order SEAL skills include:
- Respects the rights of others
- Uses thinking skills to resolve conflicts
- Plays well with others
- Shares with others
- Self-discipline
- Willpower
- Positive expression of emotions
- Follows classroom routines and rules
- Recognize and manage their feelings
- Respond appropriately to the feelings of others

Higher order virtues are developed through SEAL skills learning. These include:
- Determination
- Perseverance
- Self-control
- Honesty
- Kindness
- Obedience
- Politeness
- Respectfulness
- Compassion

- Friendship
- Generosity

SEAL, the flipside: Persistent physical aggression, high school dropout rates, adolescent delinquency, and antisocial behavior have all been associated with early childhood conduct problems. Therefore, it is incumbent upon us as early childhood educators to do all we can to insure that children start off on the right trajectory. Further, that we would doubly hard to work with children and families to correct deficiencies when children are in our care, as over time the likelihood of change diminishes and takes more effort and resources.

5. **Planning and Implementing Engaging Instruction**
   a. Instruction. Aspects of direct and explicit instruction include:
      i. Stating expectations and objectives at the beginning of each lesson.
      ii. Presenting the information to the students using modeling and demonstration.
      iii. Use scaffolding, or prompting and prompt fading. Providing students with opportunities for practice.
      iv. Be caring, but resolutely serious in your instruction.
      v. Project confidence and demonstrate that everything you ask of them has been deliberately planned in your students' best interest.
   b. Student Involved Learning. Create highly engaging instruction by providing frequent opportunities for students to respond.
   c. Materials. Have all materials organized and ready prior to the start of the lesson.
   d. Student Attention. Establish an attention getting signal.
   e. Adaptability. Adapt content and activities to students' interests and abilities.
   f. Challenge Students. Ensure students work at the appropriate level of challenge or difficulty.
   g. Autonomy & Choices. Provide opportunity to exercise autonomy and make choices.
   h. Enthusiasm. Project enthusiasm for all activities taught to students.
   i. Knowledge Transfer. Teachers should explain the applicability of what they instruct to other subjects.
   j. Preparation. Being prepared allows you to be practice proper classroom management that is more likely to be thoughtful, concrete, consistent, and implemented in a calm and supportive way.
   k. Peer Instruction & Collaboration. Use peer-facilitated instruction and collaboration.
   l. Organize the Lesson.
      i. Preparation is needed to develop an engaging lesson that moves smoothly forward and permits the teacher the opportunity to communicate with every child.

ii. You should design your lesson plans with classroom management in mind.

iii. Build teaching strategies and interventions into each lesson.

iv. Develop one-on-one and small group strategies, allowing time for social interaction and reflection.

v. Organization also involves ample preparation time arranging handouts, preparing supplies, writing on the board and taking care of myriad other tasks. By preparing in advance, you can prevent gaps during the lesson when you lose students' attention and better manage your classroom.

vi. Develop a series of activity transitions. By doing so going from one activity to another can be smooth, without losing their attention.

6. **Classroom Management Techniques**

a. Shaping Behavior. You need to be deliberate, to be assertive, and to always have a reason for everything.

b. Planned Ignoring. If an attention-seeking behavior, such as pencil tapping, is ignored, the child may first increase the intensity of the tapping but may eventually stop due to lack of reinforcement.

c. Signal Interference. Nonverbal signals, such as the use of sign language, and verbal signals, such as the reminder of the rules, can signal students to change their own behavior.

d. Proximity and Touch Control. The presence of the teacher nearby can remind students to refocus, refrain, and re-engage.

e. Involvement in the Interest Relationship. Changing examples to reflect student interests or shifting the activity can reel students back into classroom discussions. Personal attention can also serve to re-engage students.

f. Hurdle Help. Providing instructional support rather than a reprimand or redirect can sometimes help this situation.

g. Regrouping. Simply moving the players around can be an effective strategy for addressing unwanted behaviors. Teachers should take care to remove emotion from this strategy since negative attention can be reinforcing to some students.

h. Restructuring. Teachers can change an activity that is not going as planned in order to avoid or reduce undesired behaviors.

i. Supports that are embedded in the environment help students manage themselves by reinforcing expectations and promoting positive behavior even when the teacher is unavailable.

j. Documentation. Effective classroom management requires perpetual observation and documentation. Teachers need to continually assess their management strategies and adapt as needed. Documentation helps educators identify patterns and anticipate and correct recurring problems. Careful observation and documentation, meticulously writing down what has transpired, what was said, and what exactly happened lets teachers reflect upon and improve their interactions with students, as well as their overall classroom management plan.

7. **Addressing Discipline Issues**
   a. Classroom Climate. Studies show that teachers who had positive relationships with their students had almost 1/3 fewer discipline problems and rule violations over the course of the year than teachers who did not have positive relationships with their students.
   b. Non-verbal Interventions. Use nonverbal interventions such as proximity, eye contact, sign language, and facial expressions to redirect misbehavior.
   c. Minor Misbehavior. Ignore minor misbehavior, if possible.
   d. Verbal Interventions. Use brief, concise, and specific sign language and/or verbal interventions to redirect misbehavior.
   e. Teacher Communication. A final way of communicating a strong teacher presence is to calmly, clearly, and consistently reinforce rules or expectations.
      i. Yelling, moving too close to students, lecturing, displaying strong emotion, and avoiding the offending student behavior communicate teacher insecurity.
      ii. A positive classroom climate communicates to students that the teacher is calm and confident in your ability to respond to student needs; either by reinforcing the rules, redirecting misbehavior, or addressing an extreme situation.
   f. Positive Language. Use positive teacher language, and sign language, to tell the child what to do rather than what not to do.
   g. Student Engagement. If students are engaged, classroom management issues are greatly reduced.
   h. Patience. Patience on the part of the teacher is key. The teacher must react calmly, but with a firm voice.

8. **Self-Monitoring Instruction.** Teaching children to begin to internally monitor specific negative behaviors they exhibit can be the first step to eliminating these behaviors. Self-monitoring interventions include the following steps:
   a. Identifying Errant Behavior. Identification of a specific errant behavior.
   b. Student Buy-in. Soliciting buy-in from the student on the advantages of self-monitoring to help eliminate the specific behavior.
   c. Data. Developing a method for monitoring and collecting data on the behavior.

d. Self-monitoring. Teaching the student to self-monitor and helping with reminders when target behavior occurs.

e. Teacher Monitoring. Correction of the behavior, over time, with concurrent reduction and ultimately eliminating of teacher monitoring.

9. **Knowing & Supporting Your Students**

a. Strategies to Enhance Climate. Simple strategies such as proximity, eye contact, or the incorporation of students' names or interests during instruction can contribute to an overall positive classroom climate.

b. Support to Meet Expectations. Given proper instruction, motivation, and control, students will meet our high expectations for them.

c. Knowing Students. Learning more about students' lives outside of the classroom will go a long way toward successful interactions with students within classrooms. Knowing about the significant people in students' lives will give teachers insight as to the important adults to involve in the support of their education, which in turn will provide needed information about whom to seek support from when the student is in need.

d. Community. Teachers should make a point of understanding the community from which their student's come.

e. Family Involvement. Teachers and the school must actively involve families in the education of students.

  i. To encourage family involvement, all family members should feel valued and welcome in the classroom and school.

  ii. Teachers should maintain family communication with a frequency based on student need and family desire.

f. Teachers and Staff as a Resource. While the classroom teacher is not a social worker and therefore does not have responsibility or the ability to solve all of the problems families may face. However, they can serve as a trusted point person who is aware of community resources to direct families to needed services.

g. Expectations. Set high expectations for your students. The higher the expectations the greater the social, emotional, and academic growth.

h. Relationships and Classroom Management. Teachers who establish and maintain positive, trusting relationships with students can use their history of positive interactions in order to address challenges as they develop.

i. Teacher-Student Relationships. High-quality teacher-student relationships are characterized by caring and openness to student needs on one hand and by clear boundaries and consistent consequences on the other hand. The trick is finding the right balance.

10. **Encourage Helpful Hands**
   a. Student help. Students feel invested when they assist the teacher in the classroom. It also builds their self-esteem.
   b. Helping Activities. Students to help getting supplies, passing out papers, or straighten the room.
   c. Avoid Favoritism. You should be careful to let everyone help to avoid favoritism.

11. **Teach Additional Needed Skills**
   a. Other Skills. Often children come into our classroom in need of skills to succeed academically and in life, in addition to learning the subject matter. These skills include: social skills, thinking skills, study skills, test-taking skills, problem-solving skills, memory skills and self-regulation.
   b. Positive Student Change. If students are struggling to get along with peers, is it better to discipline them for what they lack? Or is it better to teach them what they need to know?

Intro to American Sign Language (ASL) usage in the Classroom: Teach the children the basic preschool age signs and common classroom phrases from the Time to Sign Preschool Sign Language Book. These signs will enhance learning, classroom behavior, and SEAL.

Benefits of using sign language with preschool children include:
   • 2-sided brain activity that increases brain functioning
      • Visual right brain usage
      • Cognitive second language left brain usage
      • Creates additional connections or synapses in the brain
      • Creates higher IQ levels in Children
   • A fun activity for child and parent/caregiver that reduces frustration and enhances bond between child and parent/caregiver
   • Enhances vocabulary, pre-literacy concept recognition and understanding and reading skills
   • Enhances fine motor coordination
   • Enables children to control their hyperactive tendencies
   • Boosts children's confidence and self-esteem
   • Raises communication awareness and abilities

Classroom benefits of sign language include:
   • Lowers children's noise levels in the classroom
   • Reduces need for teachers to raise their voice
   • Enables class to support special needs children
   • Increases children's use of manners

- Sign language gets their attention better than the spoken word
- Children pay better attention, they have to look directly at you
- Increased ability to express themselves reduces instances of misbehavior
- Provides children the ability to express emotions

Dr. Marilyn Daniels thoughts on the benefits of sign language: The added benefits of signing derive in part from its unique status as both a visual and kinetic language. There are individual memory stores for each language a person knows, even at the initial stages of acquiring the second or third language. You intake sign with your eyes, using the right side of the brain. Then like any other language, sign is processed and stored in the brain's left hemisphere. This operation creates more synapses in the brain, adding to its growth and development. It also helps to establish two memory stores in the left hemisphere for language, one for English (or the native language) and one for ASL. So children who use both develop a built-in redundancy of memory, storing the same word in two formats in two places.

Furthermore, because visual cues are taken in with the right side of the brain while language engages the left using ASL activates both sides of the brain at once. In the same way that bilingual children develop greater brain function, users of sign language build more connections or synapses in the brain than those who use English alone and because of the kinetic component of sign language, the ASL brain benefits even more than the bilingual one because of the dual-hemisphere work. Babies using sign language are simply building more brain.

Using sign language encourages language-delayed and shy children to increase their language acquisition skills in a relatively pressure-free manner. It is difficult for some children to speak well, but with sign the children are on a more level playing field and don't feel inhibited. In addition, children are more attentive simply because they have to be. When you are speaking to someone you don't really have to make eye contact, but when you're using sign language, you naturally and unconsciously focus your attention on the person signing. This improves the quality of the communication.

For a more in-depth analysis of this topic I suggest you consult my web site marilyndaniels.com or my book, *Dancing with Words: Signing for Hearing Children's Literacy*, where you will find additional information. I wish each of you and the children with whom you communicate much success in realizing the benefits of sign language.

Dr. Marilyn Daniels
Marilyn Daniels, Ph.D.
Associate Professor
Department of Speech Communication
Penn State University

Communication Developmental Milestones
(What you can expect to see in a child's communication development.)

37 to 42 Months

Engages in longer dialogue
Requests permission – "May I?"
Corrects others when they misspeak
Clarifies own conversation when misunderstood
Uses up to 800 words
Answers simple "how" questions
Uses compound sentences with "and"
Comprehends 1,200 words
Emerging understanding of location – "in front of", "behind"
Recognizes simple comparisons – hard/soft, rough/smooth
Recognizes the names of simple shapes – circle, square

43 to 48 Months

Speech is more fluid and understandable
Uses up to 1,000 – 1,500 words
Comprehends up to 1,500 – 2,000 words
Begins to understand the difference between fiction/non-fiction
Uses more details in conversation
Emerging ability to accurately discuss topics/events, e.g. "out of context"
Effectively uses vocabulary to express personal thoughts – discusses emotions and feelings
Narrative and retelling skills – able to tell and sequence story or situation events, emerging understanding of characters and character development
Emerging use of conjunctions – "because"
Emerging use of reflexive pronouns – "myself"

49 to 60 Months

Connected speech and language understandable
Uses "what do...does...did" questions
Uses 1,500 to 2,000 words
Answers simple "when" questions
Retells long story with increasing accuracy
Knows and can state full name – first, middle, last
Reflexive pronouns emerging more consistently
Comparatives vs. superlatives emerging – "-er," "-est"
Uses 5 to 8 word sentences
Developing understanding of prepositions – between, above, below, bottom
Repeats the days of the week
Emerging ability to name months – knows birthday (day and month)

December Schedule: Week 14

	Monday	Tuesday	Wednesday	Thursday	Friday
Before 9:00	Before-care, Centers Play, Breakfast/Snack, & Music & Movement				
8:55 - 9:00	Transition from Before-care to Classrooms				
9:00 – 9:25	**Reading Workshop:** Letters: o, g, l, h Sight Words: see & I Nursery Rhymes Winter	**Reading Workshop:** Letters: o, g, l, h Sight Words: see & I Nursery Rhymes Winter	**Reading Workshop:** Letters: o, g, l, h Sight Words: see & I Nursery Rhymes Winter	**Reading Workshop:** Letters: o, g, l, h Sight Words: see & I Nursery Rhymes Winter	**Reading Workshop:** Letters: o, g, l, h Sight Words: see & I Nursery Rhymes Winter
9:25 – 10:15	**Centers**				
10:15 – 10:25	Clean-up & Transition Activity				
10:25 – 10:55	**Monthly Topical Learning:** Winter Kwanzaa Hanukah	**Monthly Topical Learning:** Winter Kwanzaa Hanukah	**Monthly Topical Learning:** Winter Kwanzaa Hanukah	**Monthly Topical Learning:** Winter Kwanzaa Hanukah	**Monthly Topical Learning:** Winter Kwanzaa Hanukah
10:55 – 11:00	Bathroom Break & Transition Activity				
11:00 – 11:30	**Recess on the Playground or in the Indoor Play/Exercise Area for Inclement Weather**				
11:30 – 11:35	Wash-up & Transition Activity Back to the Classroom				
11:35 – Noon	**Circle Time:** Reindeer Winter Weather	**Circle Time:** Reindeer Winter Weather	**Circle Time:** Reindeer Winter Weather	**Circle Time:** Reindeer Winter Weather	**Circle Time:** Reindeer Winter Weather
Noon – 12:10	Bathroom Break & Transition Activity				
12:10 – 12:50	**Lunch Time**				
12:50 – 1:00	Clean-up and Transition Song				
1:00 – 2:00	**Naptime**				
2:00 – 2:25	**Math, Art & Writing:** Letters: o, g, l, h Counting: 1-20 Reindeer Shapes & Colors Sight Words: see & I	**Math, Art & Writing:** Letters: o, g, l, h Counting: 1-20 Reindeer Shapes & Colors Sight Words: see & I	**Math, Art & Writing:** Letters: o, g, l, h Counting: 1-20 Reindeer Shapes & Colors Sight Words: see & I	**Math, Art & Writing:** Letters: o, g, l, h Counting: 1-20 Reindeer Shapes & Colors Sight Words: see & I	**Math, Art & Writing:** Letters: o, g, l, h Counting: 1-20 Reindeer Shapes & Colors Sight Words: see & I
2:25 – 2:45	**Snack Time**				
2:45– 2:50	Clean-up/Transition	Clean-up/Transition	Clean-up/Transition	Clean-up/Transition	Clean-up/Transition
2:50 – 3:15	**Music/Creative Expression:** Reindeer Winter	**Music/Creative Expression:** Reindeer Winter	**Music/Creative Expression:** Reindeer Winter	**Music/Creative Expression:** Reindeer Winter	**Music/Creative Expression:** Reindeer Winter
3:15 – 3:20	Transition Activity				
3:20 – 3:55	**Recess on the Playground or in the Indoor Play/Exercise Area for Inclement Weather**				
3:55 – 4:00	Wash-up & Transition Activity Back to the Classroom				
4:00 – 4:25	**Read-aloud:** Letters: o, g, l, h Nursery Rhymes Holidays	**Read-aloud:** Letters: o, g, l, h Nursery Rhymes Holidays	**Read-aloud:** Letters: o, g, l, h Nursery Rhymes Holidays	**Read-aloud:** Letters: o, g, l, h Nursery Rhymes Holidays	**Read-aloud:** Letters: o, g, l, h Nursery Rhymes Holidays
4:30 – 4:50	**Centers**				
4:50 – 5:00	Clean-up for the Day				
5:00	Transition to Aftercare				

Week 14 Notes

Topics:
Winter
Hanukkah
Kwanzaa
Snowman
Gingerbread Man
Reindeer
Nursery Rhymes
Letters: o, g, l, h
Sight Words: see & I
Colors: Gold, Red, & Green
Counting: 1-15
Shapes: Rectangle & Cylinder

Season:
Winter

Upcoming Holidays:

Christmas

Hanukkah

Kwanzaa

New Year's Eve

See Appendices for December for songs, stories, crafts, games and activities to support the use of sign language in learning the various topics.

See the 8 Modules of the Curriculum for 8.5 x 11" topical signs and sign handouts. Take advantage of the Table of Contents to find groups of signs and the Index in the back of the book to find specific signs.

December Schedule: Week 15

	Monday	Tuesday	Wednesday	Thursday	Friday
Before 9:00	Before-care, Centers Play, Breakfast/Snack, & Music & Movement				
8:55 - 9:00	Transition from Before-care to Classrooms				
9:00 – 9:25	**Reading Workshop:** Letters: o, g, l, h Sight Words: see & I Nursery Rhymes Winter	**Reading Workshop:** Letters: o, g, l, h Sight Words: see & I Nursery Rhymes Winter	**Reading Workshop:** Letters: o, g, l, h Sight Words: see & I Nursery Rhymes Winter	**Reading Workshop:** Letters: o, g, l, h Sight Words: see & I Nursery Rhymes Winter	**Reading Workshop:** Letters: o, g, l, h Sight Words: see & I Nursery Rhymes Winter
9:25 – 10:15	**Centers**				
10:15 – 10:25	Clean-up & Transition Activity				
10:25 – 10:55	**Monthly Topical Learning:** Winter Kwanzaa Hanukah	**Monthly Topical Learning:** Winter Kwanzaa Hanukah	**Monthly Topical Learning:** Winter Kwanzaa Hanukah	**Monthly Topical Learning:** Winter Kwanzaa Hanukah	**Monthly Topical Learning:** Winter Kwanzaa Hanukah
10:55 – 11:00	Bathroom Break & Transition Activity				
11:00 – 11:30	**Recess on the Playground or in the Indoor Play/Exercise Area for Inclement Weather**				
11:30 – 11:35	Wash-up & Transition Activity Back to the Classroom				
11:35 – Noon	**Circle Time:** Snowman Winter Weather	**Circle Time:** Snowman Winter Weather	**Circle Time:** Snowman Winter Weather	**Circle Time:** Snowman Winter Weather	**Circle Time:** Snowman Winter Weather
Noon – 12:10	Bathroom Break & Transition Activity				
12:10 – 12:50	**Lunch Time**				
12:50 – 1:00	Clean-up and Transition Song				
1:00 – 2:00	**Naptime**				
2:00 – 2:25	**Math, Art & Writing:** Letters: o, g, l, h Counting: 1-20 Reindeer Shapes & Colors Sight Words: see & I	**Math, Art & Writing:** Letters: o, g, l, h Counting: 1-20 Reindeer Shapes & Colors Sight Words: see & I	**Math, Art & Writing:** Letters: o, g, l, h Counting: 1-20 Reindeer Shapes & Colors Sight Words: see & I	**Math, Art & Writing:** Letters: o, g, l, h Counting: 1-20 Reindeer Shapes & Colors Sight Words: see & I	**Math, Art & Writing:** Letters: o, g, l, h Counting: 1-20 Reindeer Shapes & Colors Sight Words: see & I
2:25 – 2:45	**Snack Time**				
2:45– 2:50	Clean-up/Transition	Clean-up/Transition	Clean-up/Transition	Clean-up/Transition	Clean-up/Transition
2:50 – 3:15	**Music/Creative Expression:** Snowman Winter	**Music/Creative Expression:** Snowman Winter	**Music/Creative Expression:** Snowman Winter	**Music/Creative Expression:** Snowman Winter	**Music/Creative Expression:** Snowman Winter
3:15 – 3:20	Transition Activity				
3:20 – 3:55	**Recess on the Playground or in the Indoor Play/Exercise Area for Inclement Weather**				
3:55 – 4:00	Wash-up & Transition Activity Back to the Classroom				
4:00 – 4:25	**Read-aloud:** Letters: o, g, l, h Nursery Rhymes Holidays	**Read-aloud:** Letters: o, g, l, h Nursery Rhymes Holidays	**Read-aloud:** Letters: o, g, l, h Nursery Rhymes Holidays	**Read-aloud:** Letters: o, g, l, h Nursery Rhymes Holidays	**Read-aloud:** Letters: o, g, l, h Nursery Rhymes Holidays
4:30 – 4:50	**Centers**				
4:50 – 5:00	Clean-up for the Day				
5:00	Transition to Aftercare				

Week 15 Notes

Topics:
Winter
Hanukkah
Kwanzaa
Snowman
Gingerbread Man
Reindeer
Nursery Rhymes
Letters: o, g, l, h
Sight Words: see & I
Colors: Gold, Red, & Green
Counting: 1-15
Shapes: Rectangle & Cylinder

Season:
Winter

Upcoming Holidays:

Christmas

Hanukkah

Kwanzaa

New Year's Eve

See Appendices for December for songs, stories, crafts, games and activities to support the use of sign language in learning the various topics.

See the 8 Modules of the Curriculum for 8.5 x 11" topical signs and sign handouts. Take advantage of the Table of Contents to find groups of signs and the Index in the back of the book to find specific signs.

December Schedule: Week 16

	Monday	Tuesday	Wednesday	Thursday	Friday
Before 9:00	Before-care, Centers Play, Breakfast/Snack, & Music & Movement				
8:55 - 9:00	Transition from Before-care to Classrooms				
9:00 – 9:25	**Reading Workshop:** Letters: o, g, l, h Sight Words: go/got Nursery Rhymes Winter Holidays	**Reading Workshop:** Letters: o, g, l, h Sight Words: go/got Nursery Rhymes Winter Holidays	**Reading Workshop:** Letters: o, g, l, h Sight Words: go/got Nursery Rhymes Winter Holidays	**Reading Workshop:** Letters: o, g, l, h Sight Words: go/got Nursery Rhymes Winter Holidays	**Reading Workshop:** Letters: o, g, l, h Sight Words: go/got Nursery Rhymes Winter Holidays
9:25 – 10:15	Centers				
10:15 – 10:25	Clean-up & Transition Activity				
10:25 – 10:55	**Monthly Topical Learning:** Winter Christmas New Year's Eve	**Monthly Topical Learning:** Winter Christmas New Year's Eve	**Monthly Topical Learning:** Winter Christmas New Year's Eve	**Monthly Topical Learning:** Winter Christmas New Year's Eve	**Monthly Topical Learning:** Winter Christmas New Year's Eve
10:55 – 11:00	Bathroom Break & Transition Activity				
11:00 – 11:30	**Recess on the Playground or in the Indoor Play/Exercise Area for Inclement Weather**				
11:30 – 11:35	Wash-up & Transition Activity Back to the Classroom				
11:35 – Noon	**Circle Time:** Gingerbread Man Winter Weather	**Circle Time:** Gingerbread Man Winter Weather	**Circle Time:** Gingerbread Man Winter Weather	**Circle Time:** Gingerbread Man Winter Weather	**Circle Time:** Gingerbread Man Winter Weather
Noon – 12:10	Bathroom Break & Transition Activity				
12:10 – 12:50	Lunch Time				
12:50 – 1:00	Clean-up and Transition Song				
1:00 – 2:00	Naptime				
2:00 – 2:25	**Math, Art & Writing:** Letters: o, g, l, h Counting: 1-20 Reindeer Shapes & Colors Sight Words: go/got	**Math, Art & Writing:** Letters: o, g, l, h Counting: 1-20 Reindeer Shapes & Colors Sight Words: go/got	**Math, Art & Writing:** Letters: o, g, l, h Counting: 1-20 Reindeer Shapes & Colors Sight Words: go/got	**Math, Art & Writing:** Letters: o, g, l, h Counting: 1-20 Reindeer Shapes & Colors Sight Words: go/got	**Math, Art & Writing:** Letters: o, g, l, h Counting: 1-20 Reindeer Shapes & Colors Sight Words: go/got
2:25 – 2:45	Snack Time				
2:45– 2:50	Clean-up/Transition	Clean-up/Transition	Clean-up/Transition	Clean-up/Transition	Clean-up/Transition
2:50 – 3:15	**Music/Creative Expression:** Holidays Gingerbread Man	**Music/Creative Expression:** Holidays Gingerbread Man	**Music/Creative Expression:** Holidays Gingerbread Man	**Music/Creative Expression:** Holidays Gingerbread Man	**Music/Creative Expression:** Holidays Gingerbread Man
3:15 – 3:20	Transition Activity				
3:20 – 3:55	**Recess on the Playground or in the Indoor Play/Exercise Area for Inclement Weather**				
3:55 – 4:00	Wash-up & Transition Activity Back to the Classroom				
4:00 – 4:25	**Read-aloud:** Letters: o, g, l, h Holidays Nursery Rhymes	**Read-aloud:** Letters: o, g, l, h Holidays Nursery Rhymes	**Read-aloud:** Letters: o, g, l, h Holidays Nursery Rhymes	**Read-aloud:** Letters: o, g, l, h Holidays Nursery Rhymes	**Read-aloud:** Letters: o, g, l, h Holidays Nursery Rhymes
4:30 – 4:50	Centers				
4:50 – 5:00	Clean-up for the Day				
5:00	Transition to Aftercare				

Week 16 Notes

Topics:
Winter
Christmas
New Year's Eve
Snowman
Gingerbread Man
Reindeer
Rhymes
Letters: o, g, l, h
Sight Words: see & I
Colors: Gold, Red, & Green
Counting: 1-15
Shapes: Rectangle & Cylinder

Season:
Winter

Upcoming Holidays:

Christmas

New Year's Eve

See Appendices for December for songs, stories, crafts, games and activities to support the use of sign language in learning the various topics.

See the 8 Modules of the Curriculum for 8.5 x 11" topical signs and sign handouts. Take advantage of the Table of Contents to find groups of signs and the Index in the back of the book to find specific signs.

December Schedule: Week 17

	Monday	Tuesday	Wednesday	Thursday	Friday
Before 9:00	Before-care, Centers Play, Breakfast/Snack, & Music & Movement				
8:55 - 9:00	Transition from Before-care to Classrooms				
9:00 – 9:25	**Reading Workshop:** Letters: o, g, l, h Sight Words: go/got Nursery Rhymes Winter	**Reading Workshop:** Letters: o, g, l, h Sight Words: go/got Nursery Rhymes Winter	**Reading Workshop:** Letters: o, g, l, h Sight Words: go/got Nursery Rhymes Winter	**Reading Workshop:** Letters: o, g, l, h Sight Words: go/got Nursery Rhymes Winter	**Reading Workshop:** Letters: o, g, l, h Sight Words: go/got Nursery Rhymes Winter
9:25 – 10:15	Centers				
10:15 – 10:25	Clean-up & Transition Activity				
10:25 – 10:55	**Monthly Topical Learning:** Winter New Year's Eve	**Monthly Topical Learning:** Winter New Year's Eve	**Monthly Topical Learning:** Winter New Year's Eve	**Monthly Topical Learning:** Winter New Year's Eve	**Monthly Topical Learning:** Winter New Year's Eve
10:55 – 11:00	Bathroom Break & Transition Activity				
11:00 – 11:30	**Recess on the Playground or in the Indoor Play/Exercise Area for Inclement Weather**				
11:30 – 11:35	Wash-up & Transition Activity Back to the Classroom				
11:35 – Noon	**Circle Time:** Winter Weather Father Time & Baby New Year	**Circle Time:** Winter Weather Father Time & Baby New Year	**Circle Time:** Winter Weather Father Time & Baby New Year	**Circle Time:** Winter Weather Father Time & Baby New Year	**Circle Time:** Winter Weather Father Time & Baby New Year
Noon – 12:10	Bathroom Break & Transition Activity				
12:10 – 12:50	**Lunch Time**				
12:50 – 1:00	Clean-up and Transition Song				
1:00 – 2:00	**Naptime**				
2:00 – 2:25	**Math, Art & Writing:** Letters: o, g, l, h Counting: 1-20 Reindeer Shapes & Colors Sight Words: go/got	**Math, Art & Writing:** Letters: o, g, l, h Counting: 1-20 Reindeer Shapes & Colors Sight Words: go/got	**Math, Art & Writing:** Letters: o, g, l, h Counting: 1-20 Reindeer Shapes & Colors Sight Words: go/got	**Math, Art & Writing:** Letters: o, g, l, h Counting: 1-20 Reindeer Shapes & Colors Sight Words: go/got	**Math, Art & Writing:** Letters: o, g, l, h Counting: 1-20 Reindeer Shapes & Colors Sight Words: go/got
2:25 – 2:45	**Snack Time**				
2:45– 2:50	Clean-up/Transition	Clean-up/Transition	Clean-up/Transition	Clean-up/Transition	Clean-up/Transition
2:50 – 3:15	**Music/Creative Expression:** New Year's Eve/Day Winter	**Music/Creative Expression:** New Year's Eve/Day Winter	**Music/Creative Expression:** New Year's Eve/Day Winter	**Music/Creative Expression:** New Year's Eve/Day Winter	**Music/Creative Expression:** New Year's Eve/Day Winter
3:15 – 3:20	Transition Activity				
3:20 – 3:55	**Recess on the Playground or in the Indoor Play/Exercise Area for Inclement Weather**				
3:55 – 4:00	Wash-up & Transition Activity Back to the Classroom				
4:00 – 4:25	**Read-aloud:** Letters: o, g, l, h New Year's Eve/Day Nursery Rhymes	**Read-aloud:** Letters: o, g, l, h New Year's Eve/Day Nursery Rhymes	**Read-aloud:** Letters: o, g, l, h New Year's Eve/Day Nursery Rhymes	**Read-aloud:** Letters: o, g, l, h New Year's Eve/Day Nursery Rhymes	**Read-aloud:** Letters: o, g, l, h New Year's Eve/Day Nursery Rhymes
4:30 – 4:50	Centers				
4:50 – 5:00	Clean-up for the Day				
5:00	Transition to Aftercare				

Week 17 Notes

Topics:
Winter
Christmas
New Year's Eve
Snowman
Gingerbread Man
Reindeer
Rhymes
Letters: o, g, l, h
Sight Words: go & got
Colors: Gold, Red, & Green
Counting: 1-15
Shapes: Rectangle & Cylinder

Season:
Winter

Upcoming Holidays:

Christmas

New Year's Eve

See Appendices for December for songs, stories, crafts, games and activities to support the use of sign language in learning the various topics.

See the 8 Modules of the Curriculum for 8.5 x 11" topical signs and sign handouts. Take advantage of the Table of Contents to find groups of signs and the Index in the back of the book to find specific signs.

January Schedule: Week 18

	Monday	Tuesday	Wednesday	Thursday	Friday
Before 9:00	Before-care, Centers Play, Breakfast/Snack, & Music & Movement				
8:55 - 9:00	Transition from Before-care to Classrooms				
9:00 – 9:25	**Reading Workshop:** Letters: u, c, b, n Sight Words: is & for Bears & Teddy Bears Presidents	**Reading Workshop:** Letters: u, c, b, n Sight Words: is & for Bears & Teddy Bears Presidents	**Reading Workshop:** Letters: u, c, b, n Sight Words: is & for Bears & Teddy Bears Presidents	**Reading Workshop:** Letters: u, c, b, n Sight Words: is & for Bears & Teddy Bears Presidents	**Reading Workshop:** Letters: u, c, b, n Sight Words: is & for Bears & Teddy Bears Presidents
9:25 – 10:15	**Centers**				
10:15 – 10:25	Clean-up & Transition Activity				
10:25 – 10:55	**Monthly Topical Learning:** Presidents Bears & Teddy Bears	**Monthly Topical Learning:** Presidents Bears & Teddy Bears	**Monthly Topical Learning:** Presidents Bears & Teddy Bears	**Monthly Topical Learning:** Presidents Bears & Teddy Bears	**Monthly Topical Learning:** Presidents Bears & Teddy Bears
10:55 – 11:00	Bathroom Break & Transition Activity				
11:00 – 11:30	**Recess on the Playground or in the Indoor Play/Exercise Area for Inclement Weather**				
11:30 – 11:35	Wash-up & Transition Activity Back to the Classroom				
11:35 – Noon	**Circle Time:** Bears & Teddy Bears Presidents	**Circle Time:** Bears & Teddy Bears Presidents	**Circle Time:** Bears & Teddy Bears Presidents	**Circle Time:** Bears & Teddy Bears Presidents	**Circle Time:** Bears & Teddy Bears Presidents
Noon – 12:10	Bathroom Break & Transition Activity				
12:10 – 12:50	**Lunch Time**				
12:50 – 1:00	Clean-up and Transition Song				
1:00 – 2:00	**Naptime**				
2:00 – 2:25	**Math, Art & Writing:** Letters: u, c, b, n Counting: 1-20 Shapes & Colors Sight Words: is & for	**Math, Art & Writing:** Letters: u, c, b, n Counting: 1-20 Shapes & Colors Sight Words: is & for	**Math, Art & Writing:** Letters: u, c, b, n Counting: 1-20 Shapes & Colors Sight Words: is & for	**Math, Art & Writing:** Letters: u, c, b, n Counting: 1-20 Shapes & Colors Sight Words: is & for	**Math, Art & Writing:** Letters: u, c, b, n Counting: 1-20 Shapes & Colors Sight Words: is & for
2:25 – 2:45	**Snack Time**				
2:45– 2:50	Clean-up/Transition	Clean-up/Transition	Clean-up/Transition	Clean-up/Transition	Clean-up/Transition
2:50 – 3:15	**Music/Creative Expression:** Bears & Teddy Bears Presidents	**Music/Creative Expression:** Bears & Teddy Bears Presidents	**Music/Creative Expression:** Bears & Teddy Bears Presidents	**Music/Creative Expression:** Bears & Teddy Bears Presidents	**Music/Creative Expression:** Bears & Teddy Bears Presidents
3:15 – 3:20	Transition Activity				
3:20 – 3:55	**Recess on the Playground or in the Indoor Play/Exercise Area for Inclement Weather**				
3:55 – 4:00	Wash-up & Transition Activity Back to the Classroom				
4:00 – 4:25	**Read-aloud:** Letters: u, c, b, n Bears & Teddy Bears Presidents	**Read-aloud:** Letters: o, g, l, h Bears & Teddy Bears Presidents	**Read-aloud:** Letters: o, g, l, h Bears & Teddy Bears Presidents	**Read-aloud:** Letters: o, g, l, h Bears & Teddy Bears Presidents	**Read-aloud:** Letters: o, g, l, h Bears & Teddy Bears Presidents
4:30 – 4:50	**Centers**				
4:50 – 5:00	Clean-up for the Day				
5:00	Transition to Aftercare				

Week 18 Notes:

Topics:
New Year
Presidents
Dinosaurs
Circus
Day and Night
Hibernation
Bears, Nature, and Habitat
Teddy Bears
Penguins & Other Arctic Animals
Letters: u, c, b, n
Sight Words: go & got
Word Chunks: -an
Counting: 1-20
Shapes: Triangle & Cone
Colors: White, Blue, & Yellow

Season:
Winter

Upcoming Holidays:

New Year's Day

President's Day

See Appendices for January for songs, stories, crafts, games and activities to support the use of sign language in learning the various topics.

See the 8 Modules of the Curriculum for 8.5 x 11" topical signs and sign handouts. Take advantage of the Table of Contents to find groups of signs and the Index in the back of the book to find specific signs.

January Schedule: Week 19

	Monday	Tuesday	Wednesday	Thursday	Friday
Before 9:00	Before-care, Centers Play, Breakfast/Snack, & Music & Movement				
8:55 - 9:00	Transition from Before-care to Classrooms				
9:00 – 9:25	**Reading Workshop:** Letters: u, c, b, n Sight Words: is & for Dinosaurs Circus	**Reading Workshop:** Letters: u, c, b, n Sight Words: is & for Dinosaurs Circus	**Reading Workshop:** Letters: u, c, b, n Sight Words: is & for Dinosaurs Circus	**Reading Workshop:** Letters: u, c, b, n Sight Words: is & for Dinosaurs Circus	**Reading Workshop:** Letters: u, c, b, n Sight Words: is & for Dinosaurs Circus
9:25 – 10:15	Centers				
10:15 – 10:25	Clean-up & Transition Activity				
10:25 – 10:55	**Monthly Topical Learning:** Dinosaurs Circus Presidents	**Monthly Topical Learning:** Dinosaurs Circus Presidents	**Monthly Topical Learning:** Dinosaurs Circus Presidents	**Monthly Topical Learning:** Dinosaurs Circus Presidents	**Monthly Topical Learning:** Dinosaurs Circus Presidents
10:55 – 11:00	Bathroom Break & Transition Activity				
11:00 – 11:30	**Recess on the Playground or in the Indoor Play/Exercise Area for Inclement Weather**				
11:30 – 11:35	Wash-up & Transition Activity Back to the Classroom				
11:35 – Noon	**Circle Time:** Dinosaurs Circus	**Circle Time:** Dinosaurs Circus	**Circle Time:** Dinosaurs Circus	**Circle Time:** Dinosaurs Circus	**Circle Time:** Dinosaurs Circus
Noon – 12:10	Bathroom Break & Transition Activity				
12:10 – 12:50	**Lunch Time**				
12:50 – 1:00	Clean-up and Transition Song				
1:00 – 2:00	**Naptime**				
2:00 – 2:25	**Math, Art & Writing:** Letters: u, c, b, n Counting: 1-20 Shapes & Colors Sight Words: is & for	**Math, Art & Writing:** Letters: u, c, b, n Counting: 1-20 Shapes & Colors Sight Words: is & for	**Math, Art & Writing:** Letters: u, c, b, n Counting: 1-20 Shapes & Colors Sight Words: is & for	**Math, Art & Writing:** Letters: u, c, b, n Counting: 1-20 Shapes & Colors Sight Words: is & for	**Math, Art & Writing:** Letters: u, c, b, n Counting: 1-20 Shapes & Colors Sight Words: is & for
2:25 – 2:45	**Snack Time**				
2:45– 2:50	Clean-up/Transition	Clean-up/Transition	Clean-up/Transition	Clean-up/Transition	Clean-up/Transition
2:50 – 3:15	**Music/Creative Expression:** Dinosaurs Circus	**Music/Creative Expression:** Dinosaurs Circus	**Music/Creative Expression:** Dinosaurs Circus	**Music/Creative Expression:** Dinosaurs Circus	**Music/Creative Expression:** Dinosaurs Circus
3:15 – 3:20	Transition Activity				
3:20 – 3:55	**Recess on the Playground or in the Indoor Play/Exercise Area for Inclement Weather**				
3:55 – 4:00	Wash-up & Transition Activity Back to the Classroom				
4:00 – 4:25	**Read-aloud:** Letters: u, c, b, n Dinosaurs Circus Presidents	**Read-aloud:** Letters: o, g, l, h Dinosaurs Circus Presidents	**Read-aloud:** Letters: o, g, l, h Dinosaurs Circus Presidents	**Read-aloud:** Letters: o, g, l, h Dinosaurs Circus Presidents	**Read-aloud:** Letters: o, g, l, h Dinosaurs Circus Presidents
4:30 – 4:50	Centers				
4:50 – 5:00	Clean-up for the Day				
5:00	Transition to Aftercare				

Week 19 Notes:

Topics:
Presidents
Dinosaurs
Circus
Day and Night
Hibernation
Bears, Nature, and Habitat
Teddy Bears
Penguins & Other Arctic Animals
Letters: u, c, b, n
Sight Words: is & for
Word Chunks: -an
Counting: 1-20
Shapes: Triangle & Cone
Colors: White, Blue, & Yellow

Season:
Winter

Upcoming Holidays:

President's Day

See Appendices for January for songs, stories, crafts, games and activities to support the use of sign language in learning the various topics.

See the 8 Modules of the Curriculum for 8.5 x 11" topical signs and sign handouts. Take advantage of the Table of Contents to find groups of signs and the Index in the back of the book to find specific signs.

January Schedule: Week 20

	Monday	Tuesday	Wednesday	Thursday	Friday
Before 9:00	Before-care, Centers Play, Breakfast/Snack, & Music & Movement				
8:55 - 9:00	Transition from Before-care to Classrooms				
9:00 – 9:25	**Reading Workshop:** Letters: u, c, b, n Sight Words: is & for Day & Night Arctic Animals	**Reading Workshop:** Letters: u, c, b, n Sight Words: is & for Day & Night Arctic Animals	**Reading Workshop:** Letters: u, c, b, n Sight Words: is & for Day & Night Arctic Animals	**Reading Workshop:** Letters: u, c, b, n Sight Words: is & for Day & Night Arctic Animals	**Reading Workshop:** Letters: u, c, b, n Sight Words: is & for Day & Night Arctic Animals
9:25 – 10:15	Centers				
10:15 – 10:25	Clean-up & Transition Activity				
10:25 – 10:55	**Monthly Topical Learning:** Day & Night Arctic Animals Presidents Dinosaurs	**Monthly Topical Learning:** Day & Night Arctic Animals Presidents Dinosaurs	**Monthly Topical Learning:** Day & Night Arctic Animals Presidents Dinosaurs	**Monthly Topical Learning:** Day & Night Arctic Animals Presidents Dinosaurs	**Monthly Topical Learning:** Day & Night Arctic Animals Presidents Dinosaurs
10:55 – 11:00	Bathroom Break & Transition Activity				
11:00 – 11:30	**Recess on the Playground or in the Indoor Play/Exercise Area for Inclement Weather**				
11:30 – 11:35	Wash-up & Transition Activity Back to the Classroom				
11:35 – Noon	**Circle Time:** Day & Night Arctic Animals	**Circle Time:** Day & Night Arctic Animals	**Circle Time:** Day & Night Arctic Animals	**Circle Time:** Day & Night Arctic Animals	**Circle Time:** Day & Night Arctic Animals
Noon – 12:10	Bathroom Break & Transition Activity				
12:10 – 12:50	**Lunch Time**				
12:50 – 1:00	Clean-up and Transition Song				
1:00 – 2:00	**Naptime**				
2:00 – 2:25	**Math, Art & Writing:** Letters: u, c, b, n Counting: 1-20 Shapes & Colors Sight Words: is & for	**Math, Art & Writing:** Letters: u, c, b, n Counting: 1-20 Shapes & Colors Sight Words: is & for	**Math, Art & Writing:** Letters: u, c, b, n Counting: 1-20 Shapes & Colors Sight Words: is & for	**Math, Art & Writing:** Letters: u, c, b, n Counting: 1-20 Shapes & Colors Sight Words: is & for	**Math, Art & Writing:** Letters: u, c, b, n Counting: 1-20 Shapes & Colors Sight Words: is & for
2:25 – 2:45	**Snack Time**				
2:45– 2:50	Clean-up/Transition	Clean-up/Transition	Clean-up/Transition	Clean-up/Transition	Clean-up/Transition
2:50 – 3:15	**Music/Creative Expression:** Day & Night Arctic Animals	**Music/Creative Expression:** Day & Night Arctic Animals	**Music/Creative Expression:** Day & Night Arctic Animals	**Music/Creative Expression:** Day & Night Arctic Animals	**Music/Creative Expression:** Day & Night Arctic Animals
3:15 – 3:20	Transition Activity				
3:20 – 3:55	**Recess on the Playground or in the Indoor Play/Exercise Area for Inclement Weather**				
3:55 – 4:00	Wash-up & Transition Activity Back to the Classroom				
4:00 – 4:25	**Read-aloud:** Letters: u, c, b, n Day & Night Arctic Animals Dinosaurs	**Read-aloud:** Letters: o, g, l, h Day & Night Arctic Animals Dinosaurs	**Read-aloud:** Letters: o, g, l, h Day & Night Arctic Animals Dinosaurs	**Read-aloud:** Letters: o, g, l, h Day & Night Arctic Animals Dinosaurs	**Read-aloud:** Letters: o, g, l, h Day & Night Arctic Animals Dinosaurs
4:30 – 4:50	Centers				
4:50 – 5:00	Clean-up for the Day				
5:00	Transition to Aftercare				

Week 20 Notes:

Topics:
Presidents
Dinosaurs
Circus
Day and Night
Hibernation
Bears, Nature, and Habitat
Teddy Bears
Penguins & Other Arctic Animals
Letters: u, c, b, n
Sight Words: is & for
Word Chunks: -an
Counting: 1-20
Shapes: Triangle & Cone
Colors: White, Blue, & Yellow

Season:
Winter

Upcoming Holidays:

President's Day

See Appendices for January for songs, stories, crafts, games and activities to support the use of sign language in learning the various topics.

See the 8 Modules of the Curriculum for 8.5 x 11" topical signs and sign handouts. Take advantage of the Table of Contents to find groups of signs and the Index in the back of the book to find specific signs.

January Schedule: Week 21

	Monday	Tuesday	Wednesday	Thursday	Friday
Before 9:00	Before-care, Centers Play, Breakfast/Snack, & Music & Movement				
8:55 - 9:00	Transition from Before-care to Classrooms				
9:00 – 9:25	**Reading Workshop:** Letters: u, c, b, n Sight Words: but/up Artic Animals Dinosaurs	**Reading Workshop:** Letters: u, c, b, n Sight Words: but/up Artic Animals Dinosaurs	**Reading Workshop:** Letters: u, c, b, n Sight Words: but/up Artic Animals Dinosaurs	**Reading Workshop:** Letters: u, c, b, n Sight Words: but/up Artic Animals Dinosaurs	**Reading Workshop:** Letters: u, c, b, n Sight Words: but/up Artic Animals Dinosaurs
9:25 – 10:15	Centers				
10:15 – 10:25	Clean-up & Transition Activity				
10:25 – 10:55	**Monthly Topical Learning:** Artic Animals Dinosaurs	**Monthly Topical Learning:** Artic Animals Dinosaurs	**Monthly Topical Learning:** Artic Animals Dinosaurs	**Monthly Topical Learning:** Artic Animals Dinosaurs	**Monthly Topical Learning:** Artic Animals Dinosaurs
10:55 – 11:00	Bathroom Break & Transition Activity				
11:00 – 11:30	**Recess on the Playground** **or in the Indoor Play/Exercise Area for Inclement Weather**				
11:30 – 11:35	Wash-up & Transition Activity Back to the Classroom				
11:35 – Noon	**Circle Time:** Artic Animals Dinosaurs	**Circle Time:** Artic Animals Dinosaurs	**Circle Time:** Artic Animals Dinosaurs	**Circle Time:** Artic Animals Dinosaurs	**Circle Time:** Artic Animals Dinosaurs
Noon – 12:10	Bathroom Break & Transition Activity				
12:10 – 12:50	**Lunch Time**				
12:50 – 1:00	Clean-up and Transition Song				
1:00 – 2:00	**Naptime**				
2:00 – 2:25	**Math, Art & Writing:** Letters: u, c, b, n Counting: 1-20 Shapes & Colors Sight Words: but/u	**Math, Art & Writing:** Letters: u, c, b, n Counting: 1-20 Shapes & Colors Sight Words: but/u	**Math, Art & Writing:** Letters: u, c, b, n Counting: 1-20 Shapes & Colors Sight Words: but/u	**Math, Art & Writing:** Letters: u, c, b, n Counting: 1-20 Shapes & Colors Sight Words: but/u	**Math, Art & Writing:** Letters: u, c, b, n Counting: 1-20 Shapes & Colors Sight Words: but/u
2:25 – 2:45	**Snack Time**				
2:45– 2:50	Clean-up/Transition	Clean-up/Transition	Clean-up/Transition	Clean-up/Transition	Clean-up/Transition
2:50 – 3:15	**Music/Creative Expression:** Artic Animals Dinosaurs	**Music/Creative Expression:** Artic Animals Dinosaurs	**Music/Creative Expression:** Artic Animals Dinosaurs	**Music/Creative Expression:** Artic Animals Dinosaurs	**Music/Creative Expression:** Artic Animals Dinosaurs
3:15 – 3:20	Transition Activity				
3:20 – 3:55	**Recess on the Playground** **or in the Indoor Play/Exercise Area for Inclement Weather**				
3:55 – 4:00	Wash-up & Transition Activity Back to the Classroom				
4:00 – 4:25	**Read-aloud:** Letters: u, c, b, n Artic Animals Dinosaurs	**Read-aloud:** Letters: o, g, l, h Artic Animals Dinosaurs	**Read-aloud:** Letters: o, g, l, h Artic Animals Dinosaurs	**Read-aloud:** Letters: o, g, l, h Artic Animals Dinosaurs	**Read-aloud:** Letters: o, g, l, h Artic Animals Dinosaurs
4:30 – 4:50	Centers				
4:50 – 5:00	Clean-up for the Day				
5:00	Transition to Aftercare				

Week 21 Notes:

Topics:
Presidents
Dinosaurs
Circus
Day and Night
Hibernation
Bears, Nature, and Habitat
Teddy Bears
Penguins & Other Arctic Animals
Letters: u, c, b, n
Sight Words: but & up
Word Chunks: -an
Counting: 1-20
Shapes: Triangle & Cone
Colors: White, Blue, & Yellow

Season:
Winter

Upcoming Holidays:

President's Day

See Appendices for January for songs, stories, crafts, games and activities to support the use of sign language in learning the various topics.

See the 8 Modules of the Curriculum for 8.5 x 11" topical signs and sign handouts. Take advantage of the Table of Contents to find groups of signs and the Index in the back of the book to find specific signs.

January Schedule: Week 22

	Monday	Tuesday	Wednesday	Thursday	Friday
Before 9:00	Before-care, Centers Play, Breakfast/Snack, & Music & Movement				
8:55 - 9:00	Transition from Before-care to Classrooms				
9:00 – 9:25	**Reading Workshop:** Letters: u, c, b, n Sight Words: but/up Artic Animals Dinosaurs	**Reading Workshop:** Letters: u, c, b, n Sight Words: but/up Artic Animals Dinosaurs	**Reading Workshop:** Letters: u, c, b, n Sight Words: but/up Artic Animals Dinosaurs	**Reading Workshop:** Letters: u, c, b, n Sight Words: but/up Artic Animals Dinosaurs	**Reading Workshop:** Letters: u, c, b, n Sight Words: but/up Artic Animals Dinosaurs
9:25 – 10:15	Centers				
10:15 – 10:25	Clean-up & Transition Activity				
10:25 – 10:55	**Monthly Topical Learning:** Artic Animals Dinosaurs	**Monthly Topical Learning:** Artic Animals Dinosaurs	**Monthly Topical Learning:** Artic Animals Dinosaurs	**Monthly Topical Learning:** Artic Animals Dinosaurs	**Monthly Topical Learning:** Artic Animals Dinosaurs
10:55 – 11:00	Bathroom Break & Transition Activity				
11:00 – 11:30	**Recess on the Playground** **or in the Indoor Play/Exercise Area for Inclement Weather**				
11:30 – 11:35	Wash-up & Transition Activity Back to the Classroom				
11:35 – Noon	**Circle Time:** Artic Animals Dinosaurs	**Circle Time:** Artic Animals Dinosaurs	**Circle Time:** Artic Animals Dinosaurs	**Circle Time:** Artic Animals Dinosaurs	**Circle Time:** Artic Animals Dinosaurs
Noon – 12:10	Bathroom Break & Transition Activity				
12:10 – 12:50	**Lunch Time**				
12:50 – 1:00	Clean-up and Transition Song				
1:00 – 2:00	**Naptime**				
2:00 – 2:25	**Math, Art & Writing:** Letters: u, c, b, n Counting: 1-20 Shapes & Colors Sight Words: but/up	**Math, Art & Writing:** Letters: u, c, b, n Counting: 1-20 Shapes & Colors Sight Words: but/up	**Math, Art & Writing:** Letters: u, c, b, n Counting: 1-20 Shapes & Colors Sight Words: but/up	**Math, Art & Writing:** Letters: u, c, b, n Counting: 1-20 Shapes & Colors Sight Words: but/up	**Math, Art & Writing:** Letters: u, c, b, n Counting: 1-20 Shapes & Colors Sight Words: but/up
2:25 – 2:45	**Snack Time**				
2:45 – 2:50	Clean-up/Transition	Clean-up/Transition	Clean-up/Transition	Clean-up/Transition	Clean-up/Transition
2:50 – 3:15	**Music/Creative Expression:** Artic Animals Dinosaurs	**Music/Creative Expression:** Artic Animals Dinosaurs	**Music/Creative Expression:** Artic Animals Dinosaurs	**Music/Creative Expression:** Artic Animals Dinosaurs	**Music/Creative Expression:** Artic Animals Dinosaurs
3:15 – 3:20	Transition Activity				
3:20 – 3:55	**Recess on the Playground** **or in the Indoor Play/Exercise Area for Inclement Weather**				
3:55 – 4:00	Wash-up & Transition Activity Back to the Classroom				
4:00 – 4:25	**Read-aloud:** Letters: u, c, b, n Artic Animals Dinosaurs	**Read-aloud:** Letters: o, g, l, h Artic Animals Dinosaurs	**Read-aloud:** Letters: o, g, l, h Artic Animals Dinosaurs	**Read-aloud:** Letters: o, g, l, h Artic Animals Dinosaurs	**Read-aloud:** Letters: o, g, l, h Artic Animals Dinosaurs
4:30 – 4:50	Centers				
4:50 – 5:00	Clean-up for the Day				
5:00	Transition to Aftercare				

Week 22 Notes:

Topics:
Presidents
Dinosaurs
Circus
Day and Night
Hibernation
Bears, Nature, and Habitat
Teddy Bears
Penguins & Other Arctic Animals
Letters: u, c, b, n
Sight Words: but & up
Word Chunks: -an
Counting: 1-20
Shapes: Triangle & Cone
Colors: White, Blue, & Yellow

Season:
Winter

Upcoming Holidays:

Valentine's Day

See Appendices for January for songs, stories, crafts, games and activities to support the use of sign language in learning the various topics.

See the 8 Modules of the Curriculum for 8.5 x 11" topical signs and sign handouts. Take advantage of the Table of Contents to find groups of signs and the Index in the back of the book to find specific signs.

February Schedule: Week 23

	Monday	Tuesday	Wednesday	Thursday	Friday
Before 9:00	Before-care, Centers Play, Breakfast/Snack, & Music & Movement				
8:55 - 9:00	Transition from Before-care to Classrooms				
9:00 – 9:25	**Reading Workshop:** Letters: k, v, e, w Sight Words: to & in Valentine's Day Chinese New Year	**Reading Workshop:** Letters: k, v, e, w Sight Words: to & in Valentine's Day Chinese New Year	**Reading Workshop:** Letters: k, v, e, w Sight Words: to & in Valentine's Day Chinese New Year	**Reading Workshop:** Letters: k, v, e, w Sight Words: to & in Valentine's Day Chinese New Year	**Reading Workshop:** Letters: k, v, e, w Sight Words: to & in Valentine's Day Chinese New Year
9:25 – 10:15	Centers				
10:15 – 10:25	Clean-up & Transition Activity				
10:25 – 10:55	**Monthly Topical Learning:** Valentine's Day Chinese New Year Dental Health	**Monthly Topical Learning:** Valentine's Day Chinese New Year Dental Health	**Monthly Topical Learning:** Valentine's Day Chinese New Year Dental Health	**Monthly Topical Learning:** Valentine's Day Chinese New Year Dental Health	**Monthly Topical Learning:** Valentine's Day Chinese New Year Dental Health
10:55 – 11:00	Bathroom Break & Transition Activity				
11:00 – 11:30	**Recess on the Playground or in the Indoor Play/Exercise Area for Inclement Weather**				
11:30 – 11:35	Wash-up & Transition Activity Back to the Classroom				
11:35 – Noon	**Circle Time:** Valentine's Day Chinese New Year	**Circle Time:** Valentine's Day Chinese New Year	**Circle Time:** Valentine's Day Chinese New Year	**Circle Time:** Valentine's Day Chinese New Year	**Circle Time:** Valentine's Day Chinese New Year
Noon – 12:10	Bathroom Break & Transition Activity				
12:10 – 12:50	**Lunch Time**				
12:50 – 1:00	Clean-up and Transition Song				
1:00 – 2:00	**Naptime**				
2:00 – 2:25	**Math, Art & Writing:** Letters: k, v, e, w Counting: 1-25 Shapes & Colors Sight Words: to & in	**Math, Art & Writing:** Letters: k, v, e, w Counting: 1-25 Shapes & Colors Sight Words: to & in	**Math, Art & Writing:** Letters: k, v, e, w Counting: 1-25 Shapes & Colors Sight Words: to & in	**Math, Art & Writing:** Letters: k, v, e, w Counting: 1-25 Shapes & Colors Sight Words: to & in	**Math, Art & Writing:** Letters: k, v, e, w Counting: 1-25 Shapes & Colors Sight Words: to & in
2:25 – 2:45	**Snack Time**				
2:45– 2:50	Clean-up/Transition	Clean-up/Transition	Clean-up/Transition	Clean-up/Transition	Clean-up/Transition
2:50 – 3:15	**Music/Creative Expression:** Valentine's Day Chinese New Year	**Music/Creative Expression:** Valentine's Day Chinese New Year	**Music/Creative Expression:** Valentine's Day Chinese New Year	**Music/Creative Expression:** Valentine's Day Chinese New Year	**Music/Creative Expression:** Valentine's Day Chinese New Year
3:15 – 3:20	Transition Activity				
3:20 – 3:55	**Recess on the Playground or in the Indoor Play/Exercise Area for Inclement Weather**				
3:55 – 4:00	Wash-up & Transition Activity Back to the Classroom				
4:00 – 4:25	**Read-aloud:** Letters: u, c, b, n Valentine's Day Chinese New Year	**Read-aloud:** Letters: o, g, l, h Valentine's Day Chinese New Year	**Read-aloud:** Letters: o, g, l, h Valentine's Day Chinese New Year	**Read-aloud:** Letters: o, g, l, h Valentine's Day Chinese New Year	**Read-aloud:** Letters: o, g, l, h Valentine's Day Chinese New Year
4:30 – 4:50	Centers				
4:50 – 5:00	Clean-up for the Day				
5:00	Transition to Aftercare				

Week 23 Notes

Topics:
Valentine's Day
Chinese New Year
Dental Health
Transportation
Five Senses
Reptiles & Amphibians
Letters: k, v, e, w
Counting: 1-20
Shape: Heart
Colors: Pink, White, & Red
Sight Words: to & in

Season:
Winter

Upcoming Holidays:

Valentine's Day

Chinese New Year

See Appendices for February for songs, stories, crafts, games and activities to support the use of sign language in learning the various topics.

See the 8 Modules of the Curriculum for 8.5 x 11" topical signs and sign handouts. Take advantage of the Table of Contents to find groups of signs and the Index in the back of the book to find specific signs.

February Schedule: Week 24

	Monday	Tuesday	Wednesday	Thursday	Friday
Before 9:00	Before-care, Centers Play, Breakfast/Snack, & Music & Movement				
8:55 - 9:00	Transition from Before-care to Classrooms				
9:00 – 9:25	**Reading Workshop:** Letters: k, v, e, w Sight Words: to & in Valentine's Day Transportation	**Reading Workshop:** Letters: k, v, e, w Sight Words: to & in Valentine's Day Transportation	**Reading Workshop:** Letters: k, v, e, w Sight Words: to & in Valentine's Day Transportation	**Reading Workshop:** Letters: k, v, e, w Sight Words: to & in Valentine's Day Transportation	**Reading Workshop:** Letters: k, v, e, w Sight Words: to & in Valentine's Day Transportation
9:25 – 10:15	Centers				
10:15 – 10:25	Clean-up & Transition Activity				
10:25 – 10:55	**Monthly Topical Learning:** Valentine's Day Dental Health Transportation	**Monthly Topical Learning:** Valentine's Day Dental Health Transportation	**Monthly Topical Learning:** Valentine's Day Dental Health Transportation	**Monthly Topical Learning:** Valentine's Day Dental Health Transportation	**Monthly Topical Learning:** Valentine's Day Dental Health Transportation
10:55 – 11:00	Bathroom Break & Transition Activity				
11:00 – 11:30	**Recess on the Playground or in the Indoor Play/Exercise Area for Inclement Weather**				
11:30 – 11:35	Wash-up & Transition Activity Back to the Classroom				
11:35 – Noon	**Circle Time:** Valentine's Day Transportation	**Circle Time:** Valentine's Day Transportation	**Circle Time:** Valentine's Day Transportation	**Circle Time:** Valentine's Day Transportation	**Circle Time:** Valentine's Day Transportation
Noon – 12:10	Bathroom Break & Transition Activity				
12:10 – 12:50	**Lunch Time**				
12:50 – 1:00	Clean-up and Transition Song				
1:00 – 2:00	**Naptime**				
2:00 – 2:25	**Math, Art & Writing:** Letters: k, v, e, w Counting: 1-25 Shapes & Colors Sight Words: to & in	**Math, Art & Writing:** Letters: k, v, e, w Counting: 1-25 Shapes & Colors Sight Words: to & in	**Math, Art & Writing:** Letters: k, v, e, w Counting: 1-25 Shapes & Colors Sight Words: to & in	**Math, Art & Writing:** Letters: k, v, e, w Counting: 1-25 Shapes & Colors Sight Words: to & in	**Math, Art & Writing:** Letters: k, v, e, w Counting: 1-25 Shapes & Colors Sight Words: to & in
2:25 – 2:45	**Snack Time**				
2:45 – 2:50	Clean-up/Transition	Clean-up/Transition	Clean-up/Transition	Clean-up/Transition	Clean-up/Transition
2:50 – 3:15	**Music/Creative Expression:** Valentine's Day Transportation	**Music/Creative Expression:** Valentine's Day Transportation	**Music/Creative Expression:** Valentine's Day Transportation	**Music/Creative Expression:** Valentine's Day Transportation	**Music/Creative Expression:** Valentine's Day Transportation
3:15 – 3:20	Transition Activity				
3:20 – 3:55	**Recess on the Playground or in the Indoor Play/Exercise Area for Inclement Weather**				
3:55 – 4:00	Wash-up & Transition Activity Back to the Classroom				
4:00 – 4:25	**Read-aloud:** Letters: u, c, b, n Valentine's Day Transportation	**Read-aloud:** Letters: o, g, l, h Valentine's Day Transportation	**Read-aloud:** Letters: o, g, l, h Valentine's Day Transportation	**Read-aloud:** Letters: o, g, l, h Valentine's Day Transportation	**Read-aloud:** Letters: o, g, l, h Valentine's Day Transportation
4:30 – 4:50	Centers				
4:50 – 5:00	Clean-up for the Day				
5:00	Transition to Aftercare				

Week 24 Notes

Topics:
Valentine's Day
Chinese New Year
Dental Health
Transportation
Five Senses
Reptiles & Amphibians
Letters: k, v, e, w
Counting: 1-20
Shape: Heart
Colors: Pink, White, & Red
Sight Words: to & in

Season:
Winter

Upcoming Holidays:

Valentine's Day

Chinese New Year

See Appendices for February for songs, stories, crafts, games and activities to support the use of sign language in learning the various topics.

See the 8 Modules of the Curriculum for 8.5 x 11" topical signs and sign handouts. Take advantage of the Table of Contents to find groups of signs and the Index in the back of the book to find specific signs.

February Schedule: Week 25

	Monday	Tuesday	Wednesday	Thursday	Friday
Before 9:00	Before-care, Centers Play, Breakfast/Snack, & Music & Movement				
8:55 - 9:00	Transition from Before-care to Classrooms				
9:00 – 9:25	**Reading Workshop:** Letters: k, v, e, w Sight Words: what/who Transportation Five Senses	**Reading Workshop:** Letters: k, v, e, w Sight Words: what/who Transportation Five Senses	**Reading Workshop:** Letters: k, v, e, w Sight Words: what/who Transportation Five Senses	**Reading Workshop:** Letters: k, v, e, w Sight Words: what/who Transportation Five Senses	**Reading Workshop:** Letters: k, v, e, w Sight Words: what/who Transportation Five Senses
9:25 – 10:15	Centers				
10:15 – 10:25	Clean-up & Transition Activity				
10:25 – 10:55	**Monthly Topical Learning:** Dental Health Transportation Five Senses	**Monthly Topical Learning:** Dental Health Transportation Five Senses	**Monthly Topical Learning:** Dental Health Transportation Five Senses	**Monthly Topical Learning:** Dental Health Transportation Five Senses	**Monthly Topical Learning:** Dental Health Transportation Five Senses
10:55 – 11:00	Bathroom Break & Transition Activity				
11:00 – 11:30	**Recess on the Playground or in the Indoor Play/Exercise Area for Inclement Weather**				
11:30 – 11:35	Wash-up & Transition Activity Back to the Classroom				
11:35 – Noon	**Circle Time:** Transportation Five Senses	**Circle Time:** Transportation Five Senses	**Circle Time:** Transportation Five Senses	**Circle Time:** Transportation Five Senses	**Circle Time:** Transportation Five Senses
Noon – 12:10	Bathroom Break & Transition Activity				
12:10 – 12:50	**Lunch Time**				
12:50 – 1:00	Clean-up and Transition Song				
1:00 – 2:00	**Naptime**				
2:00 – 2:25	**Math, Art & Writing:** Letters: k, v, e, w Counting: 1-25 Shapes & Colors Sight Words: what/who	**Math, Art & Writing:** Letters: k, v, e, w Counting: 1-25 Shapes & Colors Sight Words: what/who	**Math, Art & Writing:** Letters: k, v, e, w Counting: 1-25 Shapes & Colors Sight Words: what/who	**Math, Art & Writing:** Letters: k, v, e, w Counting: 1-25 Shapes & Colors Sight Words: what/who	**Math, Art & Writing:** Letters: k, v, e, w Counting: 1-25 Shapes & Colors Sight Words: what/who
2:25 – 2:45	**Snack Time**				
2:45 – 2:50	Clean-up/Transition	Clean-up/Transition	Clean-up/Transition	Clean-up/Transition	Clean-up/Transition
2:50 – 3:15	**Music/Creative Expression:** Transportation Five Senses	**Music/Creative Expression:** Transportation Five Senses	**Music/Creative Expression:** Transportation Five Senses	**Music/Creative Expression:** Transportation Five Senses	**Music/Creative Expression:** Transportation Five Senses
3:15 – 3:20	Transition Activity				
3:20 – 3:55	**Recess on the Playground or in the Indoor Play/Exercise Area for Inclement Weather**				
3:55 – 4:00	Wash-up & Transition Activity Back to the Classroom				
4:00 – 4:25	**Read-aloud:** Letters: u, c, b, n Transportation Five Senses	**Read-aloud:** Letters: o, g, l, h Transportation Five Senses	**Read-aloud:** Letters: o, g, l, h Transportation Five Senses	**Read-aloud:** Letters: o, g, l, h Transportation Five Senses	**Read-aloud:** Letters: o, g, l, h Transportation Five Senses
4:30 – 4:50	Centers				
4:50 – 5:00	Clean-up for the Day				
5:00	Transition to Aftercare				

Week 25 Notes

Topics:
Dental Health
Transportation
Five Senses
Reptiles & Amphibians
Letters: k, v, e, w
Counting: 1-20
Shape: Heart
Colors: Pink, White, & Red
Sight Words: what & who

Season:
Winter

See Appendices for February for songs, stories, crafts, games and activities to support the use of sign language in learning the various topics.

See the 8 Modules of the Curriculum for 8.5 x 11" topical signs and sign handouts. Take advantage of the Table of Contents to find groups of signs and the Index in the back of the book to find specific signs.

February Schedule: Week 26

	Monday	Tuesday	Wednesday	Thursday	Friday
Before 9:00	Before-care, Centers Play, Breakfast/Snack, & Music & Movement				
8:55 - 9:00	Transition from Before-care to Classrooms				
9:00 – 9:25	**Reading Workshop:** Letters: k, v, e, w Sight Words: what/who Five Senses Reptiles/Amphibians	**Reading Workshop:** Letters: k, v, e, w Sight Words: what/who Five Senses Reptiles/Amphibians	**Reading Workshop:** Letters: k, v, e, w Sight Words: what/who Five Senses Reptiles/Amphibians	**Reading Workshop:** Letters: k, v, e, w Sight Words: what/who Five Senses Reptiles/Amphibians	**Reading Workshop:** Letters: k, v, e, w Sight Words: what/who Five Senses Reptiles/Amphibians
9:25 – 10:15	Centers				
10:15 – 10:25	Clean-up & Transition Activity				
10:25 – 10:55	**Monthly Topical Learning:** Dental Health Transportation Five Senses Reptiles/Amphibians	**Monthly Topical Learning:** Dental Health Transportation Five Senses Reptiles/Amphibians	**Monthly Topical Learning:** Dental Health Transportation Five Senses Reptiles/Amphibians	**Monthly Topical Learning:** Dental Health Transportation Five Senses Reptiles/Amphibians	**Monthly Topical Learning:** Dental Health Transportation Five Senses Reptiles/Amphibians
10:55 – 11:00	Bathroom Break & Transition Activity				
11:00 – 11:30	**Recess on the Playground or in the Indoor Play/Exercise Area for Inclement Weather**				
11:30 – 11:35	Wash-up & Transition Activity Back to the Classroom				
11:35 – Noon	**Circle Time:** Five Senses Reptiles/Amphibians	**Circle Time:** Five Senses Reptiles/Amphibians	**Circle Time:** Five Senses Reptiles/Amphibians	**Circle Time:** Five Senses Reptiles/Amphibians	**Circle Time:** Five Senses Reptiles/Amphibians
Noon – 12:10	Bathroom Break & Transition Activity				
12:10 – 12:50	**Lunch Time**				
12:50 – 1:00	Clean-up and Transition Song				
1:00 – 2:00	**Naptime**				
2:00 – 2:25	**Math, Art & Writing:** Letters: k, v, e, w Counting: 1-25 Shapes & Colors S. Words: what/who	**Math, Art & Writing:** Letters: k, v, e, w Counting: 1-25 Shapes & Colors S. Words: what/who	**Math, Art & Writing:** Letters: k, v, e, w Counting: 1-25 Shapes & Colors S. Words: what/who	**Math, Art & Writing:** Letters: k, v, e, w Counting: 1-25 Shapes & Colors S. Words: what/who	**Math, Art & Writing:** Letters: k, v, e, w Counting: 1-25 Shapes & Colors S. Words: what/who
2:25 – 2:45	**Snack Time**				
2:45 – 2:50	Clean-up/Transition	Clean-up/Transition	Clean-up/Transition	Clean-up/Transition	Clean-up/Transition
2:50 – 3:15	**Music/Creative Expression:** Five Senses Reptiles/Amphibians	**Music/Creative Expression:** Five Senses Reptiles/Amphibians	**Music/Creative Expression:** Five Senses Reptiles/Amphibians	**Music/Creative Expression:** Five Senses Reptiles/Amphibians	**Music/Creative Expression:** Five Senses Reptiles/Amphibians
3:15 – 3:20	Transition Activity				
3:20 – 3:55	**Recess on the Playground or in the Indoor Play/Exercise Area for Inclement Weather**				
3:55 – 4:00	Wash-up & Transition Activity Back to the Classroom				
4:00 – 4:25	**Read-aloud:** Letters: u, c, b, n Five Senses Reptiles/Amphibians	**Read-aloud:** Letters: o, g, l, h Five Senses Reptiles/Amphibians	**Read-aloud:** Letters: o, g, l, h Five Senses Reptiles/Amphibians	**Read-aloud:** Letters: o, g, l, h Five Senses Reptiles/Amphibians	**Read-aloud:** Letters: o, g, l, h Five Senses Reptiles/Amphibians
4:30 – 4:50	Centers				
4:50 – 5:00	Clean-up for the Day				
5:00	Transition to Aftercare				

Week 26 Notes

Topics:
Dental Health
Transportation
Five Senses
Reptiles & Amphibians
Letters: k, v, e, w
Counting: 1-20
Shape: Heart
Colors: Pink, White, & Red
Sight Words: what & who

Season:
Winter

See Appendices for February for songs, stories, crafts, games and activities to support the use of sign language in learning the various topics.

See the 8 Modules of the Curriculum for 8.5 x 11" topical signs and sign handouts. Take advantage of the Table of Contents to find groups of signs and the Index in the back of the book to find specific signs.

Songs, Stories, Crafts, Games & Activities

Outcomes & Indicators

The Child Outcomes and indicators are depicted as follows:

Domain

Domain Element

      Indicators

A. Language Development

A.1 Listening & Understanding

    A.1.a. Sign language naturally demonstrates increased ability to understand and participate in conversations, stories, songs, rhythms, and games

    A.1.b. Sign language assists in the understanding and following of simple and multiple-step directions

    A.1.c. Sign language greatly increases children's receptive vocabulary

    A.1.d. Sign language assists non-English-speaking children in learning to listen to and understand English as well sign language

A.2 Speaking & Communication

    A.2.a. Sign language assists in developing increasing abilities to understand and use sign language and English to communicate information, experiences, ideas, feelings, opinions, needs, and questions for other purposes

    A.2.b. Sign language instruction teaches children the use of an increasingly complex and varied signed and spoken vocabulary

    A.2.c. Sign language assists non-English speaking children in signing and speaking English

B. Literacy

B.1 Phonological Awareness

    As teachers say and sign words together it serves as another way for children to understand and remember both the sign and the spoken word. When taught together sign instruction assists in providing the following benefits.

    B.1.a. Progresses in recognizing matching sounds in familiar words, songs, rhythms, games, stories, and other activities

    B.1.b. Associates sounds with written and signed words

    B.1.c. Children's use of sign language enhances language acquisition

B.1.d. Children's learning of sign language simultaneously with words assist in like word differentiation of emergent readers

B.2 Book Knowledge & Appreciation

B.2.a. Signing is an enjoyable activity for children that greatly enhances vocabulary, which makes learning to read easier and sometimes earlier
B.2.b. Children who are taught sign language demonstrate progress in abilities to retell, using sign words, stories from books and personal experiences
B.2.c. Children who are taught sign language demonstrate progress in abilities to act out stories in dramatic play which is a natural extension of the hand and finger movements learned in sign language

B.3 Print Awareness and Concepts

B.3.a. Children who learn to sign develop a growing understanding of the different functions of forms of print such as signs, letters, and numbers
B.3.b. When written words are presented with the verbal and sign introduction/instruction children better learn to recognize a word as a unit of print

B.4 Early Writing

B.4.a. Begins to represent stories and experiences through signs, pictures, songs, games, and in play

B.5 Alphabet Knowledge

B.5.a. Shows progress in associating the names of letters with their signs, shapes, and sounds
B.5.b. Identifies all the letters of the alphabet, especially those in their own name
B.5.c. Knows that the letters of the alphabet are a special category of visual graphics that can be individually signed and named

C. Mathematics
C.1 Number & Operations

C.1.a. Children are taught the sign language counterparts to the numbers
C.1.b. Children count numbers to assist with the retention of the number they have reached
C.1.c. Signing assists with children's ability to count beyond the number 10

C.1.d. Signing assists with children's learning to make use of one-to-one correspondence in counting objects and matching numbers of groups of objects

C.2 Geometry & Spatial Sense

C.2.a. Signing assists with the recognition and ability to describe common shapes as shape signs accurately represent common shapes such as square, triangle, or circle

C.2.b Signing assists children in developing visual and spatial awareness

D. Science

D.1 Scientific Skills & Methods

D.1.a. Signing assists children in the understanding of scientific principles such as being able to express differences (such as big/little, open/closed, and more/less)

D.1.b. Signing assists in increasing children's awareness

D.1.c. Singing assists in the growing awareness of ideas and language related to time

D.2 Scientific Knowledge

D.2.a. Signing assists in increasing awareness and beginning understanding of changes in material and cause-effect relationships

D.2.b. Signing assists in increasing awareness of ideas and language related to time and temperature

D.2.c. Signing assists in expanding knowledge of and respect for their body and the environment

D.2.d. Signing enhances children's abilities to observe, describe and discuss the natural world, materials, living things, and natural processes

E. Creative Arts

E.1 Music

E.1.a. As children sign to music they develop increased interest and enjoyment in listening, singing, signing, finger plays, games, and performances

E.2 Movement

E.2.a. Children express through sign what is felt and heard in music

E.3 Dramatic Play

E.3.a. Children express themselves dramatically through signing

F. Social & Development

F.1 Self Concept

   F.1.a. Begins to develop and express awareness of self in terms of specific abilities, characteristics and preferences through the use of signing, for example they learn to sign their name and are given a sign name they feel reflects their personality

   F.1.b. Children's successful use of sign language enhances their confidence and self-esteem

F.2 Self Control

   F.2.a. Through the use of sign language children learn to express their feelings, emotions, needs, and opinions in everyday and in difficult situations without harming themselves, others, or property

   F.2.b. Through the use of sign language children demonstrate increased capacity to follows rules and routines, and to use materials purposefully, safely and respectfully

   F.2.c. Children's use of sign language raises communication awareness, enabling them to better tell and understand how their actions and words effect others

   F.2.d. Children's and teacher's use of sign language lowers children's noise levels in the classroom enhancing the learning atmosphere

   F.2.e. Children's use of sign language teaches them to pay better attention, they need to pay attention visually, rather than just listen

   F.2.f. Children's use of sign language increase their use of manners, which can help to eliminate potential misbehavior reactions

   F.2.g Children's use of sign language fosters an atmosphere in which children ask questions before acting, for example asking if their classmate is done with the toy before taking it and angering their classmate

   F.2.h. Classroom usage of sign language engages the teachers to be present with the child, they need to be making regular eye contact and can better see in the faces of children if anything is wrong, the child is unhappy, etc.

F.3 Cooperation

   F.3.a. Children's use of sign language increases their abilities to sustain interactions with peers through the use of manners, enabling them to express their feelings and emotions, by helping, and by sharing

F.3.b. Children's use of sign language increases their abilities to use compromise and discussion in playing and resolving conflicts with classmates

F.3.c. Children's use of sign language increases their abilities to give and take in interactions; to take turns in games or using materials; and to be participatory in activities while not being overly aggressive

F.4 Social Relationships

F.4.a. Children's use of sign language increases their signing and speaking with and accepting guidance and directions from a wide range of familiar adults

F.4.b. Children and teacher's use of sign language in the classroom enables all in the classroom to develop friendships with peers, this is particularly true and key for any special needs members of the class.

F.4.c. Children's use of sign language teaches them to be especially aware when classmates are in need, upset, hurt, or angry; and in expressing empathy for others

F.5 Knowledge of Families & Communities

F.5.a. The Young Children's Signing Program incorporates family signs to assist in children's understanding of family composition

F.5.b. The Young Children's Signing Program incorporates gender signs, boy and girl, to assist in children's understanding of genders

G. Approaches to Learning

G.1 Initiative & Curiosity

G.1.a. Children's use of sign language increases participation in an increasing variety of tasks and activities

G.1.b. Children's use of sign language enhances their use of imagination and inventiveness in participation in tasks and activities

G.2 Engagement & Persistence

G.2.a Children's learning of sign language also assist them as they increase their capacity to maintain concentration over time on a task, question, or set of directions or interactions

G.3 Reasoning & Problem Solving

G.3.a. Children's learning and use of sign language assists in the recognition and problem solving through active exploration, including trial and error, and interactions and discussions with classmates and adults

H. Physical Health & Development

H.1. Fine Motor Skills

H.1 a. Children's learning of sign language develops hand and arm strength and dexterity needed to control such instruments as a hammer, scissors, tape, and a stapler

H.1.b. Children's learning of sign language develops hand-eye coordination required for use of building blocks, putting puzzles together, reproducing shapes and patterns, stringing beads, and using scissors

H.1.c. Children's learning of sign language develops drawing and art tools such as pencils, crayons, markers, chalk, paint brushes, and computers

H.1.d. Children's learning of sign language enables them to be able to pick up small objects

H.2 Gross Motor Skills

H.2.a. Children's learning of sign language coordinates movements in throwing, catching, and bouncing balls

H.3 Health Status & Practices

H.3.a. Children's learning of sign language enhances their ability to communicate health and hygiene problems to adults

H.3.b. Children's learning of sign language enhances their knowledge of health and hygiene

Appendices

December
Songs, Stories, Games & Activities

Holidays

Time to Sign Curriculum: *Signs can be found in the Family, Home, Holidays and Transportation Module; Music Module for all music; and Preschool or School Age Activity Guide for hands on activities. Stories were found in the local public library.*

Holidays - Handouts for holidays go home throughout the year as appropriate

Christmas

Activity: Reindeer Dance

Song: Jingle Bells (no music provided)

Song: We Wish You A Merry Christmas (no music provided)

Hanukkah

Song: Eight Little Candles (to the tune of "Twinkle, Twinkle, Little Star"-no music provided)

Song: I'm A Little Dreidel (use tune to "I'm a Little Teapot")

Kwanzaa

Song: Kwanzaa's Here (to the tune of "Three Blind Mice")

Props: Use Handouts, other propos to purchase Sign Language Holidays and Celebrations book (Garlic Press Co.)

Stories

December by Eve Bunting (homeless, home, family)

Topical signs to be learned: mother, live, house, made, small, Christmas, tree, spoon, star, cookie, candle, fire, coat, dad, December, sing, sleep, listen, move, tomorrow, who, hat, come, in, cold, careful, beautiful, hungry, eat, smile, share, love, merry/happy, dream, change, work.

Indicators: A.1.a, A.1.b, A.1.c, A.1.d, A.2.a, A.2.b, A.2.c, B.1.a, B.1.b, B.1.c, B.1.d, B.2.a, B.2.b, B.2.c, B.3.a, B.3.b, B.4.a, C.2.b, F.1.b, F.2.a, F.2.c, F.2.d, F.2.e, F.2.h, F.5.a, G.1.a, G.1.b, G.2.a, G.3.a, H.1.a, H.1.b.

<u>Five Little Snowmen</u> (Felt Board Fingerplays) by Liz and Dick Wilmes (weather)

Topical signs to be learned: five, little, snowmen, standing, row, each, has, hat, big, red, bow, out, came, sun, shown, all, day, one, melted, away, four, three, two

Indicators: A.1.a, A.1.b, A.1.c, A.1.d, A.2.a, A.2.b, A.2.c, B.1.a, B.1.b, B.1.c, B.1.d, B.2.a, B.2.b, B.3.a, B.3.b, B.4.a, C.1.a, C.1.b, C.1.d, C.2.b, F.1.b, F.2.d, F.2.e, F.2.h, G.1.a, G.1.b, G.2.a, H.1.a, H.1.b

<u>Hanukkah Lights, Hanukkah Nights</u> by Leslie Kimmelman (Hanukkah)

Topical signs to be learned: my, relatives, come, far away, help, celebrate, Hanukkah, family, lights, candle, tonight, first, night, aunt, sing, holiday, blessing, grandmother, sips, chicken, soup, second, third, nieces, spin dreidel, potato, latkes, sixth, kitten, plays, chocolate, money, seventh, cousins, eighth, shinning, happy, fourth, fifth.

Indicators: A.1.a, A.1.b, A.1.c, A.1.d, A.2.a, A.2.b, A.2.c, B.1.a, B.1.b, B.1.c, B.1.d, B.2.a, B.2.b, B.2.c, B.3.a, B.3.b, B.4.a, C.2.b, F.1.b, F.2.d, F.2.e, F.2.h, F.5.a, G.1.a, G.1.b, G.2.a, H.1.a, H.1.b.

<u>Jingle Babies</u> by Tom Arma (Christmas)

Topical signs to be learned: happy, snowman, round, fat, hat, busy, beautiful (pretty), angel, one, reindeer, candy cane, you, cookie, nice, sweet, little, Santa, bag, full, treats, stocking, me, you, surprises, under, tree.

Indicators: A.1.a, A.1.b, A.1.c, A.1.d, A.2.a, A.2.b, A.2.c, B.1.a, B.1.b, B.1.c, B.1.d, B.2.a, B.2.b, B.2.c, B.3.a, B.3.b, B.4.a, C.2.b, F.1.b, F.2.d, F.2.e, F.2.f, F.2.h, G.1.a, G.1.b, G.2.a, H.1.a, H.1.b.

<u>The Mitten</u> by Jan Brett (seasons, weather)

Topical signs to be learned: boy, new, mitten, white, snow, grandmother, find, make, home, safe, see, dropped, mole, inside, warm, rabbit, stop, hedgehog, owl, badger, fox, bear, mouse, sky, sneeze, animals, lost,

Indicators: A.1.a, A.1.b, A.1.c, A.1.d, A.2.a, A.2.b, A.2.c, B.1.a, B.1.b, B.1.c, B.1.d, B.2.a, B.2.b, B.3.a, B.3.b, B.4.a, C.2.b, D.1.b, D.2.b, D.2.c, D.2.d, F.1.b, F.2.d, F.2.e, F.2.h, G.1.a, G.1.b, G.2.a, H.1.a, H.1.b

<u>The Polar Express</u> by Chris Van Allsburg (Christmas, transportation)

Topical signs to be learned: Christmas, bed, listen, bells/ringing, friend, see, train, door, come, where, children, sing, eat, candy, hot, chocolate, drink, town, light, journey/travel, forest, mountain, snow, ice, big/huge, toy, made, look, sled, cheer, like, silver, smile, hug, first, shout, lost, house, sad, good-bye, merry/happy, small, box, name.

Indicators: A.1.a, A.1.b, A.1.c, A.1.d, A.2.a, A.2.b, A.2.c, B.1.a, B.1.b, B.1.c, B.1.d, B.2.a, B.2.b, B.2.c, B.3.a, B.3.b, B.4.a, C.2.b, F.1.b, F.2.d, F.2.e, F.2.h, G.1.a, G.1.b, G.2.a, H.1.a, H.1.b.

Ten Days of Christmas (Wee Sign Board Book) by Pamela Conn (Christmas)

Topical signs to be learned: Holiday signs

Indicators: A.1.a, A.1.b, A.1.c, A.1.d, A.2.a, A.2.b, A.2.c, B.1.a, B.1.b, B.1.c, B.1.d, B.2.a, B.2.b, B.2.c, B.3.a, B.3.b, B.4.a, C.1.a, C.1.b, C.1.d, C.2.b, F.1.b, F.2.d, F.2.e, F.2.h, G.1.a, G.1.b, G.2.a, H.1.a, H.1.b.

Songs

Eight Little Candles (holidays)

Indicators: A.1.a, A.1.b, A.1.c, A.1.d, A.2.a, A.2.b, A.2.c, B.1.a, B.1.c, B.1.d, B.2.a, B.2.b, B.3.a, B.4.a, C.1.a, C.1.b, C.1.d, C.2.b, E.1.a, E.2.a, F.1.b, F.2.e, F.2.h, F.3.c, G.1.a, G.1.b, H.1.a, H.1.b, H.1.d

I'm a Little Dreidel (holidays)

Indicators: A.1.a, A.1.b, A.1.c, A.1.d, A.2.a, A.2.b, A.2.c, B.1.a, B.1.c, B.1.d, B.2.a, B.2.b, B.3.a, B.4.a, C.2.b, E.1.a, E.2.a, F.1.b, F.2.e, F.2.h, F.3.c, G.1.a, G.1.b, H.1.a, H.1.b, H.1.d

Jingle Bells (holidays)

Indicators: A.1.a, A.1.b, A.1.c, A.1.d, A.2.a, A.2.b, A.2.c, B.1.a, B.1.c, B.1.d, B.2.a, B.2.b, B.3.a, B.4.a, C.2.b, E.1.a, E.2.a, F.1.b, F.2.e, F.2.h, F.3.c, G.1.a, G.1.b, H.1.a, H.1.b, H.1.d

Kwanzaa's Here (holidays)

Indicators: A.1.a, A.1.b, A.1.c, A.1.d, A.2.a, A.2.b, A.2.c, B.1.a, B.1.c, B.1.d, B.2.a, B.2.b, B.3.a, B.4.a, C.2.b, E.1.a, E.2.a, F.1.b, F.2.e, F.2.h, F.3.c, G.1.a, G.1.b, H.1.a, H.1.b, H.1.d

Over the River and Through the Woods (family, holidays)

Indicators: A.1.a, A.1.b, A.1.c, A.1.d, A.2.a, A.2.b, A.2.c, B.1.a, B.1.c, B.1.d, B.2.a, B.2.b, B.3.a, B.4.a, C.2.b, E.1.a, E.2.a, F.1.b, F.2.e, F.2.h, F.3.c, G.1.a, G.1.b, H.1.a, H.1.b, H.1.d

We Wish You a Merry Christmas (holidays)

Indicators: A.1.a, A.1.b, A.1.c, A.1.d, A.2.a, A.2.b, A.2.c, B.1.a, B.1.c, B.1.d, B.2.a, B.2.b, B.3.a, B.4.a, C.2.b, E.1.a, E.2.a, F.1.b, F.2.e, F.2.h, F.3.c, G.1.a, G.1.b, H.1.a, H.1.b, H.1.d

Games & Activities

Detective Snow (weather)

Materials: white paper, scissors, felt pen, small classroom items, small box, cotton batting.

Cut white paper in half. Make a half sheet for each child. On each sheet draw a picture or glue a picture of a small object in the classroom, such as a block, a small toy, a box of crayons, a pot in the kitchen area, a small stuffed animal, etc. Fold each sheet in half twice. Place them in a small box.

Explain that each child will become Detective Snow! Walk slowly around the classroom. Notice the many things in the classroom, where the objects are located and their size. Talk about what you are seeing. Now have the children close their eyes. The teacher places cotton batting (snow) over objects in the classroom that are pictured on the folded papers. The children open their eyes. Objects have changed shape! Do they look different? Choose a child to be Detective Snow. The child chooses a paper square from the box and identifies the picture. Detective Snow tries to remember where he or she saw the object. They search the classroom and uncover the object. The teacher replaces the snow (cotton batting) over the object. Now choose another child to be Detective Snow!

Topical signs to be learned: snow, see, find, cover.

Indicators: A.1.a, A.1.b, A.1.c, A.1.d, A.2.a, A.2.b, A.2.c, B.1.c, B.2.a, B.2.b, B.2.c, C.2.b, D.1.a, D.1.b, D.2.a, D.2.c, D.2.d, F.1.b, F.2.e, F.2.h, F.3.c, F.4.a, G.1.a, G.1.b, G.2.a, G.3.a, H.1.a, H.1.b, H.1.d, H.2.a

Hot Chocolate to Go (winter, foods)

Pour powdered milk and chocolate drink mix into a large bowl or bag and mix well. Pour into large plastic bag and seal it. Fill a cup ¾ full with hot water. Add 2 heaping tablespoons of chocolate mix and stir.

Topical signs to be learned: banana, knife, bake, raisins, dried fruit, nut, pretzel, seeds, milk, chocolate, hot, cup, spoon, bowl.

Indicators: A.1.c, A.1.d, A.2.a, A.2.b, A.2.c, B.1.c, B.2.a, C.2.b, F.1.b, F.2.b, F.2.d, F.2.e, F.2.h, F.3.c, F.4.a., G.1.a, G.2.a, H.1.a, H.1.b, H.1.c, H.1.d.

Dreidel (Hanukkah)

Materials: dreidels, tokens-rains, nuts, toothpicks, pennies, etc.; bowl (pot).

To play Dreidel, each player puts one token into the pot. One player spins the dreidel. If the dreidel lands on "N," the player receives nothing. If it lands on "G," the player receives all the tokens in the pot. If it lands on "H," the player gets half. If it lands on "S," the player adds two tokens to the pot. The game continues until one player has won all the tokens.

Topical signs to be learned: dreidel (top), bowl, game, play, N, G, H, S, all, half, nothing, two.

Indicators: A.1.a, A.1.b, A.1.c, A.1.d, A.2.a, A.2.b, A.2.c, B.1.c, B.2.a, B.2.b, B.2.c, C.2.b, F.1.b, F.2.b, F.2.c, F.2.e, F.2.h, F.3.a, F.3.c, F.4.a, G.1.a, G.1.b, G.2.a, H.1.a, H.1.b, H.1.c, H.1.d.

Greeting Card Puzzles (holidays)

Materials: old greeting cards, scissors, small plastic bags.

Cut the fronts of old greeting cards into puzzle pieces or have children cut them into puzzle pieces. Place the pieces to each card in separate plastic bags. Children put puzzles together. You can make one for each child to bring home to use.

Topical signs to be used: puzzle, scissors.

Indicators: A.1.a, A.1.b, A.1.c, A.1.d, A.2.a, A.2.b, A.2.c, B.1.c, B.2.a, B.2.b, B.2.c, C.2.b, F.1.b, F.2.b, F.2.c, F.2.e, F.2.h, F.3.a, F.3.c, F.4.a, G.1.a, G.1.b, G.2.a, H.1.c, H.1.d

Holiday Bingo (holidays)

Have the children create their own bingo boards by choosing where to place different holiday items and glue them into place. Teach them the signs for the different items on their bingo cards. They can also color, cut and paste them onto the bingo card depending on age/ability. December Seasonal items include: dreidel, menorah, stocking, snow flake, snow man, wreath, ornaments, angel, Kwanzaa cloth, basket, muhindi, candle, reindeer, sleigh, etc. This game can be altered by choosing different items for different holidays.

Topical signs to be learned: holiday signs, holiday items signs.

Indicators: A.1.a, A.1.b, A.1.c, A.1.d, A.2.a, A.2.b, A.2.c, B.1.c, B.2.a, B.2.b, B.2.c, C.2.b, F.1.b, F.2.b, F.2.c, F.2.e, F.2.h, F.3.a, F.3.c, F.4.a, F.5.a, G.1.a, G.1.b, G.2.a, G.3.a, H.1.c, H.1.d

Five Little Snowmen Fingerplay

Materials: 5 white felt snowmen, 5 red felt bows, 5 black felt hats, and 1 yellow felt sun.

Teach children this poem about snowmen, signing the key words as you go. Make the appropriate felt pieces and place them on the board as you read.

Five Little Snowman Fingerplay

Five little Snowman standing in a row,
Each had a hat and a big red bow.

Out came the sun and it shone all day,
One Little snowman melted away.

Four Little Snowman standing in a row,
Each had a hat and a big red bow.
Out Came the sun and it shone all day,
One Little snowman melted away.
Etc....

Topical signs to be learned: numbers 1-5, snow, man, little, each, hat, red, out, sun, day.

Indicators: A.1.c, A.1.d, A.2.a, A.2.b, A.2.c, B.1.a, B.1.c, B.1.d, B.2.a, B.4.a, C.1.a, C.1.b, C.1.d, C.2.b, D.1.b, D.2.a, D.2.b, D.2.c, E.1.a, F.1.b, F.2.e, F.2.h, F.3.c, F.4.a, G.1.a, G.2.a, H.1.a, H.1.b.

Floating Icebergs (science & nature)

Materials: food coloring, various shaped bowls and containers, wading or swimming pool, large freezer.

Fill the containers with water. Add food coloring. Place in the freezer and allow to freeze completely. Take the frozen container out, remove the ice, and place the icebergs in the pool. Notice how much of the ice is under water. Have the children place their hands near the iceberg and move them away. How far does the cold water extend from the ice? Watch the shape of the iceberg as it melts. Does the shape change? How long does the iceberg take to melt? Does the color and size make a difference?

Freeze objects inside your iceberg to see how long it takes for them to melt free. Do other liquids float when frozen? Try indoors in water table with toy boats.

Topical signs to be learned: ice, freeze, water, melt (fade) food, color, under, cold, shape, change, size.

Indicators: A.1.a, A.1.b, A.1.c, A.1.d, A.2.a, A.2.b, A.2.c, B.1.c, B.2.a, C.2.b, D.1.a, D.1.b, D.2.a, D.2.b, D.2.c, D.2.d, F.1.b, F.2.e, F.2.h, F.3.c, F.4.a, G.1.a, G.1.b, H.1.a, H.1.b, H.1.d.

Ice Melting Contest (science)

Materials: block of ice for each team.

Divide the group into equal teams and give each team a block of ice. At a signal, each team tries to melt the ice without scraping or breaking it. Usual methods are rubbing it, blowing on it, putting it in the sun, etc. After a certain amount of time (this depends on the original size of the block), the team with the smallest block wins. A bathroom scale comes in handy to determine this.

Topical signs to be learned: ice, melt (dissolve), time, team, blow, sun, weigh.

Indicators: A.1.a, A.1.b, A.1.c, A.1.d, A.2.a, A.2.b, A.2.c, B.1.c, B.2.a, B.2.b, B.2.c, C.2.b, D.1.a, D.1.b, D.1.c, D.2.a, D.2.b, D.2.c, D.2.d, F.1.b, F.2.d, F.2.e, F.2.g, F.2.h, , F.3.a, F.3.c, F.4.a, G.1.a, G.1.b, G.2.a, G.3.a, H.1.a, H.1.b, H.1.d.

Icy Icicles (weather)

Materials: large plastic soda bottles, food coloring, instrument with a sharp point, string.

Take the children outside to a place where they can examine icicles without the danger of being hit by a falling icicle. Encourage them to look for several areas where icicles can be found. Back in the classroom have the children discuss their discoveries with the whole group. List the locations and any other information on the chalkboard or chart paper. Divide children into groups to make icicles (optional). Give each group or child a soda bottle. Have them fill the bottles with water and a small amount of food coloring. Using an instrument with a sharp point, make a very small hole in the side of each bottle near the bottom. Hang the bottles outside in trees or other areas. As the water drips slowly from the bottles it will freeze to form icicles. Take the children outside periodically to observe their icicles. Have them compare the size of their icicles to other objects

Topical signs to be learned: ice/free, water, cold, find, talk, group, color signs, outside, slow, look at, compare, size signs, like/same.

Indicators: A.1.a, A.1.b, A.1.c, A.1.d, A.2.a, A.2.b, A.2.c, B.1.c, B.2.a, B.2.b, B.2.c, B.2.d, C.2.b, D.1.a, D.1.b, D.2.a, D.2.b, D.2.c, F.1.b, F.2.b, F.2.d, F.2.e, F.2.g, F.2.h, F.3.a, F.3.c, G.1.a, G.1.b, G.2.a, G.3.a, H.1.a, H.1.b, H.1.d.

It's Snowing (weather)

Materials: different sizes of white paper, markers, scissors.

Draw long skinny triangles on a sheet of white paper. These are icicles! Make an icicle sheet for each child. Fold small sheets of white paper in half and in half again. Make at least two folded sheets for each child.

Demonstrate how to make snowflakes! Cut out designs on the folded edge of a folded piece of paper. Round off the corners and also make cuts on this side. Open the paper and you have a snowflake! (The older children can make more folds to make more intricate designs.) A snowflake is a tiny drop of snow. Each snowflake has a beautiful and unique design!

Show an icicle sheet. Explain that icicles form in cold weather. Water drips from an object such as a tree branch. The water drop freezes and forms an icicle! Place the folded papers and icicle sheets on the table. The children cut out snowflake designs and a sheet of icicles! Print the children's names on the backs of their snowflakes and icicles.

Topical signs to be learned: snow, water, weather, cold, winter, freeze, paper, scissors.

Indicators: A.1.a, A.1.b, A.1.c, A.1.d, A.2.a, A.2.b, A.2.c, B.1.c, B.2.a, C.2.b, D.1.a, D.1.b, D.2.a,D.2.b, D.2.c, D.2.d, F.1.b, F.2.b, F.2.d, F.2.e, F.2.h, F.4.a., F.3.a, F.3.c, G.1.a, G.1.b, G.2.a, G.3.a, H.1.a, H.1.b, H.1.d.

Magnifying Snowflakes (weather)

Materials: magnifying glass, black velvet, pie pan.

Keep a piece of black velvet in the refrigerator. When there is a fresh snowfall take out the piece of black velvet and place it on top of a pie pan and run outdoors with it. Catch a few small snowflakes. Then get your magnifying or reading glass and really LOOK at a snowflake up close! Count the sides. Can you find any two that are the same?

Topical signs to be learned: snow, outside, catch, look, count, same.

Indicators: A.1.a, A.1.b, A.1.c, A.1.d, A.2.a, A.2.b, A.2.c, B.1.c, B.2.a, C.2.b, D.1.a, D.1.b, D.2.a, D.2.b, D.2.c, D.2.d, F.1.b, F.2.b, F.2.e, F.2.h, F.3.a, F.3.c, F.4.a, G.1.a, G.1.b, G.2.a, G.3.a, H.1.a, H.1.b, H.1.d.

Snow Walks (nature, weather)

Have the children pretend look out the window, and see snow falling softly to the ground. Ask them to create movements to show how they would move: How do you walk with boots and heavy coats on? How would you drive a car? How would you move on skates? How would you move on a sled quickly going down a hill? How would you move on a snowplow?

Topical signs to be learned: pretend, look, snow, move, how, walk, boots, coat, car, sled.

Indicators: A.1.a, A.1.b, A.1.c, A.1.d, A.2.a, A.2.b, A.2.c, B.1.c, B.2.a, B.2.b, B.2.c, C.2.b, D.1.a, D.1.b, D.2.a, D.2.c, E.2.a, .1.b, F.2.b, F.2.e, F.2.h, F.3.a, F.3.b, F.3.c, F.4.b, G.1.a, G.1.b, G.2.a, G.3.a, H.1.a, H.1.b, H.1.d, H.2.a.

Snowman, Snowman (weather, seasons)

Materials: 2 white felt snowman, 1 set of blue felt mittens, 1 green felt hat, 1 pair of red felt boots, 1 yellow felt scarf, and 1 orange felt carrot nose.

Based on the book "Brown Bear, Brown Bear, What Do You See?" White Snowman, White Snowman, What do you see? I see blue mittens (green hat, red boots, yellow scarf, orange carrot nose, another snowman) looking at me. Cut out felt pieces in the appropriate colors to place on the fleet board as you go through the story.

Topical signs to be learned: color signs, snow, man, what, see, look at, clothing signs, carrot.

Indicators: A.1.c, A.1.d, A.2.a, A.2.b, A.2.c, B.1.a, B.1.c, B.1.d, B.2.a, B.2.b, C.2.b, E.1.a, F.1.b, F.2.e, F.2.h, F.3.c, G.1.a, G.1.b, H.1.a, H.1.b, H.1.d.

Snowy Ideas (weather)

Materials: blue and white or silver balloons, music.

Inflate the balloons. Divide the children into two groups and have them take off their shoes. One group is the rain drops and gets blue balloons. The other group are ice crystals and get white or silver balloons. The children are going to act out the formation of snow. Tell them they are rain drops and ice crystals in a cloud, where snow falls from. Play music. The children dance around the room with their balloons. Stop the music. Have each rain drop find an ice crystal. Say and sign "It's snowing!" Now the pairs of children slowly fall to the ground. Each pair has turned into a snowflake. (When a water droplet and ice crystal attach and fall from a cloud, it turns to snow.) Play music again. Exchange the balloons. The water drops are now ice crystals and the ice crystals are water drops. Continue to become snowflakes.

Topical signs to be learned: water, ice, snow, cloud, dance, music, stop, become.

Indicators: A.1.a, A.1.b, A.1.c, A.1.d, A.2.a, A.2.b, A.2.c, B.1.c, B.2.a, B.2.b, B.2.c, C.2.b, D.1.a, D.1.b, D.2.a, D.2.c, E.1.a, E.2.a, F.1.b, F.2.b, F.2.e, F.2.h, F.3.a, F.3.b, F.4.a, F.4.b, F.3.c, G.1.a, G.1.b, H.1.a, H.1.b, H.1.d, H.2.a.

Where's Santa?" (holidays)

Materials: stuffed Santa or felt Santa, flannel board, felt pieces depicting classroom items and holiday items.

Using a stuffed Santa, hide Santa in various places around the room. Sign to the class "Where's Santa?" Have children look and find Santa. Can also be done using flannel board patterns, "hide" Santa in various places. Sign "Where's Santa?" and have children sign where he is.

Topical signs to be learned: Santa (show the outline of a beard from the chin with the claw hand), where, look for, find.

Indicators: A.1.a, A.1.b, A.1.c, A.1.d, A.2.a, A.2.b, A.2.c, B.1.c, B.2.a, B.2.b, B.2.c, B.3.a, C.1.a, C.1.b, C.1.d., C.2.b, F.1.b, F.2.b, F.2.c, F.2.d, F.2.e, F.2.h, F.3.a, F.3.c, F.4.a, G.1.a, G.1.b, G.2.a, G.3.a, H.1.b, H.1.d, H.2.a.

Crafts

Angel Pattern (holidays)

Materials: Copy paper, construction paper, scissors (if old enough), glue sticks, paper cut outs and crayons.

Have the children color and decorate an angel (older children may cut out themselves).

Topical signs to be learned: angel, white, wings, dress.

Indicators: A.1.b, A.1.c, A.1.d, A.2.a, A.2.b, A.2.c, B.1.c, C.2.b, F.1.b, F.2.b, F.2.c, F.2.d, F.2.e, F.2.h, F.3.c, G.1.a, G.1.b, G.2.a, H.1.a, H.1.b, H.1.c, H.1.d.

Birds-in-the-Snow (animals, foods)

Materials: celery, sharp knife, cream cheese, raisins, sesame or sunflower seeds.

Cut celery into short lengths and fill them with cream cheese "snow." Have the children place raisins on top of the cheese to represent birds. Then let them sprinkle on sesame or sunflower seeds for birdseed.

Topical signs to be learned: snow, birds, in, raisins, seeds, sun, flower.

Indicators: A.1.b, A.1.c, A.1.d, A.2.a, A.2.b, A.2.c, B.1.c, B.2.a, C.2.b, F.1.b, F.2.b, F.2.d, F.2.e, F.2.h, F.3.c, F.4.a., G.1.a, G.1.b, G.2.a, H.1.a, H.1.b, H.1.c, H.1.d.

Candles (holidays)

Materials: Copy paper, construction paper, scissors (if old enough), glue sticks, paper cut outs and crayons.

Have the children color and decorate a candle (older children may make the cut outs themselves). The cut out decorations should include a flame and a base.

Topical signs to be learned: candle, light, hot.

Indicators: A.1.b, A.1.c, A.1.d, A.2.a, A.2.b, A.2.c, B.1.c, C.2.b, F.1.b, F.2.b, F.2.c, F.2.d, F.2.e, F.2.h, F.3.c, G.1.a, G.1.b, G.2.a, H.1.a, H.1.b, H.1.c, H.1.d.

Candles II (holidays)

Materials: pre-cut candlesticks, oaktag squares, fingerpaint (red, yellow and orange) and smocks.

Have children finger paint flames to attach to pre-cut candlesticks.

Topical signs to be learned: candle, light, hot, paint, red, yellow, orange.

Indicators: A.1.b, A.1.c, A.1.d, A.2.a, A.2.b, A.2.c, B.1.c, C.2.b, F.1.b, F.2.b, F.2.c, F.2.d, F.2.e, F.2.h, F.3.c, G.1.a, G.1.b, G.2.a, H.1.a, H.1.b, H.1.c, H.1.d.

Christmas Tree Lights (holidays)

Materials: green construction paper, scissors, glue, red/yellow/blue tempera paint, cotton swabs.

Cut out Christmas tree shapes from the paper. Mix a few tablespoons of glue with each paint color. Have the children dip the cotton swabs in the colored glue and make dots on the trees.

Topical signs to be learned: Christmas, tree, light, red, yellow, blue, paint, glue.

Indicators: A.1.b, A.1.c, A.1.d, A.2.a, A.2.b, A.2.c, B.1.c, C.2.b, F.1.b, F.2.b, F.2.c, F.2.d, F.2.e, F.2.h, F.3.c, G.1.a, G.1.b, G.2.a, H.1.a, H.1.b, H.1.c, H.1.d.

Colorful Clay Ornaments (holidays)

Materials: ¾ cup flour, ½ cup cornmeal, ½ cup salt, hot water, food coloring, waxed paper, small plastic sandwich bags, large bowl, measuring cups, wooden spoon, newspaper, rolling pin or large can, cookie cutters, paper clips, poster paint, brushes, white glue, glitter, sequins, clear acrylic paint, ornament hooks, string or leather thong.

In a large bowl, mix together the flour, cornmeal, and salt. With a wooden spoon, stir in ¼ cup of hot tap water. Continue adding water a little at a time until the mixture looks like stiff cookie dough. Do not add too much water—dry clay works better than wet. Divide the clay into two or three batches and put each batch on a piece of waxed paper. Make a hole in the center of each batch and add a few drops of food coloring. Roll the clay and knead it to spread the food coloring evenly. Wear small plastic sandwich bags on your hands while you knead the clay to keep the food coloring from staining your hands.

Cover your work area with newspaper. Sandwich each batch of clay between two pieces of waxed paper. Using a rolling pin or a large can, roll the clay out between the waxed paper until it is ¼ to ½ inch thick. Remove the top piece of waxed paper and cut out shapes with cookie cutters. If you are making ornaments for your room, use cookie cutters of action figures and toys. For Christmas ornaments, use cookie cutters in holiday shapes. Push a partially opened paper clip gently into the top of each shape for a hanging loop. Let the clay shapes dry for 1 to 2 hours, or until they are dry to the touch. Decorate them with poster paint, or glue glitter, sequins, or other decorations onto them. Let the ornaments dry completely (it might take about 2 days), then protect them with a coat of clear acrylic paint. To hang an ornament on the Christmas tree, slip an ornament hook through the paper clip hanging loop. To hang an ornament in your room, thread a piece of string or a narrow leather thong through the top of the paper clip hanging loop.

Topical signs to be learned: salt, hot, water, corn, food coloring, bowl, measure, cup, spoon, paint, glue, string, add, roll, dry.

Indicators: A.1.b, A.1.c, A.1.d, A.2.a, A.2.b, A.2.c, B.1.c, C.2.b, F.1.b, F.2.b, F.2.c, F.2.d, F.2.e, F.2.h, F.3.c, G.1.a, G.1.b, G.2.a, H.1.a, H.1.b, H.1.c, H.1.d.

Cornstarch Clay Ornaments (holidays)

Materials: 3 cups cornstarch, 6 cups baking soda, large pan, 3 ¾ cup water, mixing spoon, dish towel, waxed paper, masking tape, rolling pin or large can, cookie cutters, knife, knitting needle or unsharpened pencil, drying rack, acrylic paint, paint brushes, colored permanent marker, spray shellac or clear acrylic sealer, ribbon or gold cord, glue, photo of child or colored pencil drawing of a Christmas scene.

Combine the cornstarch and baking soda in a large pan. Add the water. Place over low heat. Stir all the while until mixture has the consistency of mashed potatoes. Remove from heat and cover with a moistened dish towel. When the pan is cool enough to handle, remove the clay and knead it until smooth. Cover the working area with waxed paper held down by masking tape. Roll out the clay to ¼" thickness. Cut out shapes using small cookie cutters. Cut out a 1 ½" x 1 ¼" area in the center of each ornament with a knife. Make a centered hole through the top of the ornament using the point of a big knitting needle or an unsharpened pencil. Place the ornaments on a rack to dry overnight. Use acrylic paint thinned with water to paint the ornaments. Allow to dry. Use a bright colored permanent marking pen to print the date or year on the ornament. Give each dried ornament a final coat of spray shellac or clear acrylic sealer. When dry, the ornament is threaded with a short length of ribbon or gold cord through the top hole. Knot the ends of the cord to form a loop. Finally glue a tiny photo of the child or a picture they drew to the back of the ornament (so that it shows through the hole in the center of the ornament).

Topical signs to be learned: bowl, spoon, Christmas, decorate, tree, dry, paint, ribbon, glue, picture, draw.

Indicators: A.1.b, A.1.c, A.1.d, A.2.a, A.2.b, A.2.c, B.1.c, C.2.b, F.1.b, F.2.b, F.2.c, F.2.d, F.2.e, F.2.h, F.3.c, G.1.a, G.1.b, G.2.a, H.1.a, H.1.b, H.1.c, H.1.d.

Gingerbread Boy (foods)

Materials: Copy paper, construction paper, scissors, glue sticks, paper cut outs and crayons. Or Cookie dough, gingerbread man cookie cutter, icing, sprinkles, and gumdrops.

Have the children decorate a brown paper cut out of a gingerbread boy. Decorations include: cut out eyes, nose, buttons, etc. Children may use patterns or draw and cut out themselves. Or Make gingerbread cookies with icing, sprinkles, and gumdrops for decorations.

Topical signs to be learned: cookie, brown, boy, paper, decorate, eyes, nose, scissors, glue.

Indicators: A.1.b, A.1.c, A.1.d, A.2.a, A.2.b, A.2.c, B.1.c, B.2.a, C.2.b, F.1.b, F.2.b, F.2.d, F.2.e, F.2.h, F.3.c, F.4.a., G.1.a, G.1.b, G.2.a, H.1.b, H.1.c, H.1.d.

Gingerbread Boy or Girl (holidays)

Materials: Copy paper, construction paper, scissors (if old enough), glue sticks, paper cut outs and crayons.

Or

Cookie dough, gingerbread man/woman cookie cutter, icing, sprinkles, and gumdrops.

Have the children decorate a brown paper cut out of a gingerbread boy or girl. Decorations include: cut out eyes, nose, buttons, etc. (older children may cut these out from patterns).

Or

Make gingerbread cookies with icing, sprinkles, and gumdrops for decorations.

Topical signs to be learned: cookie, brown, boy.

Indicators: A.1.b, A.1.c, A.1.d, A.2.a, A.2.b, A.2.c, B.1.c, C.2.b, F.1.b, F.2.b, F.2.c, F.2.d, F.2.e, F.2.h, F.3.c, F.5.b, G.1.a, G.1.b, G.2.a, H.1.a, H.1.b, H.1.c, H.1.d.

Easy Gingerbread Houses (foods, home)

Materials: 6 double graham crackers, small serrated knife, base such as metal tray, pizza circle, or plastic platter, props such as bottles of blue or containers of paint, decorating materials such as small pretzels, vanilla wafers, pretzel rods, animal crackers, licorice whip, tinted coconut, granola, colored sugars, marshmallows, gum drops, cookies, assorted candy.

Two of the double graham crackers will be front and back walls; two will be the sides; two will be the roof. To make peaks at the tops of the walls, cut with the knife using a "sawing" motion. Spread the bottom edge of the front wall with royal icing and attach to the base. Prop with bottles of blue until the icing sets. Spread royal icing on the sides and bottom of a side wall (one long edge, two short edges). Attach the side all to the front wall and to the base. Prop with bottles of glue until icing sets. Spread the side and bottom edges of the back wall with royal icing and attach to the base and the standing side. Prop with bottles of blue until icing sets. Spread the other side wall with graham cracker with royal icing on the two side and bottom edges. Attach to the base, front wall, and back wall. Prop with bottles of blue until icing sets. Allow to set and remove and props. The last two double crackers will form the roof. Join the two crackers' long sides together with royal icing. Apply royal icing to the top edges of the front and back walls. Place the roof crackers on the wall crackers with the roof crackers forming a peak. Let set. Decorate and display.

Royal Icing

Materials: mixing bowl, electric mixer, 7 tablespoons of water, 4 tablespoons meringue powder, 7 cups powdered sugar, ½ teaspoon cream of tartar; OR 3 egg whites, 1 pound powdered sugar, ½ teaspoon cream of tartar.

Beat together water and meringue powder or egg whites. Sift together powdered sugar and cream of tartar. Place all ingredients into a mixing bowl. Beat 7 to 10 minutes or until icing holds a strong peak. It is almost impossible to specify the exact amount of sugar that your recipe needs as it depends on the size of the egg whites as well as the moisture content of your powdered sugar. Keep frosting covered with a damp cloth at all times to keep it from drying out. (When working with egg white be sure that all utensils are grease free.)

Topical signs to be learned: house, cracker, pretzel, animal, candy, cookie, wall, roof, decorate, egg, water.

Indicators: A.1.b, A.1.c, A.1.d, A.2.a, A.2.b, A.2.c, B.1.c, B.2.a, C.2.b, F.1.b, F.2.b, F.2.d, F.2.e, F.2.h, F.3.c, F.4.a., G.1.a, G.1.b, G.2.a, H.1.a, H.1.b, H.1.c, H.1.d.

Holiday Stocking (holidays)

Materials: Copy paper, construction paper, scissors (if old enough), glue sticks, paper cut outs and crayons.

Have the children color and decorate a stocking. The decorations are cut outs of holiday shapes such as a ball, reindeer, menorah, candle, etc. (older children may make the cut outs themselves).

Topical signs to be learned: stocking (sock), box, white, red.

Indicators: A.1.b, A.1.c, A.1.d, A.2.a, A.2.b, A.2.c, B.1.c, C.2.b, F.1.b, F.2.b, F.2.c, F.2.d, F.2.e, F.2.h, F.3.c, G.1.a, G.1.b, G.2.a, H.1.a, H.1.b, H.1.c, H.1.d.

Latkes/Potato Pancakes (Hanukkah)

Materials: grater, measuring spoons, mixing bowl, mixing spoon, 1 grated onion, 1 tsp. salt, 1 egg, 6 medium potatoes (washed, pared and grated), 3 T. flour, ½ tsp. baking powder, cooking oil, electric frying pan, paper towels, applesauce, sour cream, spoons and bowls.

Mix the onion, salt, and egg with the potatoes. Add flour and baking powder. Drop by spoonful into the hot oiled frying pan (be sure children are not close). Brown on both sides. Drain on paper towels. Serve with applesauce or sour cream.

Topical signs to be learned: potato, cook (also: pancake), bowl, spoon, measure, egg, Hanukkah, eat, hot.

Indicators: A.1.b, A.1.c, A.1.d, A.2.a, A.2.b, A.2.c, B.1.c, C.2.b, F.1.b, F.2.b, F.2.c, F.2.d, F.2.e, F.2.h, F.3.c, G.1.a, G.1.b, G.2.a, H.1.a, H.1.b, H.1.c, H.1.d.

Miniature Christmas Trees (holidays)

Materials: large pine cone, aluminum foil, jar lid slightly larger than the base of the pine cone, glue, paint, tinsel, sequins, glitter.

Cover the lid of a jar with aluminum foil. Glue the base of the pine cone to the top of the foil-covered lid. Use paint, glitter, sequins, or tinsel to decorate the tree.

Topical signs to be learned: Christmas, tree, decorate, glue.

Indicators: A.1.b, A.1.c, A.1.d, A.2.a, A.2.b, A.2.c, B.1.c, C.2.b, F.1.b, F.2.b, F.2.c, F.2.d, F.2.e, F.2.h, F.3.c, G.1.a, G.1.b, G.2.a, H.1.a, H.1.b, H.1.c, H.1.d.

No-Sew Stockings (holidays)

Materials: felt, scissors, fake fur scraps, glue, pinking shears, rubber cement or hot glue gun, glitter or glitter pens (optional), ribbon or yarn (optional).

Using scrap felt pieces, cut out and glue together the pieces to make little felt Christmas pictures (such as a little Santa Claus face, a wreath, a candle, a star, a toy, a Christmas tree, a bell etc.) Using pinking shears to cut from red, green, or white felt two large identical stocking shapes for each stocking. Apply a 1-inch wide strip of rubber cement along the inside of each stocking—NOT including the top edges. Let the cement dry and then, making certain that edges match, press stockings together firmly! Place the stockings flat under heavy weights (books) for one night. OR use a hot glue gun to glue the pieces together (Have an adult do this to prevent children from burning their fingers or hands). Glue a small loop of ribbon or yarn to one corner of the stocking if you wish to hang the stocking. Use white glue to adhere the felt decorations. Add (2-3") fake fur trim to the top of the stocking. Children can print their name or add other decorations to their stockings in white glue sprinkled with glitter or glitter pens.

You can give small presents or candy to the children to put in their stockings. Or the children can make the stockings as gifts for others.

Topical signs to be learned: Christmas, stocking (sock), scissors, glue, decorate, candle, star, tree, bell, red, green, white, name.

Indicators: A.1.b, A.1.c, A.1.d, A.2.a, A.2.b, A.2.c, B.1.c, C.2.b, F.1.b, F.2.b, F.2.c, F.2.d, F.2.e, F.2.h, F.3.c, G.1.a, G.1.b, G.2.a, H.1.a, H.1.b, H.1.c, H.1.d.

Paper Plate Wreath (holidays)

Materials: Paper, scissors (if old enough), glue sticks, paper cut outs and crayons.

Have the children decorate a paper plate with the center cut out (older children may cut out the center). Have ornaments, pine cones, bows and pictures they can color and attach. OR trace children's hands and cut out in various shades of green and glue together or glue to paper plate.

Topical signs to be learned: paper, plate, circle, scissors, glue, crayons, ribbon.

Indicators: A.1.b, A.1.c, A.1.d, A.2.a, A.2.b, A.2.c, B.1.c, C.2.b, F.1.b, F.2.b, F.2.c, F.2.d, F.2.e, F.2.h, F.3.c, G.1.a, G.1.b, G.2.a, H.1.a, H.1.b, H.1.c, H.1.d.

Santa Puppet (holidays)

Materials: Copy paper, construction paper, paper bag, scissors (if old enough), glue sticks, paper cut outs and crayons.

Have the children color a 2-part Santa cut out and glue it to a paper bag.
Or

Have the children put together various different shapes and color them. The hat, face, and beard for the top of the bag. The coat, belt, pants, and shoes for the bottom of the bag.

Topical signs to be learned: bag, paper, red, white, black, glue, scissors, crayon, paper.

Indicators: A.1.b, A.1.c, A.1.d, A.2.a, A.2.b, A.2.c, B.1.c, C.2.b, F.1.b, F.2.b, F.2.c, F.2.d, F.2.e, F.2.h, F.3.c, G.1.a, G.1.b, G.2.a, H.1.a, H.1.b, H.1.c, H.1.d.

Snack Food Containers (holidays)

Materials: coffee cans or other containers with plastic lids, construction paper, crayons, markers or paint; scissors, tape or glue, snack foods (granola, popcorn, snack mixes, cookies, etc.)

Cut construction paper to fit around the sides of the containers. Have the children decorate their papers with crayons, markers, or paints. Then tape or glue the papers around the sides of the containers. If desired, let children will their containers with a snack (can be something purchased or homemade). Snack food containers make great gifts for father's day, Christmas, or other special occasions.

Topical signs to be learned: paper, scissors, crayon, paint, glue, snack, give.

Indicators: A.1.b, A.1.c, A.1.d, A.2.a, A.2.b, A.2.c, B.1.c, C.2.b, F.1.b, F.2.b, F.2.c, F.2.d, F.2.e, F.2.h, F.3.c, G.1.a, G.1.b, G.2.a, H.1.a, H.1.b, H.1.c, H.1.d.

Snow and Ocean Scenes (weather, nature)

Materials: large washable table, shaving cream, small toy cars and trucks, toy animals and people, washable odds and ends, leaves, twigs, rocks, pinecones, blue food coloring, ocean and beach props.

Spray shaving cream on the table. Have the children create winter scenes. Provide props such as empty margarine containers, toy animals and people, pine tree twigs, sticks, toy cars and trucks, and cans. In the summer months, add blue food coloring and create an ocean of blue waves. Add props for a swim scenario.

Topical signs to be learned: winter, snow, summer, animal, people, tree, car, truck, ocean, swim.

Indicators: A.1.a, A.1.b, A.1.c, A.1.d, A.2.a, A.2.b, A.2.c, B.1.c, B.2.a, B.2.b, B.2.c, C.2.b, D.1.b, D.2.c, D.2.d, F.1.b, F.2.b, F.2.e, F.2.h, F.3.c, G.1.a, G.1.b, H.1.a, H.1.b, H.1.d.

Sponge Trees (Christmas)

Materials: sponges cut into Christmas tree shapes, drawing paper, green tempera paint.

Place paint, sponges, and paper out for the children to use. Have the children dip the sponges in the green paint and create designs on their paper. Older children can add details to the picture when dry.

Topical signs to be learned: Christmas, tree, paint, paper, dry, green.

Indicators: A.1.b, A.1.c, A.1.d, A.2.a, A.2.b, A.2.c, B.1.c, C.2.b, F.1.b, F.2.b, F.2.c, F.2.d, F.2.e, F.2.h, F.3.c, G.1.a, G.1.b, G.2.a, H.1.a, H.1.b, H.1.c, H.1.d.

Star of David I (holidays)

Materials: construction paper and scissors or Popsicle sticks, paint and brushes, glitter glue, glue or glue sticks, Q-tips.

Cut out two triangles and glue them together to form a Star of David. Or glue Popsicle sticks together into two triangles and glue those triangles together into a Star of David. Decorate it by using glitter glue, glitter and glue, or paint using Q-tips or paint brushes to paint.

Topical signs to be learned: paper, scissors, glue, triangle, star, paint, decorate.

Indicators: A.1.b, A.1.c, A.1.d, A.2.a, A.2.b, A.2.c, B.1.c, C.2.b, F.1.b, F.2.b, F.2.c, F.2.d, F.2.e, F.2.h, F.3.c, G.1.a, G.1.b, G.2.a, H.1.a, H.1.b, H.1.c, H.1.d.

Star of David II (Hanukkah)

Materials: construction paper triangles (two for each child), glue, paper.

Demonstrate how to place two triangles together to form a Star of David. The children create their star and glue it onto another piece of paper.

Topical signs to be learned: Hanukkah, star, glue, paper, triangle.

Indicators: A.1.b, A.1.c, A.1.d, A.2.a, A.2.b, A.2.c, B.1.c, C.2.b, F.1.b, F.2.b, F.2.c, F.2.d, F.2.e, F.2.h, F.3.c, G.1.a, G.1.b, G.2.a, H.1.a, H.1.b, H.1.c, H.1.d.

Stars (holidays)

Materials: black construction paper, sponges in the shape of stars, and smocks.

Sponge paint a night sky.

Topical signs to be learned: black, sky, star, night, paint.

Indicators: A.1.b, A.1.c, A.1.d, A.2.a, A.2.b, A.2.c, B.1.c, C.2.b, F.1.b, F.2.b, F.2.c, F.2.d, F.2.e, F.2.h, F.3.c, G.1.a, G.1.b, G.2.a, H.1.a, H.1.b, H.1.c, H.1.d.

Tree Ornaments (holidays)

Materials: Paper, scissors (if old enough), glue sticks, paper cut outs and crayons.

Have the children decorate round cut shapes using crayons, glitter, and little foil holiday shapes (older children can cut out their own shapes or decorate white Styrofoam balls). Attach strings to the top.

Topical signs to be learned: ball, string, tree, glue, crayon, and paper.

Indicators: A.1.b, A.1.c, A.1.d, A.2.a, A.2.b, A.2.c, B.1.c, C.1.a, C.1.b, C.1.d, C.2.b, F.1.b, F.2.b, F.2.c, F.2.d, F.2.e, F.2.h, F.3.c, G.1.a, G.1.b, G.2.a, H.1.a, H.1.b, H.1.c, H.1.d.

January
Songs, Stories, Games & Activities

Songs

Bear Song (bear)
(Sung to: "Row, row, row your boat")
Hug, hug, hug your bear
Squeeze him very tight
Hold him high
Help him fly
Then hug with all your might.
Indicators: A.1.a, A.1.b, A.1.c, A.1.d, A.2.a, A.2.b, A.2.c, B.1.a, B.1.c, B.1.d, B.2.a, B.2.b, B.3.a, B.4.a, C.2.b, E.1.a, E.2.a, F.1.b, F.2.e, F.2.h, F.3.c, G.1.a, G.1.b, H.1.a, H.1.b, H.1.d.

The Bear Went Over the Mountain (bears, animals)
Indicators: A.1.a, A.1.b, A.1.c, A.1.d, A.2.a, A.2.b, A.2.c, B.1.a, B.1.c, B.1.d, B.2.a, B.2.b, B.3.a, B.4.a, C.2.b, E.1.a, E.2.a, F.1.b, F.2.e, F.2.h, F.3.c, G.1.a, G.1.b, H.1.a, H.1.b, H.1.d.

Did You Ever See a Clown (Sung to the tune of Did You Ever See a Lassie?)
Did you ever see a clown,
a clown
a clown?

Did you ever see a clown,
Move this way and that?

Move this way and that way!
Move this way and that way!

Did you ever see a clown,
Move this way and that?

Add your own lines and act them out such as:
Have you ever seen an elephant...sway his trunk this way and that way...
Indicators: A.1.a, A.1.b, A.1.c, A.1.d, A.2.a, A.2.b, A.2.c, B.1.a, B.1.c, B.1.d, B.2.a, B.2.b, B.3.a, B.4.a, C.2.b, E.1.a, E.2.a, F.1.b, F.2.e, F.2.h, F.3.c, G.1.a, G.1.b, H.1.a, H.1.b, H.1.d.

Dinosaur Song (dinosaur)
Dinosaur, Dinosaur,
Turn around.
Dinosaur, Dinosaur,
Touch the ground.
Dinosaur, Dinosaur,
Shine your shoes.

Dinosaur, Dinosaur, Skidoo. Dinosaur, Dinosaur,
Go upstairs.
Dinosaur, Dinosaur,
Say your prayers.
Dinosaur, Dinosaur,
Turn out the light.
Dinosaur, Dinosaur,
Say good night.
Indicators: A.1.a, A.1.b, A.1.c, A.1.d, A.2.a, A.2.b, A.2.c, B.1.a, B.1.c, B.1.d, B.2.a, B.2.b, B.3.a, B.4.a, C.2.b, E.1.a, E.2.a, F.1.b, F.2.e, F.2.h, F.3.c, G.1.a, G.1.b, H.1.a, H.1.b, H.1.d.

The Dinosaur Went Over the Mountain (dinosaur)
Tune: For He's a Jolly Good Fellow
The dinosaur went over the mountain,
The dinosaur went over the mountain,
The dinosaur went over the mountain,
To see what he could see

To see what he could see,
To see what he could see

The other side of the mountain,
The other side of the mountain,
The other side of the mountain,
Was all that he could see

Was all that he could see,
Was all that he could see,
The other side of the mountain,
Was all that he could see!
Indicators: A.1.a, A.1.b, A.1.c, A.1.d, A.2.a, A.2.b, A.2.c, B.1.a, B.1.c, B.1.d, B.2.a, B.2.b, B.3.a, B.4.a, C.2.b, E.1.a, E.2.a, F.1.b, F.2.e, F.2.h, F.3.c, G.1.a, G.1.b, H.1.a, H.1.b, H.1.d.

Five Little Bears: Counting Up (bear)
(Have the children make the motions of climbing up the tree as if they were the bears)
One little bear
Wondering what to do
Along came another
Then there were two!
Two little bears
Climbing up a tree
Along came another
Then there were three!
Three little bears
Ate an apple core

Along came another
Then there were four!

Four little honey bears
Found honey in a hive
Along came another
Then there were five!

Indicators: A.1.a, A.1.b, A.1.c, A.1.d, A.2.a, A.2.b, A.2.c, B.1.a, B.1.c, B.1.d, B.2.a, B.2.b, B.3.a, B.4.a, C.2.b, E.1.a, E.2.a, F.1.b, F.2.e, F.2.h, F.3.c, G.1.a, G.1.b, H.1.a, H.1.b, H.1.d.

Have You Ever Seen A Penguin?

(To the Tune of Have You Ever Seen a Lassie?)

Submitted by Florence

Have you ever seen a penguin?
A penguin. . .a penguin!
Have you ever seen a penguin swim this way and that way?
Swim this way and that way . . . and this way and that way?
Have you ever seen a penguin swim this way and that? (point)

Have you ever seen a penguin?
A penguin. . .a penguin!
Have you ever seen a penguin slide this way and that way?
Slide this way and that way . . . and this way and that way?
Have you ever seen a penguin sllide this way and that? (point)

Have you ever seen a penguin?
A penguin. . .a penguin!
Have you ever seen a penguin waddle this way and that way?
Waddle this way and that way . . . and this way and that way?
Have you ever seen a penguin waddle this way and that? (point)

Have you ever seen a penguin?
A penguin. . .a penguin!

Indicators: A.1.a, A.1.b, A.1.c, A.1.d, A.2.a, A.2.b, A.2.c, B.1.a, B.1.c, B.1.d, B.2.a, B.2.b, B.3.a, B.4.a, C.2.b, E.1.a, E.2.a, F.1.b, F.2.e, F.2.h, F.3.c, G.1.a, G.1.b, H.1.a, H.1.b, H.1.d.

Penguin Waddle

(To the tune of "Hokey Pokey")

Have your children stand in a circle and do the actions to the song as you sing.

You put your right wing in, you take your right wing out,
You put your right wing in and you waddle all about.
You do the Penguin Waddle and you turn yourself around.
And that's what it's all about!

Continue singing about other body parts, such as; left wing, right foot, left foot, and head.

Indicators: A.1.a, A.1.b, A.1.c, A.1.d, A.2.a, A.2.b, A.2.c, B.1.a, B.1.c, B.1.d, B.2.a, B.2.b, B.3.a, B.4.a, C.2.b, E.1.a, E.2.a, F.1.b, F.2.e, F.2.h, F.3.c, G.1.a, G.1.b, H.1.a, H.1.b, H.1.d.

Take Me Out to the Big Top (circus)
(Sung to the tune of Take Me Out to the Ballgame)
Take me out to the Big Top,
Take me out to the show.
Buy me some peanuts and crackerjacks,
I don't care if I never go back.
Cause it's clap, clap, clap for the jugglers
and laugh, laugh, laugh for the clowns
For it's one, two, three rings of fun
at the old big top!
Indicators: A.1.a, A.1.b, A.1.c, A.1.d, A.2.a, A.2.b, A.2.c, B.1.a, B.1.c, B.1.d, B.2.a, B.2.b, B.3.a, B.4.a, C.2.b, E.1.a, E.2.a, F.1.b, F.2.e, F.2.h, F.3.c, G.1.a, G.1.b, H.1.a, H.1.b, H.1.d.

Teddy Bear Teddy Bear (bear)
(Have the children follow the motions of the song lyrics)
Teddy bear, teddy bear,
Turn around,
Teddy bear, teddy bear,
Touch the ground.
Teddy bear, teddy bear,
Dance on your toes,
Teddy bear, teddy bear.
Touch your nose.
Teddy bear, teddy bear,
Stand on your head,
Teddy bear, teddy bear,
Go to bed.
Teddy bear, teddy bear,
Say good-night,
Teddy bear, teddy bear,
Turn out the light.
Teddy bear, teddy bear,
Wake up now,
Teddy bear, teddy bear,
Take a bow.
Indicators: A.1.a, A.1.b, A.1.c, A.1.d, A.2.a, A.2.b, A.2.c, B.1.a, B.1.c, B.1.d, B.2.a, B.2.b, B.3.a, B.4.a, C.2.b, E.1.a, E.2.a, F.1.b, F.2.e, F.2.h, F.3.c, G.1.a, G.1.b, H.1.a, H.1.b, H.1.d.

Stories

10 Little Penguins by Jean-Luc Fromental
Topical signs to be learned: book, counting 10-0, ice, winter, friendly.

Indicators: A.1.a, A.1.b, A.1.c, A.1.d, A.2.a, A.2.b, A.2.c, B.1.a, B.1.b, B.1.c, B.1.d, B.2.a, B.2.b, B.2.c, B.3.a, B.3.b, B.4.a, C.2.b, D.2.c, D.2.d, F.1.b, F.2.d, F.2.e, F.2.h, G.1.a, G.1.b, G.2.a, H.1.a, H.1.b.

10 Little Penguins Stuck on the Fridge Paperback by Jean-Luc Fromental
Includes: 10 counting games with magnets.
Indicators: A.1.a, A.1.b, A.1.c, A.1.d, A.2.a, A.2.b, A.2.c, B.1.a, B.1.b, B.1.c, B.1.d, B.2.a, B.2.b, B.2.c, B.3.a, B.3.b, B.4.a, C.2.b, D.2.c, D.2.d, F.1.b, F.2.d, F.2.e, F.2.h, G.1.a, G.1.b, G.2.a, H.1.a, H.1.b.

A Picture Book of Abraham Lincoln by David A. Adler, John Wallner, and Alexandra Wallner
Topical signs to be learned: fingerspell Abraham Lincoln, hat, President.
Indicators: A.1.a, A.1.b, A.1.c, A.1.d, A.2.a, A.2.b, A.2.c, B.1.a, B.1.b, B.1.c, B.1.d, B.2.a, B.2.b, B.2.c, B.3.a, B.3.b, B.4.a, C.2.b, D.2.c, D.2.d, F.1.b, F.2.d, F.2.e, F.2.h, G.1.a, G.1.b, G.2.a, H.1.a, H.1.b.

A Picture Book of George Washington by David A. Adler, John Wallner, and Alexandra Wallner
Topical signs to be learned: fingerspell George Washington, President, father.
Indicators: A.1.a, A.1.b, A.1.c, A.1.d, A.2.a, A.2.b, A.2.c, B.1.a, B.1.b, B.1.c, B.1.d, B.2.a, B.2.b, B.2.c, B.3.a, B.3.b, B.4.a, C.2.b, D.2.c, D.2.d, F.1.b, F.2.d, F.2.e, F.2.h, G.1.a, G.1.b, G.2.a, H.1.a, H.1.b.

A Picture Book of Thomas Jefferson by David A. Adler, John Wallner, and Alexandra Wallner
Topical signs to be learned: fingerspell Thomas Jefferson, President.
Indicators: A.1.a, A.1.b, A.1.c, A.1.d, A.2.a, A.2.b, A.2.c, B.1.a, B.1.b, B.1.c, B.1.d, B.2.a, B.2.b, B.2.c, B.3.a, B.3.b, B.4.a, C.2.b, D.2.c, D.2.d, F.1.b, F.2.d, F.2.e, F.2.h, G.1.a, G.1.b, G.2.a, H.1.a, H.1.b.

Bear Loves Opposites (Bear in the Big Blue House) by Kiki Thorpe
Topical signs to be learned: book, bear, opposites, night, day, up, down, big, small.
Indicators: A.1.a, A.1.b, A.1.c, A.1.d, A.2.a, A.2.b, A.2.c, B.1.a, B.1.b, B.1.c, B.1.d, B.2.a, B.2.b, B.2.c, B.3.a, B.3.b, B.4.a, C.2.b, D.2.c, D.2.d, F.1.b, F.2.d, F.2.e, F.2.h, G.1.a, G.1.b, G.2.a, H.1.a, H.1.b.

Blueberries for Sal by Robert McCloskey
Topical signs to be learned: book, story, mother, eating, blueberries, winter, hill, mother, bear, small, big, appetite (hungry), home.
Indicators: A.1.a, A.1.b, A.1.c, A.1.d, A.2.a, A.2.b, A.2.c, B.1.a, B.1.b, B.1.c, B.1.d, B.2.a, B.2.b, B.2.c, B.3.a, B.3.b, B.4.a, C.2.b, D.2.c, D.2.d, F.1.b, F.2.d, F.2.e, F.2.h, G.1.a, G.1.b, G.2.a, H.1.a, H.1.b.

Brown Bear by Bill Martin Jr. & Eric Carle (colors, animals, bears)

Topical signs to be learned: brown, bear, what, you, see, look at, red, bird, blue, horse, black, sheep, gold, fish, purple, cat, green, frog, yellow, duck, white, dog, teacher, children, all/everyone.

Indicators: A.1.a, A.1.b, A.1.c, A.1.d, A.2.a, A.2.b, A.2.c, B.1.a, B.1.b, B.1.c, B.1.d, B.2.a, B.2.b, B.2.c, B.3.a, B.3.b, B.4.a, C.2.b, D.2.c, D.2.d, F.1.b, F.2.d, F.2.e, F.2.h, G.1.a, G.1.b, G.2.a, H.1.a, H.1.b.

Can I Have a Stegosaurus Mom? Can I? Please? by Lois Grambling and Illustrated by H. B. Lewis (dinosaurs)

After reading the story ask the children what they would do if they could have a pet Stegosaurus? Discuss which dinosaurs were meat eaters and which were plant eaters.

Topical signs to be learned: can (may I), please, dinosaurs.

Indicators: A.1.a, A.1.b, A.1.c, A.1.d, A.2.a, A.2.b, A.2.c, B.1.a, B.1.b, B.1.c, B.1.d, B.2.a, B.2.b, B.2.c, B.3.a, B.3.b, B.4.a, C.2.b, D.2.c, D.2.d, F.1.b, F.2.d, F.2.e, F.2.h, G.1.a, G.1.b, G.2.a, H.1.a, H.1.b.

Circus by Lois Ehlert
Topical signs to be learned: circus, leaping (jumping), lizards, marching, snakes, whistling, parrots, tumbling (rolling), brothers .
Indicators: A.1.a, A.1.b, A.1.c, A.1.d, A.2.a, A.2.b, A.2.c, B.1.a, B.1.b, B.1.c, B.1.d, B.2.a, B.2.b, B.2.c, B.3.a, B.3.b, B.4.a, C.2.b, D.2.c, D.2.d, F.1.b, F.2.d, F.2.e, F.2.h, G.1.a, G.1.b, G.2.a, H.1.a, H.1.b.

Circus Shapes (MathStart 1) by Stuart J. Murphy
Topical signs to be learned: circus, math, counting, shapes, colors.
Indicators: A.1.a, A.1.b, A.1.c, A.1.d, A.2.a, A.2.b, A.2.c, B.1.a, B.1.b, B.1.c, B.1.d, B.2.a, B.2.b, B.2.c, B.3.a, B.3.b, B.4.a, C.2.b, D.2.c, D.2.d, F.1.b, F.2.d, F.2.e, F.2.h, G.1.a, G.1.b, G.2.a, H.1.a, H.1.b.

The Circus Baby by Maud Petersham
Topical signs to be learned: baby, elephant, mother, try, school, manners.
Indicators: A.1.a, A.1.b, A.1.c, A.1.d, A.2.a, A.2.b, A.2.c, B.1.a, B.1.b, B.1.c, B.1.d, B.2.a, B.2.b, B.2.c, B.3.a, B.3.b, B.4.a, C.2.b, D.2.c, D.2.d, F.1.b, F.2.d, F.2.e, F.2.h, G.1.a, G.1.b, G.2.a, H.1.a, H.1.b.

Circus McGurkus 1,2,3! by Dr. Seuss
Topical signs to be learned: circus, elephant, rhymes.

Indicators: A.1.a, A.1.b, A.1.c, A.1.d, A.2.a, A.2.b, A.2.c, B.1.a, B.1.b, B.1.c, B.1.d, B.2.a, B.2.b, B.2.c, B.3.a, B.3.b, B.4.a, C.2.b, D.2.c, D.2.d, F.1.b, F.2.d, F.2.e, F.2.h, G.1.a, G.1.b, G.2.a, H.1.a, H.1.b.

The Circus Ship by Chris Van Dusen
Topical signs to be learned: circus, ship, animals, swim, chilly (cold), water, community.
Indicators: A.1.a, A.1.b, A.1.c, A.1.d, A.2.a, A.2.b, A.2.c, B.1.a, B.1.b, B.1.c, B.1.d, B.2.a, B.2.b, B.2.c, B.3.a, B.3.b, B.4.a, C.2.b, D.2.c, D.2.d, F.1.b, F.2.d, F.2.e, F.2.h, G.1.a, G.1.b, G.2.a, H.1.a, H.1.b.

Clifford at the Circus by Norman Bridwell
Topical signs to be learned: big, red, dog, help, circus, work, together
Indicators: A.1.a, A.1.b, A.1.c, A.1.d, A.2.a, A.2.b, A.2.c, B.1.a, B.1.b, B.1.c, B.1.d, B.2.a, B.2.b, B.2.c, B.3.a, B.3.b, B.4.a, C.2.b, D.2.c, D.2.d, F.1.b, F.2.d, F.2.e, F.2.h, G.1.a, G.1.b, G.2.a, H.1.a, H.1.b.

Corduroy by Don Freeman
Topical signs to be learned: book, story, small, teddy bear, waiting, store, child, friend.
Indicators: A.1.a, A.1.b, A.1.c, A.1.d, A.2.a, A.2.b, A.2.c, B.1.a, B.1.b, B.1.c, B.1.d, B.2.a, B.2.b, B.2.c, B.3.a, B.3.b, B.4.a, C.2.b, D.2.c, D.2.d, F.1.b, F.2.d, F.2.e, F.2.h, G.1.a, G.1.b, G.2.a, H.1.a, H.1.b.

Dinosaurs A to Z (Dinosaur Train) by Andrea Posner-Sanchez (dinosaurs)
Topical signs to be learned: dinosaurs.
Indicators: A.1.a, A.1.b, A.1.c, A.1.d, A.2.a, A.2.b, A.2.c, B.1.a, B.1.b, B.1.c, B.1.d, B.2.a, B.2.b, B.2.c, B.3.a, B.3.b, B.4.a, C.2.b, D.2.c, D.2.d, F.1.b, F.2.d, F.2.e, F.2.h, G.1.a, G.1.b, G.2.a, H.1.a, H.1.b.

Goldilocks and the Three Bears by Candice Ransom
Topical signs to be learned: book, counting 1-3, bears, home, girl, food, eat, bed, dinner.
Indicators: A.1.a, A.1.b, A.1.c, A.1.d, A.2.a, A.2.b, A.2.c, B.1.a, B.1.b, B.1.c, B.1.d, B.2.a, B.2.b, B.2.c, B.3.a, B.3.b, B.4.a, C.2.b, D.2.c, D.2.d, F.1.b, F.2.d, F.2.e, F.2.h, G.1.a, G.1.b, G.2.a, H.1.a, H.1.b.

How Big Were Dinosaurs? by Lita Judge (dinosaurs)
Topical signs to be learned: big, dinosaurs.
Indicators: A.1.a, A.1.b, A.1.c, A.1.d, A.2.a, A.2.b, A.2.c, B.1.a, B.1.b, B.1.c, B.1.d, B.2.a, B.2.b, B.2.c, B.3.a, B.3.b, B.4.a, C.2.b, D.2.c, D.2.d, F.1.b, F.2.d, F.2.e, F.2.h, G.1.a, G.1.b, G.2.a, H.1.a, H.1.b.

How Do Dinosaurs Eat Their Food? by Jane Yolen (foods, manners, dinosaurs, available in Spanish)

Topical signs to be learned: how, eat/food, cereal, throw, cup, pick/find, chair, spaghetti, all, bubbles, milk, oranges, no, says, please, thank you, sit, still, try, new, drop, finish, ask, more.

Indicators: A.1.a, A.1.b, A.1.c, A.1.d, A.2.a, A.2.b, A.2.c, B.1.a, B.1.b, B.1.c, B.1.d, B.2.a, B.2.b, B.2.c, B.3.a, B.3.b, B.4.a, C.2.b, F.1.b, F.2.a, F.2.b, F.2.c, F.2.d, F.2.e, F.2.f, F.2.h, G.1.a, G.1.b, G.2.a, H.1.a, H.1.b

How Do Dinosaurs Say Good Night? By Jane Yolen (home (available in Spanish)

Topical signs to be learned: how, say, good night, father, light, throw, teddy bear, shout/scream/roar, want, book, more, mother, fall, cry, no, try, kiss, quiet, hug.

Indicators: A.1.a, A.1.b, A.1.c, A.1.d, A.2.a, A.2.b, A.2.c, B.1.a, B.1.b, B.1.c, B.1.d, B.2.a, B.2.b, B.2.c, B.3.a, B.3.b, B.4.a, C.2.b, F.1.b, F.2.a, F.2.d, F.2.e, F.2.f, F.2.h, F.5.a, G.1.a, G.1.b, G.2.a, H.1.a, H.1.b.

How the Dinosaur Got to the Museum by Jessie Hartland (dinosaurs)

Topical signs to be learned: dinosaurs.

Indicators: A.1.a, A.1.b, A.1.c, A.1.d, A.2.a, A.2.b, A.2.c, B.1.a, B.1.b, B.1.c, B.1.d, B.2.a, B.2.b, B.2.c, B.3.a, B.3.b, B.4.a, C.2.b, D.2.c, D.2.d, F.1.b, F.2.d, F.2.e, F.2.h, G.1.a, G.1.b, G.2.a, H.1.a, H.1.b.

I Grew Up to Be President (Scholastic) by Laurie Calkhoven

Topical signs to be learned: fingerspell Washington, Jefferson, and Lincoln; President.

Indicators: A.1.a, A.1.b, A.1.c, A.1.d, A.2.a, A.2.b, A.2.c, B.1.a, B.1.b, B.1.c, B.1.d, B.2.a, B.2.b, B.2.c, B.3.a, B.3.b, B.4.a, C.2.b, D.2.c, D.2.d, F.1.b, F.2.d, F.2.e, F.2.h, G.1.a, G.1.b, G.2.a, H.1.a, H.1.b.

I Like It When... by Mary Murphy

Topical signs to be learned: book, story, Penguin, I, like, you, hold, my/me, hand, help, tickle, dance, with.

Indicators: A.1.a, A.1.b, A.1.c, A.1.d, A.2.a, A.2.b, A.2.c, B.1.a, B.1.b, B.1.c, B.1.d, B.2.a, B.2.b, B.2.c, B.3.a, B.3.b, B.4.a, C.2.b, D.2.c, D.2.d, F.1.b, F.2.d, F.2.e, F.2.h, G.1.a, G.1.b, G.2.a, H.1.a, H.1.b.

If I Ran a Circus by Dr Seuss

Topical signs to be learned: circus, rhymes, dream, lion.

Indicators: A.1.a, A.1.b, A.1.c, A.1.d, A.2.a, A.2.b, A.2.c, B.1.a, B.1.b, B.1.c, B.1.d, B.2.a, B.2.b, B.2.c, B.3.a, B.3.b, B.4.a, C.2.b, D.2.c, D.2.d, F.1.b, F.2.d, F.2.e, F.2.h, G.1.a, G.1.b, G.2.a, H.1.a, H.1.b.

If You Were a Penguin by Wendell & Florence Minor

Topical signs to be learned: penguin, swim, fast, ice, toboggan (sled), happy, sing, live, land, sea, you, me.

Indicators: A.1.a, A.1.b, A.1.c, A.1.d, A.2.a, A.2.b, A.2.c, B.1.a, B.1.b, B.1.c, B.1.d, B.2.a, B.2.b, B.2.c, B.3.a, B.3.b, B.4.a, C.2.b, D.2.c, D.2.d, F.1.b, F.2.d, F.2.e, F.2.h, G.1.a, G.1.b, G.2.a, H.1.a, H.1.b.

Jamberry by Bruce Degen
Topical signs to be learned: book, story, hat, shoe, canoe (small boat), bridge, berry, jam (jelly), boy, bear, star, sky, rabbits, elephants.

Indicators: A.1.a, A.1.b, A.1.c, A.1.d, A.2.a, A.2.b, A.2.c, B.1.a, B.1.b, B.1.c, B.1.d, B.2.a, B.2.b, B.2.c, B.3.a, B.3.b, B.4.a, C.2.b, D.2.c, D.2.d, F.1.b, F.2.d, F.2.e, F.2.h, G.1.a, G.1.b, G.2.a, H.1.a, H.1.b.

Last Night I Dreamed a Circus by Maya Gottfired
Topical signs to be learned: horse, rider, lion, dream, imagination, clown.

Indicators: A.1.a, A.1.b, A.1.c, A.1.d, A.2.a, A.2.b, A.2.c, B.1.a, B.1.b, B.1.c, B.1.d, B.2.a, B.2.b, B.2.c, B.3.a, B.3.b, B.4.a, C.2.b, D.2.c, D.2.d, F.1.b, F.2.d, F.2.e, F.2.h, G.1.a, G.1.b, G.2.a, H.1.a, H.1.b.

Little Bear by Else Holmelund Minarik   (family, home, available in Spanish)

Topical signs to be learned: little, bear, mother, cold, snow, wear (clothes), made, see, hat, outside, play, want, coat, pants, have; where, today, my, birthday, friends, cake, water, soup, carrot, potato, peas, tomato, hen/chicken, come, happy, thank you, smell, good, yes, duck, sit, wait, cat, cook, hot, for, big, beautiful, forget; go, moon, how, fly, can't, bird, jump, look for, sky, lunch, think, tree, look, like/same, earth, house; wish, cloud, boat, come on, red, car, fast, story, sleep, good night.

Indicators: A.1.a, A.1.b, A.1.c, A.1.d, A.2.a, A.2.b, A.2.c, B.1.a, B.1.b, B.1.c, B.1.d, B.2.a, B.2.b, B.2.c, B.3.a, B.3.b, B.4.a, C.2.b, F.1.b, F.2.a, F.2.d, F.2.e, F.2.h, F.5.a, G.1.a, G.1.b, G.2.a, G.3.a, H.1.a, H.1.b.

Mirette on the High Wire by Emily McCully
Topical signs to be learned: fear (afraid), mother, student, teacher.

Indicators: A.1.a, A.1.b, A.1.c, A.1.d, A.2.a, A.2.b, A.2.c, B.1.a, B.1.b, B.1.c, B.1.d, B.2.a, B.2.b, B.2.c, B.3.a, B.3.b, B.4.a, C.2.b, D.2.c, D.2.d, F.1.b, F.2.d, F.2.e, F.2.h, G.1.a, G.1.b, G.2.a, H.1.a, H.1.b.

Playful Little Penguins by Tony Mitton
Topical signs to be learned: book, play, little, penguins, love, play, together, snow, ice, slide, swim, splash, help, lost, seal pup (seal baby), tired, little, mother, father, sleep.

Indicators: A.1.a, A.1.b, A.1.c, A.1.d, A.2.a, A.2.b, A.2.c, B.1.a, B.1.b, B.1.c, B.1.d, B.2.a, B.2.b, B.2.c, B.3.a, B.3.b, B.4.a, C.2.b, D.2.c, D.2.d, F.1.b, F.2.d, F.2.e, F.2.h, G.1.a, G.1.b, G.2.a, H.1.a, H.1.b.

<u>Poles Apart: Why Penguins and Polar Bears will Never be Neighbors</u> by Elaine Scott
Topical signs to be learned: book, polar bears, penguins, cold, weather, same, different.
Indicators: A.1.a, A.1.b, A.1.c, A.1.d, A.2.a, A.2.b, A.2.c, B.1.a, B.1.b, B.1.c, B.1.d, B.2.a, B.2.b, B.2.c, B.3.a, B.3.b, B.4.a, C.2.b, D.2.c, D.2.d, F.1.b, F.2.d, F.2.e, F.2.h, G.1.a, G.1.b, G.2.a, H.1.a, H.1.b.

<u>Polar Bears and Penguins: A Compare and Contrast Book Paperback</u> by Katharine Hall
Topical signs to be learned: book, polar bears, penguins, cold, weather, same, different.
Indicators: A.1.a, A.1.b, A.1.c, A.1.d, A.2.a, A.2.b, A.2.c, B.1.a, B.1.b, B.1.c, B.1.d, B.2.a, B.2.b, B.2.c, B.3.a, B.3.b, B.4.a, C.2.b, D.2.c, D.2.d, F.1.b, F.2.d, F.2.e, F.2.h, G.1.a, G.1.b, G.2.a, H.1.a, H.1.b.

<u>Polar Bear, Polar Bear, What Do You Hear?</u> by Bill Martin Jr. and Eric Carle (artic animals, available in Spanish)

Topical signs to be learned: bear, what, you, hear, lion, roar (scream), hippopotamus, bird, zebra, snake, elephant, leopard, zookeeper, children, like.

Indicators: A.1.a, A.1.b, A.1.c, A.1.d, A.2.a, A.2.b, A.2.c, B.1.a, B.1.b, B.1.c, B.1.d, B.2.a, B.2.b, B.2.c, B.3.a, B.4.a, C.2.b, F.1.b, F.2.e, G.1.a, G.2.a, H.1.a, H.1.b.

<u>Spot Goes to the Circus</u> by Eric Hill
Topical signs to be learned: ball, dog, circus, kangaroo, bicycle.
Indicators: A.1.a, A.1.b, A.1.c, A.1.d, A.2.a, A.2.b, A.2.c, B.1.a, B.1.b, B.1.c, B.1.d, B.2.a, B.2.b, B.2.c, B.3.a, B.3.b, B.4.a, C.2.b, D.2.c, D.2.d, F.1.b, F.2.d, F.2.e, F.2.h, G.1.a, G.1.b, G.2.a, H.1.a, H.1.b.

<u>T Is for Terrible</u> by Peter McCarty (dinosaurs)
Topical signs to be learned: letter 'T', terrible (bad), dinosaurs.
Indicators: A.1.a, A.1.b, A.1.c, A.1.d, A.2.a, A.2.b, A.2.c, B.1.a, B.1.b, B.1.c, B.1.d, B.2.a, B.2.b, B.2.c, B.3.a, B.3.b, B.4.a, C.2.b, D.2.c, D.2.d, F.1.b, F.2.d, F.2.e, F.2.h, G.1.a, G.1.b, G.2.a, H.1.a, H.1.b.

<u>The Teddy Bear</u> by David McPhail
Topical signs to be learned: book, story, little, boy, teddy bear, together, night, sleep, next, trip, lost, friend, compassion.
Indicators: A.1.a, A.1.b, A.1.c, A.1.d, A.2.a, A.2.b, A.2.c, B.1.a, B.1.b, B.1.c, B.1.d, B.2.a, B.2.b, B.2.c, B.3.a, B.3.b, B.4.a, C.2.b, D.2.c, D.2.d, F.1.b, F.2.d, F.2.e, F.2.h, G.1.a, G.1.b, G.2.a, H.1.a, H.1.b.

Teddy Bear Tears by Jim Aylesworth
Topical signs to be learned: book, story, imagination, teddy bear, afraid, bedtime, counting 1-4, little, boy, night.
Indicators: A.1.a, A.1.b, A.1.c, A.1.d, A.2.a, A.2.b, A.2.c, B.1.a, B.1.b, B.1.c, B.1.d, B.2.a, B.2.b, B.2.c, B.3.a, B.3.b, B.4.a, C.2.b, D.2.c, D.2.d, F.1.b, F.2.d, F.2.e, F.2.h, G.1.a, G.1.b, G.2.a, H.1.a, H.1.b.

The Teddy Bears' Picnic by Michael Hague
Topical signs to be learned: book, story, woods, surprise, bear, today, eat, picnic.
Indicators: A.1.a, A.1.b, A.1.c, A.1.d, A.2.a, A.2.b, A.2.c, B.1.a, B.1.b, B.1.c, B.1.d, B.2.a, B.2.b, B.2.c, B.3.a, B.3.b, B.4.a, C.2.b, D.2.c, D.2.d, F.1.b, F.2.d, F.2.e, F.2.h, G.1.a, G.1.b, G.2.a, H.1.a, H.1.b.

Tyrone the Double Rotten Cheater by Hans Wilhelm (dinosaurs)
Topical signs to be learned: dinosaurs.

Indicators: A.1.a, A.1.b, A.1.c, A.1.d, A.2.a, A.2.b, A.2.c, B.1.a, B.1.b, B.1.c, B.1.d, B.2.a, B.2.b, B.2.c, B.3.a, B.3.b, B.4.a, C.2.b, D.2.c, D.2.d, F.1.b, F.2.d, F.2.e, F.2.h, G.1.a, G.1.b, G.2.a, H.1.a, H.1.b.

Way Up in the Arctic by Jennifer Ward
Topical signs to be learned: counting from 1-10, animal, mother, baby, sing, bear, whale, fox, rabbit, deer, walrus.
Indicators: A.1.a, A.1.b, A.1.c, A.1.d, A.2.a, A.2.b, A.2.c, B.1.a, B.1.b, B.1.c, B.1.d, B.2.a, B.2.b, B.2.c, B.3.a, B.3.b, B.4.a, C.2.b, D.2.c, D.2.d, F.1.b, F.2.d, F.2.e, F.2.h, G.1.a, G.1.b, G.2.a, H.1.a, H.1.b.

What Does the President Do? (Scholastic) by Amanda Miller
Topical signs to be learned: fingerspell Barack O'Bama, President.
Indicators: A.1.a, A.1.b, A.1.c, A.1.d, A.2.a, A.2.b, A.2.c, B.1.a, B.1.b, B.1.c, B.1.d, B.2.a, B.2.b, B.2.c, B.3.a, B.3.b, B.4.a, C.2.b, D.2.c, D.2.d, F.1.b, F.2.d, F.2.e, F.2.h, G.1.a, G.1.b, G.2.a, H.1.a, H.1.b.

When the Teddy Bears Came by Martin Waddell
Topical signs to be learned: book, story, mother, come, home, hospital, new, baby, amaze, teddy bears, friends, family, fears (afraid).
Indicators: A.1.a, A.1.b, A.1.c, A.1.d, A.2.a, A.2.b, A.2.c, B.1.a, B.1.b, B.1.c, B.1.d, B.2.a, B.2.b, B.2.c, B.3.a, B.3.b, B.4.a, C.2.b, D.2.c, D.2.d, F.1.b, F.2.d, F.2.e, F.2.h, G.1.a, G.1.b, G.2.a, H.1.a, H.1.b.

Where is Alice's Bear? by Fiona Pragoff (home, bears)
Topical signs to be learned: bear, house, crib, baby carriage, car, toy, chest.

Indicators: A.1.a, A.1.b, A.1.c, A.1.d, A.2.a, A.2.b, A.2.c, B.1.a, B.1.b, B.1.c, B.1.d, B.2.a, B.2.b, B.2.c, B.3.a, B.3.b, B.4.a, C.2.b, F.1.b, F.2.d, F.2.e, F.2.h, G.1.a, G.1.b, G.2.a, H.1.a, H.1.b.

Who Wants an Old Teddy Bear? by Ginnie Hofmann
Topical signs to be learned: book, story, rocket, birthday, grandmother, teddy bear, disappointed, night, dreams, friends.
Topical signs to be learned: Indicators: A.1.a, A.1.b, A.1.c, A.1.d, A.2.a, A.2.b, A.2.c, B.1.a, B.1.b, B.1.c, B.1.d, B.2.a, B.2.b, B.2.c, B.3.a, B.3.b, B.4.a, C.2.b, D.2.c, D.2.d, F.1.b, F.2.d, F.2.e, F.2.h, G.1.a, G.1.b, G.2.a, H.1.a, H.1.b.

Games & Activities

Brown Bear (bears, animals, colors)

Make flannel board pieces for the story then tell the story using the pieces. Once children have become familiar with the story, introduce animal signs. Retell the story by giving each child an animal and having them place it on the flannel board as you tell the story but sign the animal. Repeat process by adding color signs. Once children have mastered animals, colors and the story, retell it by signing and having the children place pieces on the flannel board in the correct order. For a change of pace, the teacher can hold onto the pieces and have the children retell the story by signing colors and animals. The teacher then has to place correct pieces on the flannel board. Have fun with it and let them correct you, after all we need to let them know we all make mistakes! You can also use Polar Bear, Polar Bear...or other books.

Topical signs to be learned: color signs, bear, bird, duck, horse, frog, cat, dog, sheep, goldfish, teacher, children, what, see, look.

Indicators: A.1.a, A.1.b, A.1.c, A.1.d, A.2.a, A.2.b, A.2.c, B.1.a, B.1.c, B.1.d, B.1.e, B.2.a, B.2.b, B.2.c, B.3.a, B.4.a, C.1.a, C.1.b, C.1.d, C.2.b, F.1.b, F.2.b, F.2.d, F.2.e, F.2.h, F.3.a, F.3.c, F.4.b, G.1.a, G.1.b, G.2.a, G.3.a, H.1.b, H.1.d.

Dinosaur Colors (dinosaurs)
Ask the children to sort the shapes by color. Make large dinosaur feet for your child to wear, from Kleenex boxes. Stomp around room like your favorite dinosaur.

Topical signs to be learned: colors, shapes, dinosaur.

Indicators: A.1.a, A.1.b, A.1.c, A.1.d, A.2.a, A.2.b, A.2.c, B.1.c, B.2.a, B.2.b, B.2.c, C.2.b, E.3.a, F.1.b, F.2.a, F.2.b, F.2.c, F.2.d, F.2.e, F.2.f, F.2.g, F.3.a, F.3.b, F.3.c, F.4.b, F.4.c, G.1.a, G.1.b, G.2.a, G.3.a, H.1.a, H.1.b, H.1.d, H.2.a.

Dinosaur Egg (dinosaurs)
Materials: plastic eggs that open, small rubber or plastic dinosaurs.

Description: Pretend with the children that the dinosaurs are in the eggs and will be hatching soon. Later give each child a dinosaur egg and tell them they are ready to hatch. Have the children open the eggs. Tell them it is their baby dinosaur to take care of. Discuss what the baby dinosaur will need to survive. Have the children pretend to do what it takes to care for their baby dinosaur.

Topical signs to be learned: colors, egg, dinosaur, food, water, bath, play, love, care.

Indicators: A.1.a, A.1.b, A.1.c, A.1.d, A.2.a, A.2.b, A.2.c, B.1.c, B.2.a, B.2.b, B.2.c, C.2.b, E.3.a, F.1.b, F.2.a, F.2.b, F.2.c, F.2.d, F.2.e, F.2.f, F.2.g, F.3.a, F.3.b, F.3.c, F.4.b, F.4.c, G.1.a, G.1.b, G.2.a, G.3.a, H.1.a, H.1.b, H.1.d, H.2.a.

Dinosaur Pets (dinosaurs)

Would a dinosaur be a good pet? Have the children vote if a dinosaur would be a good pet. Discuss with the children that a dinosaur would not be a good pet and reasons why: claws, eat a lot of food, they may not like humans, and they might hurt us.

Topical signs to be learned: pet, claws, food, eat, hurt, dinosaur.

Indicators: A.1.a, A.1.b, A.1.c, A.1.d, A.2.a, A.2.b, A.2.c, B.1.c, B.2.a, B.2.b, B.2.c, C.2.b, E.3.a, F.1.b, F.2.a, F.2.b, F.2.c, F.2.d, F.2.e, F.2.f, F.2.g, F.3.a, F.3.b, F.3.c, F.4.b, F.4.c, G.1.a, G.1.b, G.2.a, G.3.a, H.1.a, H.1.b, H.1.d, H.2.a.

Dinosaur Numbers (dinosaurs)
Materials: paper, scissors, dinosaur pictures.

Cut out ten shapes. Number them one to ten. Ask the children to line up the shapes from one to ten.

Topical signs to be learned: counting 1-10, shapes, dinosaur.

Indicators: A.1.a, A.1.b, A.1.c, A.1.d, A.2.a, A.2.b, A.2.c, B.1.c, B.2.a, B.2.b, B.2.c, C.2.b, E.3.a, F.1.b, F.2.a, F.2.b, F.2.c, F.2.d, F.2.e, F.2.f, F.2.g, F.3.a, F.3.b, F.3.c, F.4.b, F.4.c, G.1.a, G.1.b, G.2.a, G.3.a, H.1.a, H.1.b, H.1.d, H.2.a.

Dinosaur Sizing (dinosaurs)

Materials: paper, scissors, dinosaur pictures.
Cut out many different sized dinosaur. Ask the children to line up the dinosaur from largest to smallest.
Topical signs to be learned: big, small, dinosaur.

Indicators: A.1.a, A.1.b, A.1.c, A.1.d, A.2.a, A.2.b, A.2.c, B.1.c, B.2.a, B.2.b, B.2.c, C.2.b, E.3.a, F.1.b, F.2.a, F.2.b, F.2.c, F.2.d, F.2.e, F.2.f, F.2.g, F.3.a, F.3.b, F.3.c, F.4.b, F.4.c, G.1.a, G.1.b, G.2.a, G.3.a, H.1.a, H.1.b, H.1.d, H.2.a.

Face Painting
Materials: hypo-allergenic face paint, brushes, water, bowls, paper towels.

Recruit volunteers to paint a small picture on the children's cheek. Prior to the fun beginning read them one of the circus books above. Continue reading additional circus books until all the children have had their turn to get their faces painted. If a child does not want anything painted on their faces, use their hand instead.

Topical signs to be learned: face, paint, colors, beautiful, funny.

Indicators: A.1.a, A.1.b, A.1.c, A.1.d, A.2.a, A.2.b, A.2.c, B.1.c, B.2.a, B.2.b, B.2.c, C.2.b, E.3.a, F.1.b, F.2.a, F.2.b, F.2.c, F.2.d, F.2.e, F.2.f, F.2.g, F.3.a, F.3.b, F.3.c, F.4.b, F.4.c, G.1.a, G.1.b, G.2.a, G.3.a, H.1.a, H.1.b, H.1.d, H.2.a.

How Arctic Animals Survive

Each day discuss two of the following animals, while reviewing the ones learned about previously. Show students pictures about each animal as they are discussed.

Arctic Fox: Turns white to blend in with the snow. The fox has sharp teeth and claws that can dig for food. Sometimes they scavenge scraps to eat that have been left over from polar bears.

Arctic Hare: The white fur blends in with the snow and makes it very difficult to see. This rabbits strong back legs help the hare run very fast when it needs to escape from other animals. To keep warm many hares stay together in holes they dig in the snow.

Arctic Wolf: Like the artic fox it is white and its coloring blends in well with the snow. It has two thick coats of fur keep the warm. It has excellent senses of smell, sight, and hearing; and can go for long periods without food.

Beluga Whale: This mammal breathes air and needs to surface periodically. To do this it makes a great deal of noise. These sounds bounce off objects and help the Beluga locate holes in the ice so that they can breathe. Their sound detection system also helps them to find food.

Caribou: The caribou is actually a member of the deer family. It is especially well suited for the cold weather of the extreme north with thick and kinky hair. Their coats are made of hollow hair that makes it easier for them to float/swim in the water. Still the caribou moves south as winter approaches to warmer areas. It has broad hooves that can dig through snow for food.

Narwhal: Are referred to as the unicorn of the sea because they have a single long tusk that sticks out from their forehead. The narwhal can swim fast, but sometimes chooses to float on its back making it look dead. It has four inches of fat that help protect it from cold temperatures.

Polar Bear: The polar bear has water-repellent fur, with a thick layer of blubber underneath. Polar bears sometimes roll around on the ice to cool down as they can actually become hot in the frozen north.

Seal: The seal is also a mammal and it too has a layer of blubber that keeps it warm, so they spend a lot of time in the cold water. Seals have to be careful when they surface for air as they may be eaten by a polar bear.

Snowy Owl: This owl uses its keen eyesight to hunt day and night. As there are no trees in the arctic it builds nests on the ground.

Snow Geese: Snow geese, also known as the blue goose, are strong flyers that fly south for the winter. They honk very loudly, travel in huge numbers and are the most abundant geese on the planet.

Walrus: The walrus are relatively long-lived, social mammals with strong back flippers to move through the water. Both male and female walruses have tusks and have been observed using these overgrown teeth to help pull themselves out of the water.

Wolverine: The wolverine is a powerful animal that resembles a small bear but is actually the largest member of the weasel family. They are tough solitary animals, who need a lot of room to roam. Individual wolverines may travel 15 miles in a day in search of food. Wolverines eat a both meat and vegetarian fare, like plants and berries. They spray any leftover food with a terrible odor so no other animal will not be able to eat it.

Topical signs to be learned: snow, cold, fox, rabbit, wolf, whale, deer, fish, bear, seal, geese, white, walrus, wolverine.

Indicators: A.1.a, A.1.b, A.1.c, A.1.d, A.2.a, A.2.b, A.2.c, B.1.a, B.1.c, B.1.d, B.2.a, B.2.b, B.3.a, B.4.a, C.2.b, E.1.a, E.2.a, F.1.b, F.2.e, F.2.h, F.3.c, G.1.a, G.1.b, H.1.a, H.1.b, H.1.d.

Ice Cream Clowns

Materials: ice cream, sugar cones, paper plates M&M's, sprinkles, gum drops, and other assorted decorative treats. Place a scoop of ice cream onto a paper plate. Then top it off with a sugar cones placed at an angle on top, for the hat. Have your children use assorted candy to decorate the clown's face.

Topical signs to be learned: ice cream, candy, eat, manners (please and thank you), hat.

Indicators: A.1.a, A.1.b, A.1.c, A.1.d, A.2.a, A.2.b, A.2.c, B.1.c, B.2.a, B.2.b, B.2.c, C.2.b, E.3.a, F.1.b, F.2.a, F.2.b, F.2.c, F.2.d, F.2.e, F.2.f, F.2.g, F.3.a, F.3.b, F.3.c, F.4.b, F.4.c, G.1.a, G.1.b, G.2.a, G.3.a, H.1.a, H.1.b, H.1.d, H.2.a.

Let's Have a Picnic (teddy bear, foods)

Materials: Teddy Bears' Picnic by Jimmy Kennedy, picnic basket or cooler chest, ice in plastic bags, tablecloth and napkins, plates, cups, silverware, blanket to sit on, choice of good things to eat such as apple juice, chocolate chip cookies, corn on the cob, cupcakes, fried chicken, fruit salad, lemonade, peanut butter and jelly and/or tuna salad sandwiches, potato salad; entertainment, games and sports equipment such as balloons, balls, bubbles, hula hoops, kites, nerf balls, plastic wicky-tape to mark start and finish for races, ring toss, squirt guns, and music on tape or CD (optional).

Begin by reading <u>Teddy Bears' Picnic</u> by Jimmy Kennedy about teddy bears who have a wonderful picnic. To prepare a real picnic, start by making food together. Pack the food into a basket or a cooler chest. Add ice in plastic bags to keep things cool. Pack up the toys for picnic fun. Don't forget to bring a favorite teddy bear! Head out to a park, to the playground, or to the back yard for a real picnic. Spread a blanket on the ground. If there is a picnic table spread the tablecloth on the table. Set the table with silverware, plates, and cups for a picnic like the one in the book. Eat and enjoy! The teddy bears will surely want some bites too. After cleaning up, it's time for games, races, music, balloons, and bubbles. Have a grand time! You can also have an indoor picnic on the floor on a rainy day.

Topical signs to be learned: picnic, teddy bear, food, basket, pack, napkin, plate, cup, fork, knife, spoon, apple, juice, lemonade, corn, chicken, eat, toy, park, playground, table, games, balloon, ball, bubbles, kite, race, music.

Indicators: A.1.a, A.1.b, A.1.c, A.1.d, A.2.a, A.2.b, A.2.c, B.1.c, B.2.a, B.2.b, B.2.c, C.2.b, E.3.a, F.1.b, F.2.a, F.2.b, F.2.c, F.2.d, F.2.e, F.2.f, F.2.g, F.3.a, F.3.b, F.3.c, F.4.b, F.4.c, G.1.a, G.1.b, G.2.a, G.3.a, H.1.a, H.1.b, H.1.d, H.2.a.

New Year's Parade (holidays, New Year's)

Materials: construction paper, yarn, hole punch, glue, paper scraps, ribbon, tinsel glitter, other materials as desired to decorate, rhythm instruments, music.

Make small cone-shaped hats out of construction paper and attach yarn to the side for ties. Have children decorate their hats. When dry, help children put on hats and give each a rhythm instrument. Play music and let them march around the room in a New Year's Parade.

Topical signs to be learned: New Year's, hat, march, music.

Indicators: A.1.a, A.1.b, A.1.c, A.1.d, A.2.a, A.2.b, A.2.c, B.1.c, B.2.a, B.2.b, B.2.c, C.2.b, E.1.a, E.3.a, F.1.b, F.2.a, F.2.b, F.2.c, F.2.d, F.2.e, F.2.h, F.3.a, F.3.b, F.3.c, F.4.b, G.1.a, G.1.b, G.2.a, H.1.a, H.1.b, H.1.d, H.2.a.

Parachute Play

Materials: parachute, balls, foam and other soft objects.

Play some parachute games using your parachute and some soft balls and other objects. Have children take turns playing with the parachute or collecting the objects as they are thrown from the parachute.

Topical signs to be learned: parachute, balls.

Indicators: A.1.a, A.1.b, A.1.c, A.1.d, A.2.a, A.2.b, A.2.c, B.1.c, B.2.a, B.2.b, B.2.c, C.2.b, E.3.a, F.1.b, F.2.a, F.2.b, F.2.c, F.2.d, F.2.e, F.2.f, F.2.g, F.3.a, F.3.b, F.3.c, F.4.b, F.4.c, G.1.a, G.1.b, G.2.a, G.3.a, H.1.a, H.1.b, H.1.d, H.2.a.

Power of Air

Materials: balloons, brightly colored confetti, paper plate.

Place brightly colored confetti loosely on a paper plate. Blow up one of the balloons without tying it shut. Ask the children, "What is inside the balloon. Causing it to expand?" Explain to them, that it is air and that even though we can't see it, it is indeed there and can affect other things. Let the air out of the balloon next to the plate, causing the confetti to blow off the plate. Show them a picture of a windmill and describe how air can even provide us with electricity needed to light and cool/heat a house.

Topical signs to be learned: balloon, air, paper.

Indicators: A.1.a, A.1.b, A.1.c, A.1.d, A.2.a, A.2.b, A.2.c, B.1.c, B.2.a, B.2.b, B.2.c, C.2.b, E.3.a, F.1.b, F.2.a, F.2.b, F.2.c, F.2.d, F.2.e, F.2.f, F.2.g, F.3.a, F.3.b, F.3.c, F.4.b, F.4.c, G.1.a, G.1.b, G.2.a, G.3.a, H.1.a, H.1.b, H.1.d, H.2.a.

Search for Dino's (dinosaurs)

Materials: small plastic or rubber dinosaurs.

Description: Hide the dinosaurs in the room and have the children find them (or on the playground). Let each child find one dinosaur. When they have found theirs they can help other students to find one.

Topical signs to be learned: find, look, help, friends, dinosaur.

Indicators: A.1.a, A.1.b, A.1.c, A.1.d, A.2.a, A.2.b, A.2.c, B.1.c, B.2.a, B.2.b, B.2.c, C.2.b, E.3.a, F.1.b, F.2.a, F.2.b, F.2.c, F.2.d, F.2.e, F.2.f, F.2.g, F.3.a, F.3.b, F.3.c, F.4.b, F.4.c, G.1.a, G.1.b, G.2.a, G.3.a, H.1.a, H.1.b, H.1.d, H.2.a.

Teddy Bear Games (home, math)

Materials: large group of teddy bears.

Let children count the total number of teddy bears. Have the children sort the teddy bears by categories (color, size, ones with bows, etc.). Then have them count the number of bears in each category. This information can be recorded on a chalkboard or chart paper. Have the children make different sets of teddy bears (3 black bears, 2 white, etc.). Have children compare the weight of two different bears by holding one in each hand and ask them which feels heavier and which feels lighter.

Topical signs to be learned: teddy bear, count, number signs, heavy, light (weight), color signs, separate/divide.

Indicators: A.1.a, A.1.b, A.1.c, A.1.d, A.2.a, A.2.b, A.2.c, B.1.c, B.2.a, B.2.b, B.2.c, C.1.a, C.1.b, C.1.d., C.2.b, F.1.b, F.2.b, F.2.c, F.2.d, F.2.e, F.2.h, F.3.a, F.3.c, F.4.a, G.1.a, G.1.b, G.2.a, G.3.a, H.1.d, H.2.a.

Tightrope

Materials: rope.

Read the story <u>Mirette on the High Wire</u> by Emily McCully. Then lay two six feet long pieces of rope along the ground and have children take turns walking along them. Have the children pretend they are walking the tightrope like Bellini in the story.

Topical signs to be learned: rope, fear (afraid), mother, student, teacher, brave, try.

Indicators: A.1.a, A.1.b, A.1.c, A.1.d, A.2.a, A.2.b, A.2.c, B.1.c, B.2.a, B.2.b, B.2.c, C.2.b, E.3.a, F.1.b, F.2.a, F.2.b, F.2.c, F.2.d, F.2.e, F.2.f, F.2.g, F.3.a, F.3.b, F.3.c, F.4.b, F.4.c, G.1.a, G.1.b, G.2.a, G.3.a, H.1.a, H.1.b, H.1.d, H.2.a.

Crafts

Cherry Tree Picture

Use a crayon to draw a branch on white or light blue paper.

Let your child use a hole-puncher to punch circles out of red paper.

Then have him brush glue over the crayon branch and sprinkle the circle "cherries" on top of the glue.

Topical signs to be learned: cherry, tree, fingerspell George Washington, President.

Indicators: A.1.a, A.1.b, A.1.c, A.1.d, A.2.a, A.2.b, A.2.c, B.1.c, B.2.a, B.2.b, B.2.c, C.2.b, E.3.a, F.1.b, F.2.a, F.2.b, F.2.c, F.2.d, F.2.e, F.2.f, F.2.g, F.3.a, F.3.b, F.3.c, F.4.b, F.4.c, G.1.a, G.1.b, G.2.a, G.3.a, H.1.a, H.1.b, H.1.d, H.2.a.

Clown Hats

Materials: Construction paper, glue, glitter, pom poms, markers, plastic jewels, stapler.

Give each child a half-circle shape cut out of construction paper.

Let your children decorate a side with markers, glitter, plastic jewels, etc.

Fold the shape around into a clown hat, securing the edge with staples.

Glue a pom-pom to the very top. Place on children's heads and get ready to clown around. Add a clown nose and be sure to take a picture to share with their parents.

Topical signs to be learned: paper, clown, glue, hat, funny, nose, picture.

Indicators: A.1.a, A.1.b, A.1.c, A.1.d, A.2.a, A.2.b, A.2.c, B.1.c, B.2.a, B.2.b, B.2.c, C.2.b, E.3.a, F.1.b, F.2.a, F.2.b, F.2.c, F.2.d, F.2.e, F.2.f, F.2.g, F.3.a, F.3.b, F.3.c, F.4.b, F.4.c, G.1.a, G.1.b, G.2.a, G.3.a, H.1.a, H.1.b, H.1.d, H.2.a.

Dino Bones (dinosaurs)

Place plastic dinosaur shapes (pasta noodles) in the sand table. Hide them from view. Have the children search for them. Once they have found them give each child some to glue on paper. Provide sheets of paper with dinosaur outline on them. Add color with crayons.

Topical signs to be learned: find, look, color, draw, dinosaur.

Indicators: A.1.a, A.1.b, A.1.c, A.1.d, A.2.a, A.2.b, A.2.c, B.1.c, B.2.a, B.2.b, B.2.c, C.2.b, E.3.a, F.1.b, F.2.a, F.2.b, F.2.c, F.2.d, F.2.e, F.2.f, F.2.g, F.3.a, F.3.b, F.3.c, F.4.b, F.4.c, G.1.a, G.1.b, G.2.a, G.3.a, H.1.a, H.1.b, H.1.d, H.2.a.

Dinosaur Eggs (dinosaurs)
Materials: smooth rounded (egg shaped) rocks, paint.
Description: Have children paint the rocks. Once dry have them put dots or speckles of paint on them.
Topical signs to be learned: rock, paint, colors, egg, dinosaur.
Indicators: A.1.a, A.1.b, A.1.c, A.1.d, A.2.a, A.2.b, A.2.c, B.1.c, B.2.a, B.2.b, B.2.c, C.2.b, E.3.a, F.1.b, F.2.a, F.2.b, F.2.c, F.2.d, F.2.e, F.2.f, F.2.g, F.3.a, F.3.b, F.3.c, F.4.b, F.4.c, G.1.a, G.1.b, G.2.a, G.3.a, H.1.a, H.1.b, H.1.d, H.2.a.

Lincoln Log-Cabin Picture
On a piece of white or light blue paper, draw a simple house shape, using a brown crayon. Give your children strips of brown paper cut to fit inside the house shape.
Then help him glue the strips onto the house shape for logs.
Topical signs to be learned: home, wood (log), fingerspell Abraham Lincoln, President.
Indicators: A.1.a, A.1.b, A.1.c, A.1.d, A.2.a, A.2.b, A.2.c, B.1.c, B.2.a, B.2.b, B.2.c, C.2.b, E.3.a, F.1.b, F.2.a, F.2.b, F.2.c, F.2.d, F.2.e, F.2.f, F.2.g, F.3.a, F.3.b, F.3.c, F.4.b, F.4.c, G.1.a, G.1.b, G.2.a, G.3.a, H.1.a, H.1.b, H.1.d, H.2.a.

New Year's Collage (holiday, New Year's)
Materials: colored construction paper, hole punch, glue, dark blue or black construction paper, silver tinsel, brush for glue.
Make "confetti" by using a hole punch on brightly colored construction paper. Brush glue over the dark sheets of construction paper. Drop strands of tinsel on top of the glue and sprinkle small handfuls of confetti.
Topical signs to be learned: New Year's, glue, paper, color signs.
Indicators: A.1.b, A.1.c, A.1.d, A.2.a, A.2.b, A.2.c, B.1.c, C.2.b, F.1.b, F.2.b, F.2.c, F.2.d, F.2.e, F.2.h, F.3.c, G.1.a, G.1.b, G.2.a, H.1.a, H.1.b, H.1.c, H.1.d.

New Year's Paper Lanterns (holidays)
Materials: paper, scissors, glue; crayons, markers, or colored pencils (optional).
Fold an oblong sheet of paper in half, then make equal cuts from the folded edge, taking care not to snip right across the paper. Open it out and glue the edges together, then cut a small strip of paper for the handle and glue it to each side at the top. If you want to color it, it's best to do so before you open it out.

Use the paper lanterns to decorate the classroom by hanging them from the ceiling or making a string of paper lanterns and hanging them around.

Topical signs to be learned: paper, scissors, crayon, New Year's.

Indicators: A.1.b, A.1.c, A.1.d, A.2.a, A.2.b, A.2.c, B.1.c, C.2.b, F.1.b, F.2.b, F.2.c, F.2.d, F.2.e, F.2.h, F.3.c, G.1.a, G.1.b, G.2.a, H.1.a, H.1.b, H.1.c, H.1.d.

Under the Big Top Collage & Snack

Materials: construction paper, crayons, animal crackers, scissors, glue.

Description: Cut out 3 squares, 4 triangles, 3 semi-circles, and 2 stars out of construction paper or foam. Discuss the shapes with the children. Show them how to construct the circus tent. Glue 3 squares along bottom, 3 triangles on top to create roof, and connect 1 small triangle on top of roof as a flag. Have your children copy the design and glue these shapes onto piece of paper. Then give each child animal crackers and have them glue them on the picture to finish. At Amazon you can purchase the Barnum & Bailey ones. Save some for the children to eat as a snack.

Topical signs to be learned: animals, lion, elephant, giraffe, clown, tent, make, eat.

Indicators: A.1.a, A.1.b, A.1.c, A.1.d, A.2.a, A.2.b, A.2.c, B.1.c, B.2.a, B.2.b, B.2.c, C.2.b, E.3.a, F.1.b, F.2.a, F.2.b, F.2.c, F.2.d, F.2.e, F.2.f, F.2.g, F.3.a, F.3.b, F.3.c, F.4.b, F.4.c, G.1.a, G.1.b, G.2.a, G.3.a, H.1.a, H.1.b, H.1.d, H.2.a.

February

Valentine's Day

Time to Sign Curriculum: *Signs can be found in the Family, Home, Holidays and Transportation Module; Music Module for all music; and Preschool Activity Guide for hands on activities.*

Song: I'm A Little Valentine (use tune to "I'm a Little Teapot")

*Props: Use Handouts, other propos to purchase Sign Language Holidays and Celebrations book (Garlic Press Co.)

Transportation – General

Time to Sign Curriculum: *Signs can be found in the Family, Home, Holidays and Transportation Module; Music Module for all music; and Preschool Activity Guide for hands on activities. Stories were found in the local public library.*

Learn: Transportation signs- *(Review)* Airplane, car, fly, boat

Learn: Transportation signs - Airplane, bicycle, bus, car, horse, skateboard, sled, truck, walk

Activity: Body Wheels

Song: Over the River and Through the Woods

Song: Wheels on the Bus

Song: School Bus

Activity: Color letter of the week page in the activity guide

Activity: Complete letter of the week activities in the activity guide

Story: The Wheels on the Bus and Other Transportation Songs by Scholastic, Illustrated by Dick Witt (transportation general)

*Time to Sign Props: Numbers to Transportation Cards

Transportation – Car

Learn: Transportation signs – Car, bridge, bus, racing, street, wheels, wipers

Activity: Travel Starter

Song: Car Song

Song: Windshield Wiper (use Instrumental CD- "I'm a Little Teapot")

Song: The Transportation Song

Activity: Color letter of the week page in the activity guide

Activity: Complete letter of the week activities in the activity guide

Story: Little Bear by Else Holmelund Minarik (family, transportation, car)

Props: Numbers to Transportation Cards

Transportation – Trains

Learn: Transportation signs – train, track, mountain

Activity: P Train

Activity: Ride the Rails

Song: She'll Be Coming Around the Mountain

Song: I've Been Working on the Railroad

Activity: Review Alphabet; finger spell names

Story: The Little Engine that Could by Watty Piper (transportation, train)

Time to Sign Props: Numbers to Transportation Cards

Transportation – Safety

Learn: Transportation signs - Ambulance, buckle, fire engine, seat belt, stop sign, traffic light, wipers

Activities: Roly Poly Races

Activity: Color letter of the week page in the activity guide

Activity: Complete letter of the week activities in the activity guide

Song: Buckle Bear Safety Song

Song Traffic Light

Song: Windshield Wiper (use Instrumental CD- "I'm a Little Teapot")

Story: I Fly by Anne Rockwell (transportation)

Time to Sign Props: Numbers to Transportation Cards

Transportation – Water

Learn: Transportation & Water signs - Boat, bridge, row boat, sailboat

Activity: Travel Starter

Activity: Boat Adventure

Activity: Color letter of the week page in the activity guide

Activity: Complete letter of the week activities in the activity guide

Song: Row, Row, Row Your Boat

Song: Down by the Station

Story: Row, Row, Row Your Boat by Iza Trapani (transportation)

Time to Sign Props: Numbers to Transportation Cards, We See Ocean Animals Story

Stories

Fly Away Home by Eve Bunting (homelessness, transportation)

Topical signs to be learned: dad, live, home, better, street, careful, catch, blue, pants, shirt, jacket, bag, see, sleep, sit, like, walk, pilot, move, stay, bird, stop, fly, happy, bathroom, milk, juice, bus, work, carry, hamburger, mom, save, money, safe, school, mad, special, cry, sing.

Indicators: A.1.a, A.1.b, A.1.c, A.1.d, A.2.a, A.2.b, A.2.c, B.1.a, B.1.b, B.1.c, B.1.d, B.2.a, B.2.b, B.2.c, B.3.a, B.3.b, B.4.a, C.2.b, F.1.b, F.2.a, F.2.c, F.2.d, F.2.e, F.2.h, F.5.a, G.1.a, G.1.b, G.2.a, G.3.a, H.1.a, H.1.b

Freight Train by Donald Crews (transportation, available bilingual)

Topical signs to be learned: train, track, red, orange, yellow, green, cow, blue, purple, black, move, go, through, city, dark, light, gone.

Indicators: A.1.a, A.1.b, A.1.c, A.1.d, A.2.a, A.2.b, A.2.c, B.1.a, B.1.b, B.1.c, B.1.d, B.2.a, B.2.b, B.2.c, B.3.a, B.3.b, B.4.a, C.2.b, F.1.b, F.2.c, F.2.d, F.2.e, F.2.h, G.1.a, G.1.b, G.2.a, H.1.a, H.1.b

I Fly by Anne Rockwell (transportation)

Topical signs to be learned: cousin, fly (airplane), captain, pilot, chair/seat, window, look at, big, airplane, flight attendant (sign: airplane + serve + agent), seat belt, light, welcome, enjoy, loud, up, wheels, sky, city, cloud, fast, drink, up, down, road, river, field, hill (mountain), house, little, stop, slow, good, love.

Indicators: A.1.a, A.1.b, A.1.c, A.1.d, A.2.a, A.2.b, A.2.c, B.1.a, B.1.b, B.1.c, B.1.d, B.2.a, B.2.b, B.2.c, B.3.a, B.3.b, B.4.a, C.2.b, F.1.b, F.2.d, F.2.e, F.2.f, F.2.h, F.5.a, G.1.a, G.1.b, G.2.a, H.1.a, H.1.b.

If You'll Be My Valentine by Cynthia Rylant (valentine's day)

Topical signs to be learned: you, my, valentine, kiss, two, three, walk, sing, talk, write, letter, hug, better, sit, read, book, frog, play, car, look, far, fly, sky, tea, cookies, orange, funny/silly, go, love, tree, world, happy, day.

Indicators: A.1.a, A.1.b, A.1.c, A.1.d, A.2.a, A.2.b, A.2.c, B.1.a, B.1.b, B.1.c, B.1.d, B.2.a, B.2.b, B.2.c, B.3.a, B.3.b, B.4.a, C.2.b, F.1.b, F.2.d, F.2.e, F.2.f, F.2.h, F.5.a, G.1.a, G.1.b, G.2.a, H.1.a, H.1.b.

The Little Engine That Could by Watty Piper (transportation, available in Spanish)

Topical signs to be learned: little, train, happy, good, things, boys, girls, toy, animals, giraffe, bear, baby, elephant, clown, funny, blue, yellow, brown, see, cars, airplanes, books, eat, oranges, apples, red, milk, breakfast, diner, other, side, mountain, stop, shiny, new, engine, help, sad, strong, books, newspapers, world, old, tired, sleep (rest), blue, please, I, think, can, slow, started, up, faster, city.

Indicators: A.1.a, A.1.b, A.1.c, A.1.d, A.2.a, A.2.b, A.2.c, B.1.a, B.1.b, B.1.c, B.1.d, B.2.a, B.2.b, B.2.c, B.3.a, B.3.b, B.4.a, C.2.b, F.1.b, F.2.a, F.2.d, F.2.e, F.2.h, F.5.a, G.1.a, G.1.b, G.2.a, G.3.a, H.1.a, H.1.b.

Please Play Safe: Penguin's Guide to Playground Safety by Margery Cuyler

Topical signs to be learned: friend, go, playground, run, fast, right, wrong, no, walk, not, hurt, play, jump, off, wait, want, slide, climb, turn, catch, throw, ball, ready, sand, box, face, ask, help, dig, see, gentle, back, swing, stop, leave, bring.

Indicators: A.1.a, A.1.b, A.1.c, A.1.d, A.2.a, A.2.b, A.2.c, B.1.a, B.1.b, B.1.c, B.1.d, B.2.a, B.2.b, B.3.a, B.3.b, B.4.a, F.1.b, F.2.b, F.2.c, F.2.d, F.2.e, F.2.h, F.4.a, F.4.b, F.4.c, G.1.a, G.1.b, G.2.a, H.1.a, H.1.b.

Row Row Row Your Boat by Iza Trapani (transportation)

Topical signs to be learned: row, boat, down, stream, life, dream, happy, sunshine, family, oars, fly, clumsy, all your, might, water, splash, hold on, look, ahead, find, dam, wood, stop, eat, noisy, shore, rain, thunder, dry, hide, home, sky.

Indicators: A.1.a, A.1.b, A.1.c, A.1.d, A.2.a, A.2.b, A.2.c, B.1.a, B.1.b, B.1.c, B.1.d, B.2.a, B.2.b, B.2.c, B.3.a, B.3.b, B.4.a, C.2.b, F.1.b, F.2.d, F.2.e, F.2.h, G.1.a, G.1.b, G.2.a, H.1.a, H.1.b.

The Wheels on the Bus and Other Transportation Songs (Scholastic) illustrated by Dick Witt (transportation)

Topical signs to be learned: this is a song book of various transportation songs. The songs are Daisy, Daisy; Down by the Station; I've Been Working on the Railroad; Sally Go Around the Sun; She'll be Coming Around the Mountain; Yankee Doodle; Ride a Cockhorse; Row, Row, Row, Your Boat; Wheels on the Bus

Indicators: A.1.a, A.1.b, A.1.c, A.1.d, A.2.a, A.2.b, A.2.c, B.1.a, B.1.b, B.1.c, B.1.d, B.2.a, B.2.b, B.2.c, B.3.a, B.3.b, B.4.a, C.2.b, F.1.b, F.2.d, F.2.e, F.2.h, G.1.a, G.1.b, G.2.a, H.1.a, H.1.b.

Songs

Buckle Bear Song (transportation)

Indicators: A.1.a, A.1.b, A.1.c, A.1.d, A.2.a, A.2.b, A.2.c, B.1.a, B.1.c, B.1.d, B.2.a, B.2.b, B.3.a, B.4.a, C.2.b, E.1.a, E.2.a, F.1.b, F.2.b, F.2.e, F.2.h, F.3.c, G.1.a, G.1.b, H.1.a, H.1.b, H.1.d

Car Song - (transportation)

Indicators: A.1.a, A.1.b, A.1.c, A.1.d, A.2.a, A.2.b, A.2.c, B.1.a, B.1.c, B.1.d, B.2.a, B.2.b, B.3.a, B.4.a, C.2.b, E.1.a, E.2.a, F.1.b, F.2.b, F.2.e, F.2.h, F.3.c, G.1.a, G.1.b, H.1.a, H.1.b, H.1.d

Did You Ever Go A Camping (transportation)

Indicators: A.1.a, A.1.b, A.1.c, A.1.d, A.2.a, A.2.b, A.2.c, B.1.a, B.1.c, B.1.d, B.2.a, B.2.b, B.3.a, B.4.a, C.2.b, E.1.a, E.2.a, F.1.b, F.2.e, F.2.h, F.3.c, G.1.a, G.1.b, H.1.a, H.1.b, H.1.d

Down by the Station (transportation)

Indicators: A.1.a, A.1.b, A.1.c, A.1.d, A.2.a, A.2.b, A.2.c, B.1.a, B.1.c, B.1.d, B.2.a, B.2.b, B.3.a, B.4.a, C.2.b, E.1.a, E.2.a, F.1.b, F.2.e, F.2.h, F.3.c, G.1.a, G.1.b, H.1.a, H.1.b, H.1.d

I'm a Little Valentine (holidays)

Indicators: A.1.a, A.1.b, A.1.c, A.1.d, A.2.a, A.2.b, A.2.c, B.1.a, B.1.c, B.1.d, B.2.a, B.2.b, B.3.a, B.4.a, C.2.b, E.1.a, E.2.a, F.1.b, F.2.e, F.2.h, F.3.c, G.1.a, G.1.b, H.1.a, H.1.b, H.1.d

I've Been Working on the Railroad (transportation)

Indicators: A.1.a, A.1.b, A.1.c, A.1.d, A.2.a, A.2.b, A.2.c, B.1.a, B.1.c, B.1.d, B.2.a, B.2.b, B.3.a, B.4.a, C.2.b, E.1.a, E.2.a, F.1.b, F.2.e, F.2.h, F.3.c, G.1.a, G.1.b, H.1.a, H.1.b, H.1.d

Little Red Caboose (transportation)

Indicators: A.1.a, A.1.b, A.1.c, A.1.d, A.2.a, A.2.b, A.2.c, B.1.a, B.1.c, B.1.d, B.2.a, B.2.b, B.3.a, B.4.a, C.2.b, E.1.a, E.2.a, F.1.b, F.2.e, F.2.h, F.3.c, G.1.a, G.1.b, H.1.a, H.1.b, H.1.d

Row, Row, Row Your Boat (transportation)

Indicators: A.1.a, A.1.b, A.1.c, A.1.d, A.2.a, A.2.b, A.2.c, B.1.a, B.1.c, B.1.d, B.2.a, B.2.b, B.3.a, B.4.a, C.2.b, E.1.a, E.2.a, F.1.b, F.2.e, F.2.h, F.3.c, G.1.a, G.1.b, H.1.a, H.1.b, H.1.d

Safety Belts (transportation)

Indicators: A.1.a, A.1.b, A.1.c, A.1.d, A.2.a, A.2.b, A.2.c, B.1.a, B.1.c, B.1.d, B.2.a, B.2.b, B.3.a, B.4.a, C.2.b, E.1.a, E.2.a, F.1.b, F.2.b, F.2.e, F.2.h, F.3.c, G.1.a, G.1.b, H.1.a, H.1.b, H.1.d

Traffic Light (transportation)

Indicators: A.1.a, A.1.b, A.1.c, A.1.d, A.2.a, A.2.b, A.2.c, B.1.a, B.1.c, B.1.d, B.2.a, B.2.b, B.3.a, B.4.a, C.2.b, E.1.a, E.2.a, F.1.b, F.2.e, F.2.h, F.3.c, G.1.a, G.1.b, H.1.a, H.1.b, H.1.d

Transportation Song (transportation)

Indicators: A.1.a, A.1.b, A.1.c, A.1.d, A.2.a, A.2.b, A.2.c, B.1.a, B.1.c, B.1.d, B.2.a, B.2.b, B.3.a, B.4.a, C.2.b, E.1.a, E.2.a, F.1.b, F.2.e, F.2.h, F.3.c, G.1.a, G.1.b, H.1.a, H.1.b, H.1.d

Wheels on the Bus (transportation)

Indicators: A.1.a, A.1.b, A.1.c, A.1.d, A.2.a, A.2.b, A.2.c, B.1.a, B.1.c, B.1.d, B.2.a, B.2.b, B.3.a, B.4.a, C.2.b, E.1.a, E.2.a, F.1.b, F.2.e, F.2.h, F.3.c, G.1.a, G.1.b, H.1.a, H.1.b, H.1.d

Windshield Wiper (transportation)

Indicators: A.1.a, A.1.b, A.1.c, A.1.d, A.2.a, A.2.b, A.2.c, B.1.a, B.1.c, B.1.d, B.2.a, B.2.b, B.3.a, B.4.a, C.2.b, E.1.a, E.2.a, F.1.b, F.2.e, F.2.h, F.3.c, G.1.a, G.1.b, H.1.a, H.1.b, H.1.d

Games & Activities

Bus Scene (transportation)

Materials: large sheet of butcher or craft paper to make a bus mural, markers, crayons, or pencils, tape, stapler or pushpins, scissors; bus props such as baby car seat, chairs, blocks or boxes to sit on, dolls or toys as passengers, newspaper, magazines, books, plastic jar for collecting fares, poker chips for play money, real steering wheels, shopping bag, backpack, package.

Design the bus wall scenery on a large piece of butcher paper but in a bus shape (don't forget wheels). Draw big rectangles to indicate windows. In each window, draw or paste a picture of a scene that someone might see if looking out the bus windows (real life or completely imaginary or fantasy). Attach the bus mural to the wall with the wheels just touching the floor, just beside the bus, set up the seats (At least four but no more than ten). Now play bus! The driver collects fares, passengers come and go whenever they reach their stops. Everyone sings "The Wheels on the Bus"!

You can play taxi, train, airplane, or other mode of transportation. You can add dress-up clothes to the pretend scene of the people riding the transportation.

Topical signs to be learned: bus, wheels, drive, wipers, draw, window, door, seat/chair, money, pay, people, come, go, sit, book, bag, backpack.

Indicators: A.1.a, A.1.b, A.1.c, A.1.d, A.2.a, A.2.b, A.2.c, B.1.c, B.2.a, B.2.b, B.2.c, C.2.b, E.3.a, F.1.b, F.2.a, F.2.b, F.2.c, F.2.d, F.2.e, F.2.f, F.2.g, F.2.h, F.3.a, F.3.b, F.3.c, F.4.b, F.4.c, G.1.a, G.1.b, G.2.a, G.3.a, H.1.a, H.1.b, H.1.d, H.2.a.

Boat Floats (transportation)

Materials: large shallow pan of water, sponges, scissors, one large block, 2" twigs, dish, heavy rock (optional).

Fill the pan half full of water. Cut the sponges in half. Explain that the water is ocean in water in a place called a harbor, which is a special place for boats. Let each child choose a sponge as their boat and place it in the harbor. Place the wooden block in the pan for a dock, talk about what a dock is for. Place twigs on the rug and allow each child to choose one, these are their twig people. Have them walk them along the dock and place them in their boat. Talk about places the boats and twig people might go and what they might do out in their boats on the ocean. Remove a boat and place it on a dish. Ask the children if the boat is moving and what it needs to move. Now place the boat back on the water. Boats need water. They are built to float. They provide transportation on water. Send a sponge and a twig person home with each child so they can float their boats at home and find harbors for them.

To demonstrate how boats can sink, place a sponge in a pan of water. Explain that the boat is pushing down on the water. Place on hand in the air, palm down. Move the hand towards the rug. Move the other hand, palm up, to meet the hand moving down. When the hands meet, stop. The bottom hand is the water pushing up on the boat, keeping the boat from sinking. Now place a heavy rock on the sponge. The boat is pushing down on the water with greater force and the water cannot hold it up. Place your palms together and push your top palm down to make the bottom hand sink to the floor. Take turns placing the rock on the boat and sinking it.

Topical signs to be learned: boat, water, ocean, people, move, heavy,

Indicators: A.1.a, A.1.b, A.1.c, A.1.d, A.2.a, A.2.b, A.2.c, B.1.c, B.2.a, B.2.b, B.2.c, C.2.b, F.1.b, F.2.b, F.2.c, F.2.d, F.2.e, F.2.h, F.3.a, F.3.c, F.4.a, G.1.a, G.1.b, G.2.a, G.3.a, H.1.a, H.1.d, H.2.a.

The Caboose is on the Loose (transportation)

This game can have 10-50+ players (At least three "trains" and one "caboose" needed.)

Have the participants get into groups of three. If there are a few left over, they will become loose cabooses. If everyone is in a group of three, ask one group to become the loose cabooses. Make sure there is a caboose for every two or three trains. Each group of three will form a train, with one person behind another. The person behind puts his hands on the waist of the person in front. On the command "start," the trains chug around the area and the cabooses quickly seek a train to join. This means that they attach to the last person in the train by taking hold of the person's waist. When they do so, they yell "Go!" This is the signal for the engine, or the first person in the train to disconnect, thereby becoming a loose caboose. The trains move to keep this from happening, trying to dodge the cabooses. This, of course, should be done in a defined area, or you may find trains head for destinations unknown. The game goes on until players start to tire, about a few minutes.

Topical signs to be learned: group, train, caboose, 3, behind, start, join, go, first, person.
Indicators: A.1.a, A.1.b, A.1.c, A.1.d, A.2.a, A.2.b, A.2.c, B.1.c, B.2.a, B.2.b, B.2.c, C.2.b, F.1.b, F.2.b, F.2.c, F.2.e, F.2.h, F.3.a, F.3.c, F.4.a, G.1.a, G.1.b, G.2.a, H.1.d, H.2.a.

Car Car (transportation)

Players pair up by height (is someone is left over, there can be a group of three). Partners stand with an arm's length facing the same direction, one in front of the other. The one in the back is the driver. The car must put their arms up in from of themselves in a relaxed manner, creating bumpers. The car closes its eyes and the driver puts his hands on their shoulders and begins to guide the car carefully, avoiding crashing into other cars. After a few minutes, everyone stops and switches: car becomes driver, driver becomes car. So if you are the driver first, you had better treat your car right if you expect similar treatment. If the game gets too rough you can have "police" car introduced to stop people and give them tickets, or you could have a tow truck to tow crashed cars to the garage where they must stay for at least a minute for repairs.

Topical signs to be learned: car, other, drive, stop, people, give, police, truck, fix.
Indicators: A.1.a, A.1.b, A.1.c, A.1.d, A.2.a, A.2.b, A.2.c, B.1.c, B.2.a, B.2.b, B.2.c, C.2.b, F.1.b, F.2.b, F.2.c, F.2.e, F.2.h, F.3.a, F.3.c, F.4.a, G.1.a, G.1.b, G.2.a, H.1.d, H.2.a.

Car Wash (transportation)

Game can have 5-35 players, although for 25 or more players make more car washes as needed.

The players form two parallel lines facing each other, about 3 feet apart. They can kneel, crouch, or stand, depending on the softness of the surface and the inclination of the participants. Ask the players to practice motions a carwash makes, such as spraying, brushing, and towel drying. Then tell them that they are going to be the car wash (and the cars, for that matter). Each car/player gets an opportunity to say what kind of car he is and the kind of cleaning he needs—vigorous or gentle, depending on the condition he is in. For instance, an old Chevy that has been driving through mud will need a lot of cleaning, but a new Bentley right off the showroom floor will need only a light dusting. Just for fun, you can have a fantasy wash where players can be anything they want: a frog, a double-decker bus, even a cat on a hot tin roof. Whatever.

Topical signs to be learned: car, wash, line, stand, practice, motions (move), make, say, what, kind, clean, need, gentle, old, new.
Indicators: A.1.a, A.1.b, A.1.c, A.1.d, A.2.a, A.2.b, A.2.c, B.1.c, B.2.a, B.2.b, B.2.c, C.2.b, F.1.b, F.2.b, F.2.c, F.2.e, F.2.h, F.3.a, F.3.c, F.4.a, G.1.a, G.1.b, G.2.a, H.1.d, H.2.a.

Choo Choo (transportation)

Trains are not only a good from of transportation, they are also good places to meet people. And on this train, you can meet a lot of people who will cheer your name.

The game starts in a circle. The leader, after explaining that it is a name game that is easier to do than to explain, starts chugging along moving and sounding like a steam engine. He stops in front of a person, asks her name, and then gives her a little cheer using her name, such as "Edna, Edna, Edna, Edna, Edna!" At the same time, he also makes body movements, which may vary with each added person. Or you can use the person's name sign in the cheer. The leader then invites the person to join the train by turning his back to her and putting her hands on this waist (or shoulders). Once a person joins the train, she can make train sounds and motions, too. When they come to the next person, they ask his name and when they hear it, they both give a cheer. That person is then asked to join and the game continues. After the train has about seven people, split the train in two. For a large group, repeat splitting as many times as necessary until everyone is given a cheer within a few minutes.

Topical signs to be learned: train, meet, circle, game, leader, ask, name, cheer, body, movement (move), join, continue (go on), next, person.

Indicators: A.1.a, A.1.b, A.1.c, A.1.d, A.2.a, A.2.b, A.2.c, B.1.c, B.2.a, B.2.b, B.2.c, C.2.b, F.1.b, F.2.b, F.2.c, F.2.e, F.2.h, F.3.a, F.3.c, F.4.a, G.1.a, G.1.b, G.2.a, H.1.d, H.2.a.

Cockpit (transportation)

Materials: box (the size of a two-drawer file cabinet), two 3-foot dowels, butcher paper, yarn, tempera paint, shallow tins for painting, paintbrushes, scissors, masking tape, glue, colored markers, pencils and crayons, sharp instrument for cutting (for adult use only).

Place the box on its side. Completely remove the bottom of the box (save this piece of cardboard for the steering yoke.) Tape the two ends of the box closed. Cut a windshield in one side of the box. Cut two holes in the front top corners of the box. Draw two airplane steering yokes on the extra cardboard and cut out. Punch holes in the center of each steering yoke, and punch four holes beneath the windshield. Align the holes on each steering yoke with the holes beneath the windshield. Tie the yokes to the box with yearn. Paint the cockpit instrument panel. Cut a long strip of butcher paper the width of the windshield. Mark lines to make sections on the butcher paper that are the same length as the windshield. Draw pictures of destinations on the sections of the butcher paper. Tape the ends of the butcher paper to the dowels, leaving space at the top of the dowel to insert into the holes in the top of the box. Insert the dowels in the holes in the top of the box and scroll.

Now have fun flying your airplane!

Topical signs to be learned: airplane, box, paint, scissors, glue, pencil, crayon, draw, picture.

Indicators: A.1.a, A.1.b, A.1.c, A.1.d, A.2.a, A.2.b, A.2.c, B.1.c, B.2.a, B.2.b, B.2.c, C.2.b, E.3.a, F.1.b, F.2.a, F.2.b, F.2.c, F.2.d, F.2.e, F.2.f, F.2.g, F.3.a, F.3.b, F.3.c, F.4.b, F.4.c, G.1.a, G.1.b, G.2.a, G.3.a, H.1.a, H.1.b, H.1.d, H.2.a.

Cutting Roads (transportation)

Materials: white paper, black marker, scissors, plastic bags.

Draw lines spaced 1" apart down a sheet of white paper with a black marker. These are roads. Make at least one sheet per child. Or have older children make their own roads.

Give each child a sheet of roads, scissors, and a plastic bag. Trace the roads with your finger, count the roads, then have the children cut out the roads on their papers. Mark each road with the child's name or have them write their name on their roads. Have children place all the roads end to end. Make patterns with the roads, count the roads, etc. Place the roads in the plastic bag so the children can bring them home to build roads at home.

You can also tape a large piece of butcher paper onto a wall and tape pieces of road onto the paper as well as pictures of cards from magazines or that children draw.

Topical signs to be learned: road/street, car, scissors, count, number signs, write, name, bring, home.

Indicators: A.1.b, A.1.c, A.1.d, A.2.a, A.2.b, A.2.c, B.1.c, C.1.a, C.1.b, C.1.d, C.2.b, F.1.b, F.2.b, F.2.c, F.2.d, F.2.e, F.2.h, F.3.c, G.1.a, G.1.b, G.2.a, G.3.a, H.1.a, H.1.b, H.1.c, H.1.d.

How far will the car go? (transportation)

Materials: toy car, yarn or rulers and yardsticks.

Have the children examine the toy car. Ask for predictions of whether the car would roll the farthest on a bare surface, on a rug, or on cement. Have the children roll the car on different surfaces and measure with the yarn the distance the car traveled. You can also use rules and yardsticks to measure the distance. Talk about which surface the car traveled the farthest. Talk about how the surfaces are the same or different. Talk about types of roads and surfaces that are easy and hard to drive/skate/ride a bike on.

Topical signs to be learned: car, go, far, smooth, hard, measure, same, different, road/street.

Indicators: A.1.a, A.1.b, A.1.c, A.1.d, A.2.a, A.2.b, A.2.c, B.1.c, B.2.a, B.2.b, B.2.c, C.2.b, F.1.b, F.2.b, F.2.c, F.2.d, F.2.e, F.2.h, F.3.a, F.3.c, F.4.a, G.1.a, G.1.b, G.2.a, G.3.a, H.1.a, H.1.d, H.2.a.

My Ship is Loaded (transportation)

Materials: one ball per group

Have the group sit in a circle formation. One person starts the activity by rolling the ball to another student, saying and signing "My ship is loaded with bananas" (or any other cargo he or she wishes) Sign: my + boat + have...). The second player receiving the ball has to repeat what the first student said and signed and add another item to the list. "My ship is loaded with bananas and cups." She then rolls the ball to another player. Each player who receives the ball has to repeat what the other players have said and add another item. When a player fails to repeat all the cargo, the ball is given to the player on their right as the game continues. This activity can be played with the entire group sitting in a large circle, or you can divide them into smaller groups. Besides encouraging group interaction, this game can also be used to help everyone learn the names and name signs of the others in the group. Instead of saying an object, the first person says their name and signs their name sign. The other students that receive the ball must repeat all the names and name signs given.

Topical signs to be learned: ball, roll, sit in circle, my, ship/boat, add, name, name signs.

Indicators: A.1.a, A.1.b, A.1.c, A.1.d, A.2.a, A.2.b, A.2.c, B.1.c, B.2.a, B.2.b, B.2.c, C.2.b, F.1.a, F.1.b, F.2.b, F.2.c, F.2.e, F.2.h, F.3.a, F.3.c, F.4.a, F.5.a, G.1.a, G.1.b, G.2.a, G.3.a, H.1.c, H.1.d

Pull the Sled (transportation)

Have the children work with partners. One child will pull the sled; the other will be the sled in the snow. The "sled" puts his or her hands on the puller's waist to represent a rope. The puller drags the sled through the snow until they come to a hill. They have trouble getting up the hill. When they reach the top of the hill, the puller moves behind the sled, and the sled runs quickly down the hill.

Topical signs to be learned: sled, snow, run, up, down, hill (mountain).

Indicators: A.1.a, A.1.b, A.1.c, A.1.d, A.2.a, A.2.b, A.2.c, B.1.c, B.2.a, B.2.b, B.2.c, C.2.b, F.1.b, F.2.b, F.2.c, F.2.e, F.2.h, F.3.a, F.3.c, F.4.b, G.1.a, G.1.b, G.2.a, H.1.d, H.2.a.

Railroad Train (transportation)

Materials: cardboard boxes (at least 2 feet long), paper punch, paper tickets, triangle or bell, whistle, shakers or maracas, books on trains.

Share a book or books about trains with the children. Line cardboard boxes up behind each other, the front is the engine and the rest are passenger cars. One child can play engineer, one can be given a triangle or bell to signal the start of the train, another can make wheel sounds and so on. Pieces of paper can be distributed as tickets and then collected by a conductor (These can be made by the children before this activity).

Topical signs to be learned: train, book, ride, sit, ticket, give.

Indicators: A.1.a, A.1.b, A.1.c, A.1.d, A.2.a, A.2.b, A.2.c, B.1.c, B.2.a, B.2.b, B.2.c, C.2.b, F.1.b, F.2.b, F.2.c, F.2.e, F.2.h, F.3.a, F.3.c, F.4.b, G.1.a, G.1.b, G.2.a, H.1.d, H.2.a.

Red Light, Green Light (transportation)

One player stands on an imaginary line and is It. The rest of the players in a straight line some distance away, each trying to be the first to cross the finish line and win. It turns their back to the players and yells "Green Light!" At this signal all the players hurry toward the finish line. But as soon as It yells "Red light!" and spins around to face the other players, they must all freeze. Anyone It catches moving is sent back to the starting line. The first player to cross the finish line wins and becomes It for the next game.

Topical signs to be learned: cross, line, hurry, freeze, catch, light, red, green, start, stop, go, line, finish, win, spin.

Indicators: A.1.a, A.1.b, A.1.c, A.1.d, A.2.a, A.2.b, A.2.c, B.1.c, B.2.a, B.2.b, B.2.c, C.2.b, F.1.b, F.2.b, F.2.c, F.2.e, F.2.h, F.3.a, F.3.c, F.4.b, G.1.a, G.1.b, G.2.a, H.1.d, H.2.a.

Rescue (emergencies)

This is a very noisy game and should not be played if it is likely to bother neighbors or other classes.

One child is "It" and the rest can go anywhere in the area where the doors are open. As soon as "It" touches another player, that player has to stand still and shout for "Rescue!" He can't move until another player comes along and touches him, so the smart "It" hangs around and grabs the others as they attempt a rescue. The game ends when everyone except "It" is standing stock-still shouting for rescue!

Topical signs to be learned: door, open, touch, stand, still, shout, rescue (safety), can't, move, other.

Indicators: A.1.a, A.1.b, A.1.c, A.1.d, A.2.a, A.2.b, A.2.c, B.1.c, B.2.a, B.2.b, C.2.b, E.3.a, F.1.b, F.2.a, F.2.b, F.2.c, F.2.d, F.2.e, F.2.h, F.3.a, F.3.c, F.4.a, G.1.a, G.1.b, G.2.a, H.1.d, H.2.a.

Rocket Ship Trip (transportation)

Materials: paper rockets or rocket toys, jar of marbles.

Bring all the rocket ships to an area such as a rug and stand them up. This is earth. Talk about rocket ships (their uses, who uses them, why, etc.).

Take a trip to the moon. Pass the jar of marbles around. Each child gives it a few strong shakes to start their rocket engine. Now count down from ten to one. When you get to one, everyone says, "Blast off!" Slowly move the rocket ships from earth around the room. Move silently. Space is very quiet. Say "I see the moon" and slowly head towards the paper moon on the wall. When the rockets have passed the moon, head back to earth and slowly land the ships.

Topical signs to be learned: rocket, earth, moon, star, astronaut, travel, numbers 1-10, quiet, see.

Indicators: A.1.b, A.1.c, A.1.d, A.2.a, A.2.b, A.2.c, B.1.c, C.1.a, C.1.b, C.1.d, C.2.b, F.1.b, F.2.b, F.2.c, F.2.d, F.2.e, F.2.h, F.3.c, G.1.a, G.1.b, G.2.a, H.1.b, H.1.d.

Seasonal Transportation (weather, transportation)

Materials: magazines, catalogs or pictures printed from the internet, scissors, glue, poster board or construction paper.

Cut out pictures of seasonal transportation (snowplows, sleds, skis, snow mobiles, snow shoes, row boats, sailboats, RVs, convertibles, hot-air balloons, trucks, motorcycles, bicycles, tricycles, skateboards, roller skates, horses). Mount the pictures on construction paper or poster board.

Discuss the word "transportation." Show the pictures of different transportation and have children identify them. Show the signs for the different types of transportation (or have children show you the signs if they already know them). Ask what type of weather is best for each vehicle and use weather signs. Ask them what would happen if we traveled on a sled on skis on a hot, sunny day or in a row boat on a rainy day, etc. Then have the children pick one way of traveling and take an imaginary trip on a snowy, rainy, sunny, or windy day. You can also have pictures of different types of weather and have children match the transportation pictures with the weather pictures.

Topical signs to be learned: transportation signs, weather signs, picture.

Indicators: A.1.a, A.1.b, A.1.c, A.1.d, A.2.a, A.2.b, A.2.c, B.1.c, B.2.a, B.2.b, B.2.c, C.2.b, D.1.b, D.2.b, D.2.c, D.2.d, F.1.a, F.1.b, F.2.b, F.2.c, F.2.e, F.2.h, F.3.a, F.3.c, F.4.a, G.1.a, G.1.b, G.2.a, G.3.a, H.1.a, H.1.d.

Smoke Crawl (fire & police)

Explain to the children that if there is a lot of smoke that they should crawl instead of walk. Have the children practice crawling.

Topical signs to be learned: smoke, walk, don't, down.

Indicators: A.1.a, A.1.b, A.1.c, A.1.d, A.2.a, A.2.b, A.2.c, B.1.c, B.2.a, B.2.b, B.2.c, C.2.b, F.1.b, F.2.a, F.2.b, F.2.c, F.2.d, F.2.e, F.2.h, F.4.a, G.1.a, G.2.a, H.1.d, H.2.a.

Telephone Smart (emergencies)

Materials: construction paper, marker, scissors.

Discuss using the telephone with children. Explain how using the telephone is for calling help. Introduce the emergency numbers in your area. Have the children practice saying the numbers. Explain children can dial "0" for the operator to receive help, as well. Use the following activities to help children remember the emergency numbers:

Draw each number on large sheets of construction paper. Place the sheets on a paper on the rug about half an arm's length apart. Have the children jump from number to number, repeating the numbers out loud.

Cut three small squares of paper. Print one number on each paper. Hide the squares around the room. Have the children hunt for the numbers and place them in order.

Repeat the emergency numbers with the children three times in a row. Clap as you say each number. Have the children think of different ways to move as you say the numbers. They can march, twist, hope, or rock.

Topical signs to be learned: emergency, 9-1-1, telephone, help, jump, find, number signs.

Indicators: A.1.a, A.1.b, A.1.c, A.1.d, A.2.a, A.2.b, A.2.c, B.1.c, B.2.a, B.2.b, B.2.c, C.1.a, C.2.a, C.2.b, F.1.b, F.2.a, F.2.b, F.2.c, F.2.d, F.2.e, F.2.h, F.2.e, F.4.a, G.1.a, G.2.a, H.1.d.

Traffic Course (transportation)

Materials: riding toys, playground or indoor gym, carpet sample scraps, chalk, masking tape, ropes, string, washable paint (for making roads and streets); cardboard boxes, chairs, coat racks, crayons, heavy paper or newsprint, paint easels, paints, brushes (for making traffic signs); traffic cones, wide markers; clothespins, crepe paper, fabric scraps, flags, newspaper, ribbons, sewing trim, stapler, streamers, tape, yarn (for decorating riding toys); broom dustpan.

Read about cars and trucks for enjoyment. Build an obstacle or traffic course on a playground or large indoor area. Sweep the area clean of rocks glass or debris. Spread out and arrange materials to indicate roads, paths, or streets from the list above. Have cross streets, one way streets, and speedways. Next put up signs made from boxes, posted on chairs or easels, or sticking on traffic cones. Begin with two or three signs and add others as needed. Signs to make are Bridge Ahead, Carpool Lane, Do Not Enter, Exit Only, Gas Ahead, Left Turn Only, One Way, Park, Speed Limit __mph, Stop, Yield. Drive riding toys through the traffic plan, paying attention to signs and rules. You can have a police officer who gives tickets to those violating the traffic rules. As a culmination, decorate the vehicles and have a parade through the course, with all traffic except the main street blocked off, of course. Play parade music if desired.

Topical signs to be learned: transportation vehicle signs, chalk, crayon, chair, paper, paint, flag, road/street, traffic, traffic light, stop, police officer, ticket, bridge, parade, music.

Indicators: A.1.a, A.1.b, A.1.c, A.1.d, A.2.a, A.2.b, A.2.c, B.1.c, B.2.a, B.2.b, B.2.c, C.2.b, F.1.b, F.2.b, F.2.c, F.2.e, F.2.h, F.3.a, F.3.c, F.4.b, G.1.a, G.1.b, G.2.a, H.1.d, H.2.a.

Traffic Light (transportation)

Explain what each color means, sing "Traffic Light" song and then teach a few other traffic signs (slow down, stop, go).

Topical signs to be learned: traffic light, red, yellow, green, stop, slow, go, fast.

Indicators: A.1.a, A.1.b, A.1.c, A.1.d, A.2.a, A.2.b, A.2.c, B.1.c, B.2.a, B.2.b, B.2.c, C.2.b, F.1.b, F.2.b, F.2.c, F.2.e, F.2.h, F.3.a, F.3.c, F.4.b, G.1.a, G.1.b, G.2.a, H.1.b, H.1.d.

Train Sequence (transportation, math)

Materials: construction paper train cars, construction paper engine and caboose, sticky dots or marker.

Place dots or numbers on train cars. The children arrange the cars from smallest number or number of dots to largest number or number of dots.

Topical signs to be learned: train, caboose, number signs.

Indicators: A.1.a, A.1.b, A.1.c, A.1.d, A.2.a, A.2.b, A.2.c, B.1.c, B.2.a, B.2.b, B.2.c, B.3.a, C.1.a, C.1.b, C.1.d., C.2.b, F.1.b, F.2.b, F.2.c, F.2.d, F.2.e, F.2.h, F.3.a, F.3.c, F.4.a, G.1.a, G.1.b, G.2.a, G.3.a, H.1.b, H.1.d.

Trucking Shapes (transportation, shapes)

Materials: construction paper, poster board, glue.

Make a truck out of construction paper for each shape you are doing. Glue the truck shape to a piece of poster board but do not glue the top strip of the truck bed, leaving a pocket for the shapes. Glue a different shape to the bed of each truck. Help the children trace or draw and color different shapes. Encourage the children to match their shapes to the right shape on a truck and put their shape into the right truck.

Topical signs to be learned: shape signs, same, different.

Indicators: A.1.a, A.1.b, A.1.c, A.1.d, A.2.a, A.2.b, A.2.c, B.1.c, B.2.a, B.2.b, B.2.c, C.2.a, C.2.b, F.1.b, F.2.b, F.2.c, F.2.d, F.2.e, F.2.h, F.3.a, F.3.c, F.4.a, G.1.a, G.1.b, G.2.a, G.3.a, H.1.d, H.2.a.

Vacations (transportation)

Materials: paper, pen, pencil or markers.

Discussion. Send home a note asking parents to send in a picture from their family vacation. Display pictures on wall under caption *"Summer Fun"*. Have children tell you something special about their vacation. Write and post the sentence under their picture. Talk about different vacations the children experienced.

Topical signs to be learned: send, home, picture, family, summer, fun, tell, special, write.

Indicators: A.1.a, A.1.b, A.1.c, A.1.d, A.2.a, A.2.b, A.2.c, B.1.c, B.2.a, B.2.b, B.2.c, B.3.a, B.3.b, B.4.a, B.5.a, B.5.b, B.5.c, C.2.b, F.1.b, F.2.a, F.2.b, F.2.c, F.2.e, F.2.h, F.3.a, F.3.c, F.4.a, F.5.a, G.1.a, G.1.b, G.2.a, H.1.c, H.1.d.

Crafts

Barges (transportation)

Materials: several clean Styrofoam meat trays, hole punch, and yarn.

Punch a hole in opposite ends of each of several foam meat trays. Connect the trays with yarn to make a barge.

Topical signs to be learned: boat, string.

Indicators: A.1.b, A.1.c, A.1.d, A.2.a, A.2.b, A.2.c, B.1.c, C.2.b, F.1.b, F.2.b, F.2.c, F.2.d, F.2.e, F.2.h, F.3.c, G.1.a, G.1.b, G.2.a, H.1.a, H.1.b, H.1.c, H.1.d.

Box Train (transportation)

Materials: shoe boxes, cardboard, scissors, glue, heavy string, pencil, brass paper fasteners, spools, small bell, cardboard tubes, oatmeal or salt box, tempera paint and paint brushes (optional).

Engine: To make a shoe-box engine, find two boxes, one just enough smaller to fit snugly inside the other. For the cab, cut away about 1/3 of the smaller box. Cut holes in the sides for windows. Insert the larger section of the smaller box upright in the bigger box, with open sides facing back. Attach a brass fastener in front of the large box for a headlight. Use drinking glasses for patterns, cut six disks from cardboard and attach with brass paper fasteners for wheels. No measure the depth of the cab box and cut away this amount from the large box lid. Glue or tape the lid to its own box, in front of the cab. Glue two spools into position for smokestacks. Glue or tie together two matchsticks or use a small stick and tie on a small bell. This engine is large enough to carry men, dolls, or animals, If wheels are not fastened too tightly, they will roll.

> Box Cars: Use boxes with lids for box cars. Cut doors in the sides large enough to insert toys. To hold door shut, use brass fasteners on the doors far enough apart to be held with a rubber band.

> Gondolas: Use a lidless box. Cut out and attach cardboard wheels with brass fasteners.

> Flat Cars: The lids left over from the gondolas can be used. Cut out and attach wheels with brass fasteners.

> Tankers: Use oatmeal or salt boxes glued to show box lids. Cut out cardboard wheels and fasten with brass fasteners.

Tie cars and engine together with heavy string. To permit uncoupling, punch a small hole for the string. Cut a narrow slit from this hole up to another large enough hole to permit knot to slip through. To add more realism these can be painted with poster paints, but this should be done before assembling. Paint different names, symbols, and slogans on the sides, similar to those on real trains.

Topical signs to be learned: train, shoe box, wheels, scissors, glue, paint, windows, measure, bell, door, string.

Indicators: A.1.b, A.1.c, A.1.d, A.2.a, A.2.b, A.2.c, B.1.c, C.2.b, F.1.b, F.2.b, F.2.c, F.2.d, F.2.e, F.2.h, F.3.c, G.1.a, G.1.b, G.2.a, H.1.a, H.1.b, H.1.c, H.1.d.

Boats (transportation)

Walnut Boat

Materials: walnut shell or split peach stone, toothpick, paper, scissors, glue or clay.

Push a one-inch length of toothpick through a tiny triangle of paper for a sail. Drop a blob of glue into the walnut shell or peach stone and prop the sail in this until set, or use a very tiny ball of clay stuck fast.

Bottle-Cap Boat

Materials: Bottle cap or milk cap, toothpick, paper.

Push a one-inch length of toothpick through a tiny triangle of paper for a sail. Attach this to the cork inside a soft-drink bottle cap or a waxed milk cap.

Box Boat

Materials: cream or milk cartons of any size, scissors, foil or paint and brushes.

Press in the pouring spout and cut out one side of cream or milk carton. Push one end out slightly to form a prow. Glue foil to the sides to cover advertising or paint.

Bark Boat

Materials: chunks of bark in varying sizes from 3-4 inches long to as big as you can handle (Pin bark (mulch) is available at garden shops), sticks, leaves, an oyster shucker/awl/ice pick, small cup hooks and string (optional).

Bore a small hole in the center of the piece of bark to hold the mast for the sail. If you have a very large piece of bark, you may want to have more than one mast. Have the children bore the holes. Depending on the sharpness of the tools they're using, they will need more or less supervision. Thread a large leaf onto a stick, and place the stick in the hole. If you want to attach string so the children can pull their boats (or not lose them downstream!), screw a small cup hook into the front edge and tie on a string.

Sail the boats in a big tub of water or water table or, better yet, take the children to a creek or stream and really let them sail!

Topical signs to be learned: boat, sailboat, sailing, paper, scissors, triangle, glue, paint, leaves.

Indicators: A.1.b, A.1.c, A.1.d, A.2.a, A.2.b, A.2.c, B.1.c, C.2.b, F.1.b, F.2.b, F.2.c, F.2.d, F.2.e, F.2.h, F.3.c, G.1.a, G.1.b, G.2.a, H.1.a, H.1.b, H.1.c, H.1.d.

Egg Carton Train (transportation)

Materials: Cardboard Egg Carton, paint, paint brush, circle stickers, cardboard tubes, and other collage materials.

Give each of your children a row of six egg cups cut lengthwise from a cardboard egg carton. Have the children turn their egg carton sections upside down and paint them to make trains. When the cartons are dry, have the children add details such as round sticker wheels or cardboard-tube smokestacks.

Topical signs to be learned: train, paint, dry, dry, wheels, smoke stack.

Indicators: A.1.b, A.1.c, A.1.d, A.2.a, A.2.b, A.2.c, B.1.c, C.2.b, F.1.b, F.2.b, F.2.c, F.2.d, F.2.e, F.2.h, F.3.c, G.1.a, G.1.b, G.2.a, H.1.a, H.1.b, H.1.c, H.1.d.

Grow Your Own Valentine (holidays)

Materials: cellulose sponges (pink or red if possible), scissors, small red construction paper hearts, glue, toothpicks, marker, tray or dish to put the sponges in, grass seed-any quick germinating kind, mister or spray bottle, white paper bowls or jar lids.

Be sure to start this project 7-10 days before you want to send them home.

Cut sponges into heart shapes about 3-4 inches wide. Write each child's name on a small construction paper heart or have them write their own names on the hearts. Glue the hearts to a toothpick and stick it in a sponge. Have the children wet the sponges and place them on a tray or saucer. Sprinkle the grass seed over the tops of the sponges, covering the surface. Keep the heart gardens in a sunny window and water each day using a mister or spray bottle. The grass should sprout quickly and grow tall and green. Wait until it gets at least an inch or more tall before sending them home. Add more little hearts—one or two per garden. Glue the hearts to the top of the toothpicks and stick the other end into the sponge. Send the heart gardens home on Valentine's Day. Use heavy weight white paper bowls or clean jar lids to support the garden on its way home.

Topical signs to be learned: heart, Valentine, grass, grow, water, sun, name, give.

Indicators: A.1.a, A.1.b, A.1.c, A.1.d, A.2.a, A.2.b, A.2.c, B.1.c, B.2.a, B.2.b, B.2.c, C.2.b, D.1.b, D.2.c, D.2.d, F.1.b, F.2.b, F.2.d, F.2.e, F.2.h, F.3.a, F.3.c, F.4.b, G.1.a, G.1.b, G.2.a, G.3.a, H.1.b, H.1.d, H.2.a.

Hot Air Balloons (transportation)

Materials: Balloon, paper mache' paint, glue, string, cup or berry basket, and smocks.

Paper mache' a blown up balloon. When dry, paint it, glue 3 pieces of string at the bottom & connect a paper cup with holes punched in the top (or use a berry basket) & tie.

Topical signs to be learned: balloon, hot, paint, glue, string, basket, cup, dry.

Indicators: A.1.b, A.1.c, A.1.d, A.2.a, A.2.b, A.2.c, B.1.c, C.2.b, F.1.b, F.2.b, F.2.c, F.2.d, F.2.e, F.2.h, F.3.c, G.1.a, G.1.b, G.2.a, H.1.a, H.1.b, H.1.c, H.1.d.

Hot Air Balloon II (transportation)

Materials: white poster board, crayons or markers, paper lunch bag, and yarn.

Cut a large balloon shape from a white poster board & have kids decorate both sides with crayons or markers. Cut a paper lunch bag about 1/3 from the bottom for the basket. Punch 2 holes on the bottom of the balloon shape & on the short side of the lunch sack. Attach basket with yarn.

Topical signs to be learned: balloon, crayon, glue, string, basket.

Indicators: A.1.b, A.1.c, A.1.d, A.2.a, A.2.b, A.2.c, B.1.c, C.2.b, F.1.b, F.2.b, F.2.c, F.2.d, F.2.e, F.2.h, F.3.c, G.1.a, G.1.b, G.2.a, H.1.a, H.1.b, H.1.c, H.1.d.

Paper Rockets (transportation)

Materials: different colored construction paper, scissors, white paper, tape, star stickers.

Cut a 2" x 4" colored construction paper rectangle for each child. Cut a large moon shape from the white paper. Tape it on a wall.

Place colored construction paper and pieces of tape on the table. Each child chooses a piece of paper and puts star stickers on it. Roll the sheet of paper to make a tube and tape the ends together. This is the rocket ship body. Place the rectangular pieces of paper on the table. Each child chooses one and forms a cone shape. Tape the ends together. Tape the cone over one end of the rocket ship body.

Topical signs to be learned: paper, scissors, rectangle, rocket, earth, moon, star, astronaut.

Indicators: A.1.b, A.1.c, A.1.d, A.2.a, A.2.b, A.2.c, B.1.c, C.2.b, F.1.b, F.2.b, F.2.c, F.2.d, F.2.e, F.2.h, F.3.c, G.1.a, G.1.b, G.2.a, H.1.a, H.1.b, H.1.c, H.1.d.

Passport, Please (transportation, travel)

Materials: paper, markers or crayons, glue or stapler, instant camera, scissors, rubber stamps and stamp pad (optional), clear contact paper (optional)

Cut two pieces of paper 4 x 8". Glue or staple the two pieces together and fold in half to make a booklet. On the front with markers or crayons have each child write their name and "PASSPORT" on the front and below that a made up passport number. On the firsts inside page on separate lines write first name, last name, town, and country. On the opposite page glue a photo or draw a self-portrait and draw a box around it. Cover the photos or pictures with clear contact paper for protection, if desired. Children can use rubber stamps to stamp their passports before entering or when leaving the plane.

Topical signs to be learned: paper, scissors, write, name, first, last, country, number, picture, glue, draw.

Indicators: A.1.b, A.1.c, A.1.d, A.2.a, A.2.b, A.2.c, B.1.c, C.2.b, F.1.b, F.2.b, F.2.c, F.2.d, F.2.e, F.2.h, F.3.c, G.1.a, G.1.b, G.2.a, H.1.a, H.1.b, H.1.c, H.1.d.

Rocket Ship -Box (transportation)

Materials: 3-4 large cardboard boxes, duct tape, paint, paintbrushes, colored construction paper, star stickers, tape, poster board or butcher paper, scissors or box cutter (adult use only).

Tape the boxes on top of each other with duct tape. If the boxes are large enough, cut an opening on the bottom box large enough for a child. Paint the boxes. Cut out shapes from colored construction paper and tape them on or inside the boxes for control buttons. Place starts on the box. Make a giant cone shape from the poster board or butcher paper and tape it to the top of the boxes.

Topical signs to be learned: rocket, box, paint, paper, star.

Indicators: A.1.b, A.1.c, A.1.d, A.2.a, A.2.b, A.2.c, B.1.c, C.2.b, F.1.b, F.2.b, F.2.c, F.2.d, F.2.e, F.2.h, F.3.c, G.1.a, G.1.b, G.2.a, H.1.a, H.1.b, H.1.c, H.1.d.

Sailboat (ocean, transportation) Materials: Margarine tub, clay, paper, crayons and markers, and straw.

Press a ball of clay in the bottom of a margarine tub. Insert a straw in the clay; then tape a decorated paper into the top of the straw.

Topical signs to be learned: sailboat, paper.

Indicators: A.1.b, A.1.c, A.1.d, A.2.a, A.2.b, A.2.c, B.1.c, C.2.b, F.1.b, F.2.b, F.2.c, F.2.d, F.2.e, F.2.h, F.3.c, G.1.a, G.1.b, G.2.a, H.1.a, H.1.b, H.1.c, H.1.d.

Sailing Along (transportation)

Materials: white construction paper, marker, scissors, empty milk cartons, straws, tape, crayons, water table or large pan of water, masking tape.

Draw a large triangle on a sheet of white construction paper and cut it out to make a sail. Make one for each child (or trace triangles onto construction paper and give to children to cut out). Cut milk cartons 3" from the bottom. Tape a straw against the inside of the carton to make a mast for the sailboat. Have children decorate their sails with crayons. When finished with the sails, tape them to the mast.

Children can take turns placing their boat in the water table or large pan of water and making them sail. Children can name their boats and place the name on a piece of masking tape on the side of their boat.

You can also have children draw people on construction paper and cut them out to go sailing in their boats.

Topical signs to be learned: boat, sailboat, water, ocean, water table, name, paper, scissors, crayon.

Indicators: A.1.b, A.1.c, A.1.d, A.2.a, A.2.b, A.2.c, B.1.c, C.2.b, F.1.b, F.2.b, F.2.c, F.2.d, F.2.e, F.2.h, F.3.c, G.1.a, G.1.b, G.2.a, H.1.a, H.1.b, H.1.c, H.1.d.

Shamrocks (St. Patrick's Day)

Materials: pre-drawn shamrock shapes, pistachio pudding and smocks.

Use pistachio pudding to paint shamrocks, can be on copy paper with shamrock shape or on pre-cut shamrock shape.

Topical signs to be learned: green, paper, St. Patrick's Day.

Indicators: A.1.b, A.1.c, A.1.d, A.2.a, A.2.b, A.2.c, B.1.c, C.2.b, F.1.b, F.2.b, F.2.c, F.2.d, F.2.e, F.2.h, F.3.c, G.1.a, G.1.b, G.2.a, H.1.a, H.1.b, H.1.c, H.1.d.

Shoe Box Train (transportation)

Materials: show boxes, tempera paints, paintbrushes, construction paper, scissors, glue.

Have children paint their shoe box(s). When the paint is dry, cut out construction paper wheels and windows and glue them to the show box train.

Topical signs to be learned: train, box, paint, paper, scissors, glue, window, wheel, circle, square/rectangle.

Indicators: A.1.b, A.1.c, A.1.d, A.2.a, A.2.b, A.2.c, B.1.c, C.2.b, F.1.b, F.2.b, F.2.c, F.2.d, F.2.e, F.2.h, F.3.c, G.1.a, G.1.b, G.2.a, H.1.a, H.1.b, H.1.c, H.1.d.

Spool Painting (transportation)

Materials: construction paper, scissors, tempera paint, Styrofoam trays or paint trays, spools.

Cut construction paper into simple bus shapes or other vehicle shape. Have children use the spools to make wheel shapes with the paint all over their vehicles.

Topical signs to be learned: wheel, bus (or other vehicle), circle, paint.

Indicators: A.1.b, A.1.c, A.1.d, A.2.a, A.2.b, A.2.c, B.1.c, C.2.b, F.1.b, F.2.b, F.2.c, F.2.d, F.2.e, F.2.h, F.3.c, G.1.a, G.1.b, G.2.a, H.1.a, H.1.b, H.1.c, H.1.d.

String of Hearts (holidays)

Materials: colored construction paper, black felt pen, scissors, yarn, hole punchers, tape.

Cut 4" x 4" squares of construction paper, at least 10 for each child. Draw a heart shape on each square. Cut a 3' piece of yarn for each child. Place the paper hearts and scissors on the work surface. Have children cut out the hearts and make their hearts into a pile. Using a hole punch, making a hole at the top of the hearts. String the hearts on the yearn. When a string of hearts is finished, the teacher can tie or tape each heart in place on the string, about an inch or two apart. Have child print their name or you print their name on one of the hearts. The strings of hearts can be used to decorate the classroom. You can have children count how many hearts are on each string of hearts.

Topical signs to be learned: heart, scissors, paper, string, number signs.

Indicators: A.1.b, A.1.c, A.1.d, A.2.a, A.2.b, A.2.c, B.1.c, C.1.a, C.1.b, C.1.d, C.2.b, F.1.b, F.2.b, F.2.c, F.2.d, F.2.e, F.2.h, F.3.c, G.1.a, G.1.b, G.2.a, H.1.a, H.1.b, H.1.c, H.1.d.

Train Cars (Transportation)

Materials: construction paper rectangle for each child, crayons, 2 wheels per child, glue.

Decorate rectangles with crayons. Glue on wheels.

Topical signs to be learned: rectangle, wheels, car, crayon, glue.

Indicators: A.1.b, A.1.c, A.1.d, A.2.a, A.2.b, A.2.c, B.1.c, C.1.a, C.1.b, C.1.d, C.2.b, F.1.b, F.2.b, F.2.c, F.2.d, F.2.e, F.2.h, F.3.c, G.1.a, G.1.b, G.2.a, H.1.a, H.1.b, H.1.c, H.1.d.

Transportation Mural (transportation)

Materials: large rolled bulletin board paper, crayons and markers, old magazines, and glue.

Using the rolled paper have students plan and draw a scene. Share the jobs - one can draw a train track while another draws a road, another clouds, maybe a lake, house or trees. On days to come have them gradually fill up the mural with cut and paste vehicles, airplanes, trains, cars, boats, trucks or even hot air balloons from old magazines!

Topical signs to be learned: paper, plan, draw, share, transportation signs, scissors.

Indicators: A.1.b, A.1.c, A.1.d, A.2.a, A.2.b, A.2.c, B.1.c, C.1.a, C.1.b, C.1.d, C.2.b, F.1.b, F.2.b, F.2.c, F.2.d, F.2.e, F.2.h, F.3.c, G.1.a, G.1.b, G.2.a, H.1.a, H.1.b, H.1.c, H.1.d.

Valentine's Card (Valentine's Day)

Materials: pre-cut hearts, red paint and smocks.

Have children make thumbprints on heart shapes and label with "Thumbbody Loves You".

Topical signs to be learned: heart, love, you, red, paint.

Indicators: A.1.b, A.1.c, A.1.d, A.2.a, A.2.b, A.2.c, B.1.c, C.1.a, C.1.b, C.1.d, C.2.b, F.1.b, F.2.a, F.2.b, F.2.c, F.2.d, F.2.e, F.2.h, F.3.c, F.5.a G.1.a, G.1.b, G.2.a, H.1.a, H.1.b, H.1.c, H.1.d.

Valentine Hearts (holidays)

Materials: red, white and pink construction paper; scissors, white glue or glue sticks, paper doilies, red felt pen, scraps of wrapping paper, foil papers, etc.

Show the children how to cut hearts on a fold. Fold the paper, and along the fold draw an "elephant's ear." Cut this out on the fold to create a symmetrical heart. Vary the size to make larger or smaller hearts. Glue different color and size hearts on top of each other, on doilies, etc. Let the children have fun. Write messages with a red felt pen or have children write the messages themselves.

Topical signs to be learned: Valentine, heart, red, white, pink, scissors, glue, write, love.

Indicators: A.1.b, A.1.c, A.1.d, A.2.a, A.2.b, A.2.c, B.1.c, C.1.a, C.1.b, C.1.d, C.2.b, F.1.b, F.2.b, F.2.c, F.2.d, F.2.e, F.2.h, F.3.c, G.1.a, G.1.b, G.2.a, H.1.a, H.1.b, H.1.c, H.1.d.

Wheel Mural (transportation)

Materials: paper towels, Styrofoam trays or other dish for paint, toys with wheels, brown craft paper, pasta wheel shapes, glue.

Place a paper towel on one side of a tray as a blotter and paint on the other side. Have the children place a toy in the paint and then make wheel tracks on the paper. Compare the wheel tracks. Then given wheel pasta and have them glue them onto their paper to decorate their wheel murals.

Topical signs to be learned: wheel, paint, car, truck.

Indicators: A.1.b, A.1.c, A.1.d, A.2.a, A.2.b, A.2.c, B.1.c, C.1.a, C.1.b, C.1.d, C.2.b, F.1.b, F.2.b, F.2.c, F.2.d, F.2.e, F.2.h, F.3.c, G.1.a, G.1.b, G.2.a, H.1.a, H.1.b, H.1.c, H.1.d.

Year Round Topical Areas and Activities

ABC's

Time to Sign Curriculum: Signs can be found in the Language Arts Module; Music Module for all music and Preschool Activity Guide for hands on activities.

Learn: ABC's (slowly sign ABC song) and basic signs (diaper, eat, drink, more, hurt)

Learn: Alphabet Fingerspelling (A-Z)

Activity: Show and Tell-First Signs book or individual items

Activity: Hokey Pokey to ABC's

Activity: Fingerspell First Letter of Children's Names

Song: ABC's Song

Activity: Name Game

Activity: Body Letters

Story: 1,2,3, to the Zoo: A Counting Book by Eric Carle (zoo, animals, math)

Time to Sign Props: Alphabet cards, ABC Wall poster and Infant Cards

ABC's With Animals

Time to Sign Curriculum: Signs can be found in the Food, Farm, Garden and Animals Module; Music Module for all music and Preschool Activity Guide for hands on activities.

Learn: Farm Animals and then teach basic signs (baby, I/me, no, yes, please)

Learn: Alphabet Fingerspelling (A-Z)

Song: Animals of the Farm

Song: ABC's song

Song: Bingo

Song/Chant: Who Came to Class Today? (use own tune-no music provided)

Play: Favorite Animal Initials

Learn: Animal signs – Animal Alphabet Cards

Art Activity: Use cotton balls and glue for children to create their favorite animals

Story: Brown Bear by Martin Jr. & Eric Carle (colors, animals)

Time to Sign Props: Alphabet cards, ABC Wall poster, We See Stories (Bugs, Farm, Ocean, Pets, and Jungle) Infant Cards

Clothing

Time to Sign Curriculum: Signs can be found in the Language Arts Module; Music Module for all music; and Preschool Activity Guide for hands on activities.

Learn: Clothing signs - Hat, shoes, socks, shirt

Learn: Clothing signs - Dress, hat, pants, scarf, shirt, shoes, socks, sweater

Activity: Scarf Starter

Activity: My Bare Feet

Activity: Wonder Shoes

Activity: Color letter of the week page in the activity guide

Activity: Complete letter of the week activities in the activity guide

Song: Shirts, Pants, Shoes & Socks (to the tune of "Head, Shoulders, Knees and Toes"- no music provided)

Story: All by Myself by Aliki (clothing)

Fun Foods

Time to Sign Curriculum: Signs can be found in the Food. Farm, Garden and Animals Module; Music Module for all music and Preschool Activity Guide for hands on activities.

Learn: Milk, crackers, cookies, thirsty

Learn: Fun Food Signs - Ice cream, cake, cookies, milk, soda, cheese, crackers, French fries, pizza, chicken, hot dog, macaroni, raisin, hungry, delicious, thirsty

Song: A Filled Up Picnic Basket (To the tune of "A Tisket, a Tasket"-no music provided)

Activity: My Favorite - Food

Activity: Gum Drop Pass

Song: If You're Hungry and You Know It

Story: The Very Hungry Caterpillar by Eric Carle (insects, days of the week, food)

Time to Sign Props: Healthy Foods Poster

Movement Songs

Time to Sign Curriculum: Signs can be found in the Sports, Recreation and Arts Module; Music Module for all music; and Preschool Activity Guide for hands on activities.

Learn: Jump, Move, Dance, Music

Activity: Jumping Beans

Song: Five Little Monkeys

Activity: Pattern Formation

Activity: Color letter of the week page in the activity guide

Activity: Complete letter of the week activities in the activity guide

Song: The Ants Go Marching In

Song: March & Sing (to the tune of "Mulberry Bush")-no music provided

Song Music: Touch Your Nose (use own tune-no music provided)

Song: Head, Shoulders, Knees and Toes (use it's tune-no music provided)

Social-Emotional Academic Learning Signs (SEAL)

Time to Sign Curriculum: Signs can be found in the Character Module; Music Module for all music and Preschool Activity Guide for hands on activities.

Learn: Emotion signs - Love, happy, sad, yes, no

Learn: Emotion signs - Afraid/scared, angry/mad, excited, feelings, happy, love

Activity: Cat Warm Up

Activity: Happy or Sad

Song: If You're Happy and You Know It

Activity: My Emotions

Song: Tell Me Why?

Song: The More We Sign Together

Activity: Color letter of the week page in the activity guide

Activity: Complete letter of the week and Emotions activities in the activity guide

Art Activity: Children will create a card to give to someone in the class showing their emotions for that person (ex: happy, silly, funny, sad...)

Story: Baby Faces by DK Publishing (emotions)

Story: Arnie and the New Kid by Nancy Carlson (feelings)

Time to Sign Props: Emotions Poster, Seal Social Skills Poster, and Infant Cards

Stories

Farm Flu by Teresa Bateman (community)

Topical signs to be learned: mom, farmer, farm, wet, dry, out, town, milk, cow, flu, sick, helped, bed, tissues, head, tea, pillows, dawn, chickens, soup, barnyard, chores, pig, turkeys, donkey, snacks, popcorn, relax, chess and checkers (games), sheep, little room, cleaned, rest (sleep), night, under, house, stop, listen, TV, toys, bed, miracle, magic, slow.

Indicators: A.1.a, A.1.b, A.1.c, A.1.d, A.2.a, A.2.b, A.2.c, B.1.a, B.1.b, B.1.c, B.1.d, B.2.a, B.2.b, B.3.a, B.3.b, B.4.a, C.2.b, F.1.b, F.2.d, F.2.e, F.2.h, G.1.a, G.1.b, G.2.a, H.1.a, H.1.b.

Games and Activities

Classroom Books (school)

Materials: Polaroid camera, film, magazines, crayons, paper.

Ideas that you might include are the following: name of child, birth date, mom and dad's names, sibling's names, pets they have, favorite toys they enjoy playing with, magazine cut outs of interests, space for a photo and a personal drawing. You can take a Polaroid photograph of each child to place on their page and let the children decide what information they would like to add.

One additional item you might wish to include would be a space in the back of the book for comments from the parents after they have viewed the book with their child.

Allow one child to take the book home on Monday and return it to class by Friday the same week. Share any personal comments that your parents have written in the book with the class when the book is returned.

Don't forget you are part of your classroom book as well; you must have a page like everyone else.

Topical signs to be learned: picture, book, name, birthday, family signs, alphabet, pet signs, favorite.

Indicators: A.1.b, A.1.c, A.1.d, A.2.a, A.2.b, A.2.c, B.1.a, B.1.b, B.1.c, B.1.d, B.2.a, B.2.b, B.3.a, B.3.b, B.4.a, B.5.a, B.5.b, C.2.b, F.1.a, F.1.b, F.2.b, F.2.c, F.2.d, F.2.e, F.2.h, F.3.c, F.4.a., F.5.a, G.1.a, G.1.b, G.2.a, H.1.a, H.1.b, H.1.c, H.1.d.

I Spy (school, colors, shapes)

Have the children sit in a circle. Teach or review colors and shapes. Have the children take turns, or raise their hands when they know the answer, finding items throughout the classroom when you give them the color and the shape of the item in sign. (Can also be played to other topical areas such as animals and transportation signs.)

Topical signs to be learned: colors, shapes, sit in circle, I, see, find.

Indicators: A.1.a, A.1.b, A.1.c, A.1.d, A.2.a, A.2.b, A.2.c, B.1.c, B.2.a, B.2.b, B.2.c, C.2.a, C.2.b, F.1.b, F.2.b, F.2.c, F.2.d, F.2.e, F.2.h, F.3.c, F.4.b, G.1.a, G.1.b, G.2.a, H.1.a, H.1.b, H.1.d.

Simon Says

Play Simon Says with a twist. Review basic signs and numbers needed to play the game Simon Says. Then give them instructions using ASL.

> Sample
>
> Simon Says touch toes
>
> Simon Says touch nose
>
> Simon Says jump 3 times
>
> Place hands on shoulders (eliminated)

Topical signs to be learned: say, touch, hands, face, jump, stop, spin, number signs, etc.

Indicators: A.1.a, A.1.b, A.1.c, A.1.d, A.2.a, A.2.b, A.2.c, B.1.c, B.2.a, B.2.b, C.2.b, F.1.b, F.2.a, F.2.b, F.2.c, F.2.d, F.2.e, F.2.h, F.3.c, F.4.b, G.1.a, G.1.b, G.2.a, H.1.a, H.1.b, H.1.d., H.2.a.

Crafts

Fingerpainted Ocean (nature, ocean)

Materials: big display wall with empty floor space nearby, large craft or butcher paper, tempera paint, liquid starch, pushpins, tape, stapler, glue, blue cellophane (optional), paper and paper scraps, pens, crayons, paint, paint brushes, art tools for "finger" paintings such as forks, kitchen utensils, rubber gloves, scraps of wood, sponges, variety of paint brushes; props (optional): beach blanket, crown, fishing pole, sand and sand toys, rocks and shells, swim-flippers, sunken model ship, treasure chest.

Spread a huge sheet of paper out on the floor. The paper should be large enough to cover the wall. Pour puddles of liquid starch on the paper. Sprinkle dry or pour liquid tempera paint into the puddles of starch. For authentic looking ocean, the colors painted at the top of the mural should be lighter, and those deeper in the ocean should be progressively darker. Fingerpaint and use other tools to swirl and create designs in the ocean. Fingernails, the edge of spatulas or rulers, combs, forks, rubber gloves, and other utensils add texture and design to the Fingerpainted Ocean. Let dry. Cover the dry painting with blue cellophane, if desired. The cellophane gives the painting a three-dimensional look. Hang the ocean mural on the wall at the child height, with the lower edge touching the floor if possible. Or suspend a wire from one corner of the room to the other with eye hooks, then staple the mural to this wire. Use the suspended wire for other hanging projects throughout the year. Create cut-out sea-life, such as crabs, octopus, sand dollars, starfish, fish, sharks, and whales. Attach these to the ocean painting. Place props near the mural to complete the imaginative space, or play in the ocean area as it is.

Topical signs to be learned: paper, paint, ocean, dry, ocean animals signs, play.

Indicators: A.1.a, A.1.b, A.1.c, A.1.d, A.2.a, A.2.b, A.2.c, B.1.c, B.2.a, C.2.b, D.1.b, D.2.c, D.2.d, F.1.b, F.2.b, F.2.d, F.2.e, F.2.h, F.3.c, F.4.a., G.1.a, G.1.b, G.2.a.

Fine & Performing Arts
Songs, Stories, Games & Activities

Arts

Time to Sign Curriculum: Signs can be found in the Sports, Recreation and Arts Module; Music Module for all music; and Preschool Activity Guide for hands on activities.

Learn: Art signs – colors, dance, drum, music

Learn: Art signs - Acting, art, band, basket, camera, colors, dance, draw, drum, guitar, music, paint, puppets, violin, xylophone

Activity: Leonardo's Warm Up

Song: Color Song

Song: Colors (Use instrumental-Farmer in the Dell)

Activity: Air Band

Activity: Color letter of the week page in the activity guide

Activity: Complete letter of the week activities in the activity guide

Story: Angelina Ballerina by Katharine Holabird (fine & arts)

Stories

Angelina Ballerina by Katharine Holabird (fine & performing arts)

Topical signs to be learned: love, dance, all, time, forget, do, mother, time clean up, ready, school, want, go, dream, breakfast, stand, bed, hat, sad, funny, practice, fast, can't, catch, idea, box, name, dress, pink, ready, lesson, jump, girl, congratulations, good, work, help, everyday.

Indicators: A.1.a, A.1.b, A.1.c, A.1.d, A.2.a, A.2.b, A.2.c, B.1.a, B.1.b, B.1.c, B.1.d, B.2.a, B.2.b, B.2.c, B.3.a, B.3.b, B.4.a, C.2.b, F.1.b, F.2.d, F.2.e, F.2.h, F.5.a, G.1.a, G.1.b, G.2.a, H.1.a, H.1.b.

Brown Rabbit's Shape Book by Alan Baker (colors, shapes)

Topical signs to be learned: Brown, rabbit, red, triangle, shape, rectangle, square, box, underneath, inside, circle, five, flat, balloons, different, colors, big, round, orange, oval, egg, away, flew, green, long, purple, smaller, pear, long, curly.

Indicators: A.1.a, A.1.b, A.1.c, A.1.d, A.2.a, A.2.b, A.2.c, B.1.a, B.1.e, B.2.a, B.2.b, B.2.c, B.2.c, B.3.a, B.4.a, H.1.a, and H.1.b

Draw Me a Star by Eric Carle (fine & performing arts)

Topical signs to be learned: draw, star, artist, good, said, sun, warm, tree, beautiful, people, house, strong, dog, big, cat, bird, butterfly, flower, red, yellow, blue, purple, cloud, rain, rainbow, night, dark, moon, sky

Indicators: A.1.a, A.1.b, A.1.c, A.1.d, A.2.a, A.2.b, A.2.c, B.1.a, B.1.b, B.1.c, B.1.d, B.2.a, B.2.b, B.2.c, B.3.a, B.3.b, B.4.a, C.2.b, F.1.b, F.2.d, F.2.e, F.2.h, G.1.a, G.1.b, G.2.a, H.1.a, H.1.b.

I Ain't Gonna Paint No More by Karen Beaumont (arts, colors)

Topical signs to be learned: day, mother, painting, pictures, wall, door, hear, scream/shout, you, not, more, (can sign "continue" for "no more"), I/me, say, way, red, my, head, can't, rest, hand, black, back, egg, still, what.

Indicators: A.1.a, A.1.b, A.1.c, A.1.d, A.2.a, A.2.b, A.2.c, B.1.a, B.1.b, B.1.c, B.1.d, B.2.a, B.2.b, B.2.c, B.3.a, B.3.b, B.4.a, C.2.b, F.1.b, F.2.d, F.2.e, F.2.h, F.5.a, G.1.a, G.1.b, G.2.a, H.1.a, H.1.b.

Little Blue & Little Yellow by Leo Lioni (colors, family)

Topical signs to be learned: little, blue, yellow, papa, mama, many, friends, best, play, hide and seek, "Ring around the Rosie", sit, rows, school, run, jump, looked, here, there, everywhere, hugged, green, ran, chased, orange, climbed, mountain, tired, cried.

Indicators: A.1.a, A.1.b, A.1.c, A.1.d, A.2.a, A.2.b, A.2.c, B.1.a, B.1.e, B.2.a, B.2.b, B.2.c, B.2.c, B.3.a, B.4.a, H.1.a, and H.1.b

Stagestruck by Tomie DePaola (fine & performing arts)

Topical signs to be learned: girl, boy, wonderful, class, play/act, school, sit, still/quiet, mother, read, story, friend, please, talk, pay attention, pick, lesson, fun, bow, happy, ask, who, mouse, peas, rabbit, stand, do, funny, laugh, sad, principle, began, bad, garden, good, scary, audience, clap, proud, thank you, sorry, hear.

Indicators: A.1.a, A.1.b, A.1.c, A.1.d, A.2.a, A.2.b, A.2.c, B.1.a, B.1.b, B.1.c, B.1.d, B.2.a, B.2.b, B.2.c, B.3.a, B.3.b, B.4.a, C.2.b, F.1.b, F.2.d, F.2.e, F.2.h, F.5.a, G.1.a, G.1.b, G.2.a, H.1.a, H.1.b.

Zin! Zin! Zin! A Violin by Lloyd Moss (fine & performing arts, counting)

Topical signs to be learned: (note: instruments are signed like they are played) numbers 1-10, horn/trumpet, sing, yellow, join, friend, hello, bow, count, silver, place, pick, make, black, wood, number, please, come, clown, laugh, others, group, see, all, start, ready, love, good-bye, new, clap, again, good night.

Indicators: A.1.a, A.1.b, A.1.c, A.1.d, A.2.a, A.2.b, A.2.c, B.1.a, B.1.b, B.1.c, B.1.d, B.2.a, B.2.b, B.2.c, B.3.a, B.3.b, B.4.a, C.1.a, C.1.b, C.1.d, C.2.b, F.1.b, F.2.d, F.2.e, F.2.h, G.1.a, G.1.b, G.2.a, H.1.a, H.1.b.

Fine & Performing Arts Games and Activities

Chain Stories (fine & performing arts)

Have the group sit in a circle or in concentric circles, or if only two people are playing sit across from each other. One person says a word, then the next person adds a word, until there's a complete sentence. Try not to pause. There are no wrong answers in this game. Just say the first word that pops into your head and see if the story makes sense. It's ok if the person after you doesn't say what you thought they would say. It's okay if you're not sure what the person before you is thinking. Continue until some type of story emerges. Perhaps stop for a moment to ask what has happened so far, or what some think may happen next. Then continue adding words and sentences together. The next step could be the one-sentence chain story. Each person adds a sentence to whatever came before in the circle. Or you can play One Word Story Ball. Instead of telling the story in a circle, toss a ball to someone as you say one word. They say the next word in a sentence as they toss the ball to someone else, and so on.

Topical signs to be learned: sit in circle, say, tell, continue, word, add, story, what happened, next, sentence.

Indicators: A.1.a, A.1.b, A.1.c, A.1.d, A.2.a, A.2.b, A.2.c, B.1.c, B.2.a, B.2.b, B.2.c, B.4.a, C.2.b, E.3.a, F.1.b, F.2.b, F.2.e, F.2.h, F.3.a, F.3.c, F.4.b, G.1.a, G.1.b, G.2.a, G.3.a, H.1.b, H.1.d.

Characters of the Space (fine & performing arts)

An actor should always be familiar with the space in which he or she is acting. This activity helps you get to know your space, as well as warm up your body, and practice using your body in different ways.

Walk around in the space you're in. Keep walking, only now you're pretending you're walking through pudding. Think about what it feels like and how your body would move through pudding. For example, you might move more slowly because pudding is thicker than air. After a while, pretend the space has turned into clouds. Think about what that feels like, and how you might walk through clouds. The space can turn into all sorts of things. Someone is appointed the caller and whenever she calls out, it will change the way you move.

Suggestions for different kinds of spaces: honey, snow, water, mashed potatoes, outer space, popcorn, wind, feathers, mud, fire, taffy, pea soup, tar.

Indicators: A.1.a, A.1.b, A.1.c, A.1.d, A.2.a, A.2.b, A.2.c, B.1.c, B.2.a, B.2.b, B.2.c, C.2.b, E.3.a, F.1.b, F.2.a, F.2.b, F.2.e, F.2.h, F.3.a, F.3.c, F.4.b, G.1.a, G.1.b, G.2.a, G.3.a, H.1.b, H.1.d, H.2.a.

Colors

Circle game. Use the color cards to help teach the children the signs for colors. Have the children take turns telling you the color then show them the sign. The color signs can be reused again and again to reinforce the learning of colors and their signs.

Indicators: A.1.c, A.1.d, A.2.a, A.2.b, A.2.c, G.1.a, G.2.a, H.1.a, and H.1.b

Color Games I

Have the children sit with you in a circle. Teach/review the color signs that make up your rainbow. Have the children repeat all the signs to the leader as they are demonstrated. Children each select, or are assigned, a color. The children take turns going around the circle clockwise demonstrating the sign for their chosen color. The leader begins the game by signing their color then that of another person. The person they have 'called', signs their sign then that of another in the circle. In about 5 minutes they should have learned all the color signs. Assist anyone who needs help with the signs, especially the last to go to insure they succeed. Praise the children for their success.

Indicators: A.1.c, A.1.d, A.2.a, A.2.b, A.2.c, G.1.a, G.2.a, H.1.a, and H.1.b

Color Games II

Have the children sit with you in a circle. Teach/review the color signs for the various items to be picked up off the floor, as well as please and thank you. Have the children repeat all the signs to the leader as they are demonstrated. Go around the circle having each child take a turn picking an item out of the center of the circle. They sign the color of the item and then place it in the box/bag. (The teacher signs 'thank you' each time a child places an item in the bag/box.) In the first round, have all the children sign the appropriate color sign for every item put away. In the second round, have only the child whose turn it is sign the color. Assist anyone who needs help with the signs to insure success. End the game by having everyone do the rainbow sign together. Additional rounds: add the name of the item as well as the color. Assist anyone who needs help with the signs, especially the last to go to insure they succeed. Praise the children for their success.

Indicators: A.1.c, A.1.d, A.2.a, A.2.b, A.2.c, G.1.a, G.2.a, H.1.a, and H.1.b

Color Games III

Have the children sit with you in a circle. Show the children the colors and rainbow sign cards to teach/review the color signs that make up your rainbow. Have the children repeat all the signs to the leader as they are demonstrated. The children take turns going around the circle clockwise selecting a sign card and showing it to the other children. They display the sign shown on the chosen card. The children take turns going around the circle until all the cards have been used up. (If there are more children than colors, then the cards are placed back in the pile in the middle of the circle for reuse.) End the game by having all the children go through the color signs once again and finish with the rainbow sign. In about 5 minutes they should have learned all the color signs. Assist anyone who needs help with the signs, especially the last to go to insure they succeed. Praise the children for their success.

Indicators: A.1.c, A.1.d, A.2.a, A.2.b, A.2.c, G.1.a, G.2.a, H.1.a, and H.1.b

Color Games IV

Have the children sit with you in a circle. Show the children the colors and rainbow sign cards to teach/review the color signs that make up your rainbow. Have the children repeat all the signs to the leader as they are demonstrated. The children take turns going around the circle clockwise selecting a sign card and showing it to the other children. They create the sign they just picked and the sign(s) of the other children who have already gone. For example, the first person selects red, so she makes the red sign. The second person selects blue. So they do the red and blue signs. And so on. (If there are more children than colors, then the cards are placed back in the pile in the middle of the circle for reuse.) End the game by having all the children go through the color signs once again as they were selected and finish with the rainbow sign. In about 5 minutes they should have learned all the color signs. Assist anyone who needs help with the signs, especially the last to go to insure they succeed. Praise the children for their success.

Indicators: A.1.c, A.1.d, A.2.a, A.2.b, A.2.c, G.1.a, G.2.a, H.1.a, and H.1.b

Color Games V

Either you have an even amount of children or the leader has to play so that everyone has a partner. Start by playing any of the Games 1-4 Rainbow Color Games. When done, have the children pick a color card slip. They have to be quite during this phase of the game. When the leader says go, they will have to make their selected color's sign. Without talking they have to find the others who have the same color. The game ends when they get together with all their same color sign partners and make the rainbow sign. Assist anyone who needs help with the signs or finding their group to insure success. Praise the children for their signing.

Indicators: A.1.c, A.1.d, A.2.a, A.2.b, A.2.c, G.1.a, G.2.a, H.1.a, and H.1.b

Colors, Let's Look At Colors

Play "Find me the color..." and sign the color you want the children to find.

Indicators: A.1.c, A.1.d, A.2.a, A.2.b, A.2.c, G.1.a, G.2.a, H.1.a, and H.1.b

Color Vote

Review color signs they previously learned and have them "vote" for their favorite color. To vote, they need to sign their favorite color sign. When everyone has voted, graph results and help the children determine a winner! Materials: color pictures and signs, and graph of colors.

Indicators: A.1.c, A.1.d, A.2.a, A.2.b, A.2.c, G.1.a, G.2.a, H.1.a, and H.1.b

Concentration Activity: I'm Going to the Game (sports & recreation)

Players build a list by naming items they would take to a game. Each player must name all the things the previous players have said and then add an item.

Example: Leader: I'm going to the game and I'm going to take binoculars.

Player 1: I'm going to the game and I'm going to take binoculars and a seat cushion.

You can play this for any type of activity or outing such as going on vacation, or going to the park etc.

Topical signs to be learned: name, game, all, things, before, add, I, go, bring.

Indicators: A.1.a, A.1.b, A.1.c, A.1.d, A.2.a, A.2.b, A.2.c, B.1.c, B.2.a, B.2.b, B.2.c, C.2.b, F.1.b, F.2.b, F.2.e, F.2.h, F.3.a, F.3.c, F.4.b, G.1.a, G.1.b, G.2.a, G.3.a, H.1.b, H.1.d.

Human Xylophone (fine & performing arts)

Have the children line up in a group of eight. Ask the first person in line to sing a very low note. Have them memorize the sound they have just made. Then have the next person in line make a sound just slightly higher (help them with examples if necessary) and memorize it. Then the third, forth, and so on. Have them go through what they have memorized in order from the lowest to the highest. Now you have created a human xylophone and it is time to play. Have the rest of the children take turns playing the xylophone. This is done by having the human xylophone children hold their hands out. As the other children touch their hands they make their memorized sound. Each person should continue to sing the note for as long as their hand is being touched. Children can try to play familiar favorites such as *Mary Had A Little Lamb* on the human xylophone.

Topical signs to be learned: line up, song, music, xylophone, numbers one - eight, hear, share, band, please, thank you.

Indicators: A.1.a, A.1.b, A.1.c, A.1.d, A.2.a, A.2.b, A.2.c, B.1.c, B.2.a, B.2.b, B.2.c, C.2.b, E.1.a, F.1.b, F.2.b, F.2.e, F.2.h, F.3.a, F.3.c, F.4.b, G.1.a, G.1.b, G.2.a, G.3.a, H.1.b, H.1.d.

Let's Play Buried Treasure (fine & performing arts)

Materials: gold, silver or other metallic spray or brush-on paints; glitter, glitter paint, glitter glue, sequins, box for treasure chest, newspaper to protect table during painting, paint and brushes, paper and pens for drawing map, used wet tea bag, items for pretend treasure: beads and hobby jewels, chocolate coins wrapped in foil, large buttons, old jewelry, plastic beads on strings, play money, small figurines or statues, small rocks, or small wood scraps.

Prepare the treasure. Some suggestions are paint the rocks gold and silver, cover the wood scraps with glitter, paint the small statues gold, or cover large buttons with glitter paint. Dry the painted items. Spread out the other items and decide what will be in the treasure chest that will be buried. Select a wooden or cardboard box for the treasure chest. The treasures can be hidden or buried in the chest, or the chest can be used to collect them after each one is found. Decorate the chest with markers and paint in any design. Find a place to bury the treasures like a sandbox, soft dirt in the garden, or behind a couch. Draw a treasure map that leads the seekers to the buried treasure. Wipe the map with a wet, used tea bag to make it look like old parchment. Find the treasure! Bury the treasure again in a new place and start all over again.

You can pretend to be pirates. Dress like pirates (eye patch, skull cap, rolled-up pants, scars, earrings), talk like pirates (Away me hearties! Ahoy there! Surrender ye swabs! Scupper that ship! Land ho!) and sing like pirates (Yo ho, yo ho, the pirate's life for me...). Or you can design flags, make sea biscuits, and write with invisible ink.

Topical signs to be learned: gold, silver, paint, paper, pens, money, statue, box, hide, find, pretend.

Indicators: A.1.a, A.1.b, A.1.c, A.1.d, A.2.a, A.2.b, A.2.c, B.1.c, B.2.a, B.2.b, B.2.c, C.2.b, E.3.a, F.1.a, F.1.b, F.2.a, F.2.b, F.2.c, F.2.d, F.2.e, F.2.f, F.2.g, F.3.a, F.3.b, F.3.c, F.4.b, F.4.c, F.5.a, G.1.a, G.1.b, G.2.a, G.3.a, H.1.a, H.1.b, H.1.d, H.2.a.

Magic Land (fine & performing arts)

Say, "Today we are going to make believe we are TV actors. Let's talk about what you saw on TV this week." Have children discuss TV shows they saw, telling what happened in the story, who the characters were, etc. Select on TV show/story mentioned by the children that has a high interest level and develop the story line (or retell the story). Review the acting situation and the rules for actors and audience. Select various children to be the characters in the play. Then say, "Now we're going to act out this story." Narrate the story, stopping at various points to let the children act and speak their parts. You man want to repeat the dramatization with different actors, so that each child has a chance to play a part in the story.

Topical signs to be learned: magic, tv, actor, see, happen, story, character, audience, narrate.

Indicators: A.1.a, A.1.b, A.1.c, A.1.d, A.2.a, A.2.b, A.2.c, B.1.c, B.2.a, B.2.b, B.2.c, C.2.b, E.3.a, F.1.a, F.1.b, F.2.a, F.2.b, F.2.c, F.2.d, F.2.e, F.2.f, F.2.g, F.3.a, F.3.b, F.3.c, F.4.b, F.4.c, F.5.a, G.1.a, G.1.b, G.2.a, G.3.a, H.1.a, H.1.b, H.1.d, H.2.a.

Mirroring (fine & performing arts)

This provides a chance to work on observation and control.

In pairs, stand facing each other as if you were seeing your reflection in a mirror. First, one person of the pair makes slow, distinct motions and facial movements, and the partner mirrors these movements as accurately as possible and at the same pace. Remember, the mirror image uses the opposite part of the body. So, if the first person moves the right hand, then the mirror image moves the left. Then let the other person initiate the movements.

For a variation, select a sport and perform actions appropriate for dressing to participate in that sport. Sports such as baseball, football, track, swimming, tennis and ice skating are good to try.

Topical signs to be learned: slow, movement, face, same, choose, sport, action, clothing signs, sport signs.

Indicators: A.1.a, A.1.b, A.1.c, A.1.d, A.2.a, A.2.b, A.2.c, B.1.c, B.2.a, B.2.b, B.2.c, C.2.b, E.3.a, F.1.a, F.1.b, F.2.b, F.2.e, F.2.h, F.3.a, F.3.c, F.4.b, G.1.a, G.1.b, G.2.a, G.3.a, H.1.b, H.1.d, H.2.a.

My Own TV (fine & performing arts)

Materials: appliance cardboard box, strong and large (big enough to crawl inside); felt pen or dark crayon, sharp knife (adult use only), stickers or labels (optional), masking or duct tape.

Draw a TV screen on one side of the box. Draw it as large as possible. Draw additional TV parts such as knobs, buttons, speakers. Stickers or labels can also be used for this step. Cut out the hole for the screen with the knife (adult only). Fold the flaps out on bottom of the box. Tape the box flaps to the floor to help keep the box from wiggling and collapsing. Crawl into the box and pretend to be on television.

More ideas: Make up a commercial. Hold an empty cereal box, toy, or other prop to sell. Sing a song or act out a favorite book or story. Ask a friend to change the "channel" for a new "program." Use an old cabinet-style TV set with all the parts removed.

Topical signs to be learned: television, movies, box, pen, crayon, draw.

Indicators: A.1.a, A.1.b, A.1.c, A.1.d, A.2.a, A.2.b, A.2.c, B.1.c, B.2.a, B.2.b, B.2.c, B.4.a, C.2.b, E.3.a, F.1.a, F.1.b, F.2.a, F.2.b, F.2.c, F.2.d, F.2.e, F.2.f, F.2.g, F.3.a, F.3.b, F.3.c, F.4.b, F.4.c, F.5.a, G.1.a, G.1.b, G.2.a, G.3.a, H.1.a, H.1.b, H.1.d, H.2.a.

Pass it Along (fine & performing arts)

Like a game of charades, this game is played in teams. It is the most fun when at least six people play, with at least three players on each team.

Each team lines up, with players either sitting or standing. The team that goes first decides what they will pass along. Will it be a piano? A feather? A crying baby? A hot slice of pizza? The funnier the made-up passed-along object, the more fun the game. The first player on the team pretends to pick up the object using exaggerated motions, and passes it to the next player, who passes it to the next player. The other team tries to guess what the object is. If the second team can't figure it out after three or four guesses, the first team reveals the object. Then the second team thinks of an object and passes it along while the first team tries to guess what it is.

Topical signs to be learned: game, team, pretend, pass, guess, wrong.

Indicators: A.1.a, A.1.b, A.1.c, A.1.d, A.2.a, A.2.b, A.2.c, B.1.c, B.2.a, B.2.b, B.2.c, C.2.b, E.3.a, F.1.a, F.1.b, F.2.b, F.2.e, F.2.h, F.3.a, F.3.c, F.4.b, G.1.a, .G.1.b, G.2.a, G.3.a, H.1.b, H.1.d, H.2.a.

Slide Show (fine & performing arts, drama)

Here's a way to make a vacation slide show very interesting.

One person is the presenter; everyone else is part of the slide show. The presenter begins telling the story of her vacation. Throughout the story, the presenter says, "next slide please." The other players strike a pose just like people in a photo from a vacation. The presenter uses this group pose to tell a story. The players keep their pose, as if they are an actual slide, until the presenter says, "next slide, please." Then the players change their pose, and the presenter continues the story of her vacation, explaining this new pose as if it where the very next slide from her vacation. The presenter can set up how the players will pose by saying something like, "in my next slide you will see us climbing the mountain. Next slide please," and the players pose as if they are climbing a mountain. Or the presenter can let the players create a picture on their own by giving the next slide no introduction. In this case, the presenter must somehow work this new pose into the story. Continue the scene until the presenter has finished the story of her vacation.

Topical signs to be learned: tell, story, next, photo, use, change, explain, finished.

Indicators: A.1.a, A.1.b, A.1.c, A.1.d, A.2.a, A.2.b, A.2.c, B.1.c, B.2.a, B.2.b, B.2.c, B.4.a, C.2.b, E.3.a, F.1.b, F.2.b, F.2.e, F.2.h, F.3.a, F.3.c, F.4.b, G.1.a, .G.1.b, G.2.a, G.3.a, H.1.b, H.1.d, H.2.a.

Spinning Feelings (fine & performing arts, emotions)

Materials: plastic coffee can lid, heavy paper plate, square of cardboard, brass bracket, pencil, scissors, permanent markers, index cards.

To construct the spinner: Cut an arrow from the plastic coffee can lid. Punch a hole in it with the points of a pair of scissors and set aside. Trace the paper plate with a pencil on a square of cardboard. Cut the cardboard 1" to 2" larger than the traced circle. Poke a hole through the center of the paper plate with a pencil point or scissors tips, and another hole through the center of the cardboard square. Join the plate and the square with a brad/brass bracket. To do this, push the brad/brass bracket through the plastic arrow, through the plate, through the cardboard, and open it to the back of the cardboard. Now spin the plate. If it does not spin, make the hole in the plate larger or loosen the brad/bracket a little.

To make the feelings circle: Draw two lines crossing each other directly through the center of the plate to divide it into four equal pie shapes. First draw light pencil lines, and when happy with the lines, go over them with a permanent marker. In the first pie shape space, draw a happy face. In the next space, draw a sad face. Draw a surprised face and an angry face in the last two spaces. Other feelings faces could be drawn instead of any of these four, such as: sleepy, bored, goofy, giddy, dreamy, thrilled, melancholy.

To make the situation cards: Write situations, such as any similar to the following: a goat is eating your shoe, a space ship landed in your backyard, it's lunch time, nothing to eat but candy bars for breakfast, lunch, and dinner!; telephone call for you, two monsters are at your door.

To play: Pick a situation card and then spin the spinner to see which emotion you must portray when acting out that situation.

Topical signs to be learned: plate, paper, scissors, pencil, write, draw, face, emotion signs, act.

Indicators: A.1.a, A.1.b, A.1.c, A.1.d, A.2.a, A.2.b, A.2.c, B.1.c, B.2.a, B.2.b, B.2.c, C.2.b, E.3.a, F.1.b, F.2.a, F.2.b, F.2.e, F.2.h, F.3.a, F.3.c, F.4.b, G.1.a, .G.1.b, G.2.a, G.3.a, H.1.b, H.1.d, H.2.a.

Talking Ball (fine & performing arts)

Materials: ball

Sit in a circle (or across from each other if there are two people playing). One person holds the ball and, while they hold the ball, they are the storyteller. The storyteller begins telling a story about anything. After a few sentences, the storyteller tosses the ball to someone else. Now they are the new storyteller. The new storyteller continues the story where the old storyteller left off. The second person must build off the story that was started by the first person. After a few sentences, the ball is passed again and the story continues with a new storyteller. Keep tossing the ball until the story comes to an end. You can only talk if you are holding the talking ball. You can toss the ball at the end of a sentence or in the middle. If the ball toss is in the middle, the new storyteller continues the story exactly from where the first person stopped. Listen closely to the story, so when it's your turn to be the storyteller, everything makes sense.

Topical signs to be learned: ball, sit in circle, pass (give), story, tell, storyteller (narrator), sentence, few, end, listen, throw.

Indicators: A.1.a, A.1.b, A.1.c, A.1.d, A.2.a, A.2.b, A.2.c, B.1.c, B.2.a, B.2.b, B.2.c, B.4.a, C.2.b, F.1.b, F.2.b, F.2.e, F.2.h, F.3.a, F.3.c, F.4.b, G.1.a, .G.1.b, G.2.a, G.3.a, H.1.b, H.1.d, H.2.a.

Through the Door (fine & performing arts)

Choose on player to be the director. Everyone else makes a line backstage (or out the door or behind the screen). The director should not be able to see the players and should not know their order in line. The director calls out a character. It can be a famous person or a type of worker. For example, the director may call out, "cheerleader." The first player in line comes out and walks across the stage (or room) as a cheerleader. She may speak if she wants to, but the most important thing is to walk like a cheerleader. After she has walked across the stage or room, she goes back through the door and to the end of the line. The director then calls out another character, such as "Captain Hook," and the next actor in line comes out as Captain Hook, walks across the stage/room, then gets back in line. The game continues until everyone has played a number of characters. This game can get humorous because the players don't know what character they will be asked to play, and the director doesn't know who is next in line. The director may call out, "Snow White," and a boy may be next, or the director may call out "a mouse" and the tallest person in the group may be next. The player must give his or her best performance, no matter how different the part may be. For ideas of characters, think of your favorite stories, famous people, or different types of work people perform. Or you can play Reverse Through the Door where the players decide what character they are performing and the director has to guess who he or she is.

Topical signs to be learned: character, act, like, through, door, walk, line (line-up).

Indicators: A.1.a, A.1.b, A.1.c, A.1.d, A.2.a, A.2.b, A.2.c, B.1.c, B.2.a, B.2.b, B.2.c, C.2.b, F.1.b, F.2.a, F.2.b, F.2.e, F.2.h, F.3.a, F.3.c, F.4.b, G.1.a, .G.1.b, G.2.a, G.3.a, H.1.b, H.1.d, H.2.a.

Water Walking (fine & performing arts)

This may be done in pantomime first and then later with improvised sounds and exclamations. Everyone stands and walks in a circle. Imagine water flowing into the room, first covering your feet, thighs, and then your waist, neck, and finally over the top of your head—but you discover that you can breathe underwater. Adjust your body movements and gestures according to the changing depth of the water. Then each person becomes a sea creature. After a few moments more, the water recedes slowly. Change your movement in reverse with the lowering of the water.

Topical signs to be learned: walk, circle, water, cover, under, change, movement/move, sea animal.

Indicators: A.1.a, A.1.b, A.1.c, A.1.d, A.2.a, A.2.b, A.2.c, B.1.c, B.2.a, B.2.b, B.2.c, C.2.b, D.2.c, E.3.a, F.1.b, F.2.b, F.2.e, F.2.h, F.3.a, F.3.c, F.4.b, G.1.a, .G.1.b, G.2.a, G.3.a, H.1.b, H.1.d, H.2.a.

Fine & Performing Art Crafts

Art Shirts (school, art)

Materials: old adult size t-shirt from home, paints, brushes.

Have the children decorate an old t-shirt that they can use as a smock for future art projects. Help them to paint their name on it.

Topical signs to be learned: shirt, decorate, paint, color signs, name, alphabet signs, art.

Indicators: A.1.b, A.1.c, A.1.d, A.2.a, A.2.b, A.2.c, B.1.c, B.5.a, B.5.b, B.5.c, C.2.b, F.1.b, F.2.b, F.2.c, F.2.d, F.2.e, F.2.h, F.3.c, F.4.a., G.1.a, G.1.b, G.2.a, H.1.a, H.1.b, H.1.c, H.1.d.

Ball Painting (fine & performing arts)

Materials: paper, round cake pan or plastic container, scissors, paint, spoon, small, rubber balls.

Cut paper to fit cake pan or use plastic container big enough to fit paper. Place the paper in the pan/container. Spoon a small amount of paint on the paper. Put the rubber balls in the pan. Have the children make an inclined plane by tilting the pan back and forth. The rubber balls will roll around and create designs. Remove the paper from the pan, and let the paint dry.

Topical signs to be learned: paper, paint, ball, dry.

Indicators: A.1.a, A.1.b, A.1.c, A.1.d, A.2.a, A.2.b, A.2.c, B.1.c, B.2.a, B.2.b, B.2.c, C.2.b, F.1.b, F.2.b, F.2.d, F.2.e, F.2.h, F.3.c, F.4.a, G.1.a, .G.1.b, G.2.a, H.1.b, H.1.c, H.1.d.

Button Mosaic (math, fine & performing arts)

Materials: cardboard, buttons, glue, craft paper.

Cut a square of cardboard, 4" x 4" or 8" x 8" as desired. Lay out buttons in a design. If there are gaps between the buttons, first cover the cardboard with craft paper and then glue on the buttons. If the buttons make a solid pattern, simply cover the board with glue and place the buttons in position. Talk about the different colors, patterns, and shapes the children are making with the buttons.

Topical signs to be learned: glue, shape, signs, color signs.

Indicators: A.1.b, A.1.c, A.1.d, A.2.a, A.2.b, A.2.c, B.1.c, B.2.a, C.2.b, F.1.b, F.2.b, F.2.d, F.2.e, F.2.h, F.3.c, F.4.a, G.1.a, .G.1.b, G.2.a, H.1.a, H.1.b, H.1.c, H.1.d.

Can Drums (fine & performing arts)

Materials: Various assortment of different size cans (cleaned), packaging tape, stickers, construction paper, markers, glue, chopsticks.

Get each child to bring in 3 cans from home. Switch them around so they each can have a various assortment of sizes. Cut out construction paper large enough to cover each of the cans. Decorate with markers and stickers then glue onto the cans. Turn them upside down and place together, then use packing tape to tape them all together. Have the children tap with their fingers to produce different sounds. Now try it with chopsticks (warn them not to tap too hard or they will break). Now we are ready to play. Compare the sounds each of the different drums make. Play the drums to one of your classes favorite songs having half the class play the drums, while the other half sign. Then switch and play again.

Topical signs to be learned: Music, song, drums, paper, glue, scissors, colors, hear, share, please, thank you.

Indicators: A.1.b, A.1.c, A.1.d, A.2.a, A.2.b, A.2.c, B.1.c, B.2.a, C.2.b, E.1.a, F.1.b, F.2.b, F.2.d, F.2.e, F.2.h, F.3.c, F.4.a, G.1.a, .G.1.b, G.2.a, H.1.a, H.1.b, H.1.c, H.1.d.

Chalk and Sandpaper Letters - (alphabet, art)

Preparations: Cut sandpaper into desired sizes and pour water into containers. Have the children dip colored chalk into water and then draw designs on the sandpaper. Encourage them to use several different colors.

Materials: Sandpaper of different textures cut into different letters, shallow containers, water.

Indicators: A.1.a, A.1.b, A.1.c, A.1.d, A.2.a, A.2.b, A.2.c, F.2.b, F.4.a., G.1.a, and G.2.a

Colors Book (art, colors)

Each month designate a page to decorate with pictures and/or items pertaining to the color of the month. You can also use "baggies" for items that cannot be glued into the book.

Materials: white construction paper, collage items and/or pictures depicting the color of the month. Have children bring in a picture from home to go into the book.

Indicators: A.1.a, A.1.b, A.1.c, A.1.d, A.2.a, A.2.b, A.2.c, F.2.b, F.4.a., G.1.a, and G.2.a

Crayon Etching (art, colors)

Fill the paper with heavy blotches of crayon or a crayon design. Color heavily over the whole paper with black crayon. Plan a picture or design. You might sketch it on scrap paper first. Use a sharp object to scratch the design on the black crayon. The black will come off and the colors will show through wherever you scratch. Try scratching sharp lines and larger areas too. Gently polish the picture to finish it. Use another piece of paper, a tissue, or a paper towel for polishing.

Materials: paper, tagboard, or paper plates (any shape), crayons, nail or un-bent paper clip
Indicators: A.1.a, A.1.b, A.1.c, A.1.d, A.2.a, A.2.b, A.2.c, F.2.b, F.4.a., G.1.a, and G.2.a

Crayon Scratching (art, colors)

Color a design on the white paper with various colors of crayons. Color darkly. After the page is covered with color, color over the whole thing with black crayon. Press down hard so all of the other colors are covered by the black. Use the paper clip or pen to scratch out your own fireworks display!

Materials: crayons of various colors, one must be black, white paper, paper clip or used up pen.
Indicators: A.1.a, A.1.b, A.1.c, A.1.d, A.2.a, A.2.b, A.2.c, F.2.b, F.4.a., G.1.a, and G.2.a

Flowerpot Bells (fine & performing arts)

Materials: 3 different size clay flowerpots, 3 – 1 foot lengths of heavy cord, wooden spoon, long thin board 1" (w) x 2" (h) x 18" (l) , hammer (adult use only), nails(adult use only).

Group project (4). Have the children tie a large knot on one end of the 1 foot lengths of cord. Thread the cord through the hole in the bottom of the flower pot, with the knot on the inside and long piece of cord coming through the hole with the pot sitting upside down on the table. Nail the cords evenly apart so that the bells have at least 2" of space in between each. Now we are ready to play. Compare the sounds each of the different flowerpot bell makes. Play the bells to one of your classes favorite songs having ¼ the class play the bells, while the others sign. Then switch and play three more songs until everyone gets a turn.

Topical signs to be learned: music, song, bells, hear, share, please, thank you.

Indicators: A.1.b, A.1.c, A.1.d, A.2.a, A.2.b, A.2.c, B.1.c, B.2.a, C.2.b, E.1.a, F.1.b, F.2.b, F.2.d, F.2.e, F.2.h, F.3.c, F.4.a, G.1.a, .G.1.b, G.2.a, H.1.a, H.1.b, H.1.c, H.1.d.

Jingle Bracelet (fine & performing arts)

Materials: 1 ft. lengths of ribbon, large wooden beads, jingle bells.

Have the children string the beads and 3 jingle bells onto the ribbon, being sure to have an equal amount of beads (4 or so) between each bell. Tie both ends together in a square knot so that the bells and beads stay close together. Compare the sounds of each bracelet by having the children shake them, tap them on their other hand and thigh. Have half of the children use their bracelet to compliment the class singing and signing the familiar song *"Jingle Bells"*. Then switch and sign, sing and play again.

Topical signs to be learned: music, song, band, bell, colors, hear, share, please, thank you.

Indicators: A.1.b, A.1.c, A.1.d, A.2.a, A.2.b, A.2.c, B.1.c, B.2.a, C.2.b, E.1.a, F.1.b, F.2.b, F.2.d, F.2.e, F.2.h, F.3.c, F.4.a, G.1.a, .G.1.b, G.2.a, H.1.a, H.1.b, H.1.c, H.1.d.

Jug Shaker (fine & performing arts)

Materials: ½ gallon plastic jug (milk, juice) with handle and lid, jingle bells, medium sized plastic or wooden beads, duck or packaging tape, glue, stickers.

Have the children work in groups of 4. Have them fill their jugs from ¼ to ½ full with beads and jingle bells. Glue the lid on, adding tape for extra support. Have the children decorate the jugs as they wish with stickers. Compare the noise made by each of the jugs. Shake them along to familiar tunes as you sing them. Now we are ready to play. Compare the sounds each of the different jug shakers make. Play the shaker jugs to one of your classes favorite songs having ¼ of the class play the shaker jugs, while the others sign. Then switch and play three more songs until everyone gets a turn.

Topical signs to be learned: music, song, band, colors, hear, share, please, thank you.

Indicators: A.1.b, A.1.c, A.1.d, A.2.a, A.2.b, A.2.c, B.1.c, B.2.a, C.2.b, E.1.a, F.1.b, F.2.b, F.2.d, F.2.e, F.2.h, F.3.c, F.4.a, G.1.a, .G.1.b, G.2.a, H.1.a, H.1.b, H.1.c, H.1.d.

Junque Collage (fine & performing arts)

Materials: white glue thinned with a little water, base for collage such as Styrofoam tray, egg carton lid, cardboard, etc.; junque; feathers, spools, buttons, corks, ribbons, plastic flowers, fabric scraps, wood scraps, etc.

Spread all the junk on the table or in small shallow containers. Have children choose an object or objects to glue on the base. Dip the object into the glue and glue it, holding tight, to the base. Continue selecting objects and gluing them onto the base until the collage is finished.

Topical signs to be learned: glue, water, egg, share, finish.

Indicators: A.1.b, A.1.c, A.1.d, A.2.a, A.2.b, A.2.c, B.1.c, B.2.a, C.2.b, F.1.b, F.2.b, F.2.d, F.2.e, F.2.h, F.3.c, F.4.a, G.1.a, .G.1.b, G.2.a, H.1.a, H.1.b, H.1.c, H.1.d.

Musical Kazoo (fine & performing arts)

Materials: Toilet tissue tube, 4" x 4" colorful cellophane square, rubber band, markers, stickers, scissors

Use markers and stickers to decorate the tube. Place the cellophane around one end of the tube and hold it in place with a rubber band. Have the children blow in the uncovered end to hear the sound. Then have the children add a hole or two, with scissors, to the tube and play, covering and uncovering the holes. Now we are ready to play. Compare the sounds each of the different kazoo makes. Play the kazoos to one of your classes favorite songs having half the class play the kazoos, while the other half sign. Then switch and play the song again or play another class favorite.

Topical signs to be learned: music, song, horn, band, paper, glue, scissors, colors, hear, share, please, thank you.

Indicators: A.1.b, A.1.c, A.1.d, A.2.a, A.2.b, A.2.c, B.1.c, B.2.a, C.2.b, E.1.a, F.1.b, F.2.b, F.2.d, F.2.e, F.2.h, F.3.c, F.4.a, G.1.a, .G.1.b, G.2.a, H.1.a, H.1.b, H.1.c, H.1.d.

Paper Plate Tambourine (fine & performing arts)

Materials: Heavy duty paper plate, jingle bells, single hole, paper punch, tempura paint, art brushes, markers, glitter, glue, yarn.

Have the children punch 3 sets of 2 evenly spaced holes around the paper plate. Decorate with glitter, markers or paint. Use yarn to tie 3 jingle bells to the plate. Once dry we are ready to make music. Now we are ready to play. Compare the sounds each of the different tambourine makes. Play the tambourine to one of your classes favorite songs having half the class play the tambourine, while the other half sign. Then switch and play the song again or play another class favorite.

Topical signs to be learned: music, song, band, bells, paper plate, glue, scissors, colors, hear, share, please, thank you.

Indicators: A.1.b, A.1.c, A.1.d, A.2.a, A.2.b, A.2.c, B.1.c, B.2.a, C.2.b, E.1.a, F.1.b, F.2.b, F.2.d, F.2.e, F.2.h, F.3.c, F.4.a, G.1.a, .G.1.b, G.2.a, H.1.a, H.1.b, H.1.c, H.1.d.

Pie Tin Cymbals (fine & performing arts)

Materials: Aluminum pie tins, small door knobs (or cork), screws, washer, nail, screwdriver.

Push the nail through the center of the pie tin to make a small hole. Place a screw through the washer, then through the pie tray (facing outside). Then put a knob on the bottom of the pie tin, screwing it onto the outward facing screw. Tighten with screw driver. Each child makes two. Gently hit them together. Now we are ready to play.

Compare the sounds each of the different cymbals makes. Play the cymbals to one of your classes favorite songs having half the class play the cymbals, while the other half sign. Then switch and play the song again or play another class favorite.

Topical signs to be learned: music, song, band, hear, please, thank you.

Indicators: A.1.b, A.1.c, A.1.d, A.2.a, A.2.b, A.2.c, B.1.c, B.2.a, C.2.b, E.1.a, F.1.b, F.2.b, F.2.d, F.2.e, F.2.h, F.3.c, F.4.a, G.1.a, .G.1.b, G.2.a, H.1.a, H.1.b, H.1.c, H.1.d.

Popcorn Maraca (fine & performing arts)

Materials: Plastic film canisters with lid, Popsicle sticks, popcorn kernels, rice, dry beans, construction paper, glue, musical stickers, markers, tempura paint, paint brushes.

Have each child make 2 maracas. Fill the film canisters about ¼ full of with either rice, popcorn kernels or dry beans. Cut a hole in the lid to insert the Popsicle stick (may be best for teacher to do ahead of time). Put a small amount of glue into the lid outer rim of the lid, then close the lid securely to the film canister. Then have the children write their names on one end of the Popsicle stick. Insert the end without the name into the canister and glue where it enters the canister. Cut out a piece of construction paper to go around and cover the film canister, glue onto the canister, and let dry for a moment. Decorate with paint, markers or stickers as children wish. Let sit long enough to insure Popsicle stick is secure than make music. Now we are ready to play. Compare the sounds each of the different maraca makes. Play the maraca to one of your classes favorite songs having half the class play the maraca, while the other half sign. Then switch and play the song again or play another class favorite.

Topical signs to be learned: music, song, drums, paper, popcorn, rice, paint, glue, scissors, colors, hear, share, please, thank you.

Indicators: A.1.b, A.1.c, A.1.d, A.2.a, A.2.b, A.2.c, B.1.c, B.2.a, C.2.b, E.1.a, F.1.b, F.2.b, F.2.d, F.2.e, F.2.h, F.3.c, F.4.a, G.1.a, .G.1.b, G.2.a, H.1.a, H.1.b, H.1.c, H.1.d.

Puppets (fine & performing arts)

Elephant Puppet (fine & performing arts)

Materials: felt, scissors, needle, thread, googly eyes, button.

Cut out two elephant shapes from pieces of felt. They must be large enough to fit onto your hand and the trunk should be just a little wider than your finger. Remember also to allow room for the seam. Now sew the two pieces together, all around the head and trunk, leaving just the opening for your hand. Cut out and stitch on ears, eyes, and tusks. The trunk can be worked with your longest finger.

Finger Puppets (fine & performing arts)

Materials: paper or felt, glue or tape (or needle and thread), markers or crayons, paper scraps, other items to decorate puppets.

Roll a piece of paper around your finger so that it fits quite well without falling off every time you move it. Stick the paper together. Or roll a piece of felt around your finger that fits well without falling off every time you move it and glue it or stitch it. Decorate with markers, crayons, paper scraps, or other items.

Finger Puppet Theatre (fine & performing arts)

Materials: strong paper plate, scissors, construction paper scraps, glue, sticky dot or white label (optional), permanent marker.

Cut a slit in the middle portion of the paper plate. With scraps of construction paper, cut shapes and things to create a scene on the plate with trees, clouds, or any other ideas. Glue them on the plate (Items can cover the slit, but must be cut apart to keep the slit open.) Take a permanent marker and draw a face on the pointer finger. A plain sticky dot or a white label can be drawn on first and then stuck to the finger, if preferred. Hold the plate upright and insert fingers through the slit of the plate for an instant puppet theatre. You can make puppets on Popsicle sticks, tongue depressors, coffee stir sticks, or straws instead of fingers, if preferred.

Lighted Box Puppet Stage (fine & performing arts)

Materials: cardboard boxes, two the same size; pencil, ruler, scissors, paint and brushes, masking and regular tape, flashlight.

Select one box. Cut away the top flaps and save for scraps. Draw a stage opening on the front of the box, making a rectangle from the base approximately two-thirds of the way up. Make the opening fairly large, but leave some room on the sides to keep the stage sturdy. Cut out the pieces (may need adult help). Paint the box inside and out with any chosen colors. Add painted decorations around the stage opening, if desired. Paint a sign for the puppet stage, like "Theatre Magnificent," "Puppet Show," or "Eric's Best Stage Shows." Let dry completely. When dry, cut lighting holes in the sides of the theatre. During a show, shine a flashlight through the holes to spotlight a puppet. You can cover the flashlight with colored cellophane held in place by a rubber band to change the lighting to different colors and effects. A lighted show may take two or more people to perform.

With cardboard from the second box and flap scraps, draw and paint scenery for the puppet stage. When dry, cut the scenery out with adult help. Depending on the store, the scenery might include a cottage, trees, or the inside of a house. The scenery will hang from the sticks into the stage area. Tape the top of each piece of scenery onto a long thing stick. Make each stick longer than the width of the box so it will rest on the top of the box. Cut little nicks in the left and right top edges of the box for the sticks to rest in so the scenery hangs down into the stage area.

Painted Hand Puppet (fine & performing arts)

Materials: face paints such as BioColor (use nontoxic paints that peel or wash off easily), brushes, markers (water-based and nontoxic), any puppet theatre, soap, water, old towel, old shirt (optional), rubber band or tape (optional), scissors (optional).

Experiment first with markers and paints to see how they work on skin. Then wash off paint and marker lines. Dry. Decide whether to make each finger into a puppet, making five puppets, or to make the entire hand into one puppet. With markers or paints, decorate fingers or hand as a puppet. See how the hand can be a full-face view or a side view. Notice how each finger can be a different character. To dress the hand puppet, create a "Sleeve Costume" by cutting the sleeve off an old shirt and secure it with a rubber band or piece of tape around the wrist. The sleeve will end near the elbow. Put on a show with any puppet theatre. When done, wash hands in soapy water and dry with an old towel. Sometimes paints can take a day or two to completely wear off.

Puppeteer (fine & performing arts)

Materials: sofa or table, tablecloth and chairs, or 2 straight-backed chairs, a book, a clothesline or rope, and a blanket or sheet, puppets, and props.

There are three ways to make a stage. If there's room behind a sofa, you can hide back there and ask the audience to sit in front of it on the floor. If you have props and scenery you want to use, you'll need a stage with a real floor. A table works well—just pull a tablecloth down long enough to hide behind. The audience can sit on the opposite side of the table, where they won't be able to see you. If you want to build a simple puppet theatre yourself, take a pair of straight-backed chairs and place them a few feet away from each other. Tie a piece of clothesline or rope between them and set a few heavy books in each chair for balance. Then hang a blanket or sheet from the clothesline to make a curtain.

Lights, puppets, action. Send your puppets out on stage and give your show. Remember to use different voices for all the puppets, and move the one who's talking a little bit, so the audience can follow the action. Your show can be as simple or as complex as you want it to be. One or two puppets can sing a song or two, or you can use a crowd of them to tell a long, fanciful story. You can work by yourself behind the stage, or you can use as many other co-puppeteers as will fit behind your stage.

Sock Puppet (fine & performing arts)

Materials: old sock, needle and thread or fabric glue, materials for decorating such as beads, buttons, felt scraps, fringes, googly craft eyes, masking tape, old jewelry, pompoms, rickrack, rug scraps, stick-on dots, yarn.

Pull the sock over the non-drawing hand, positioning the heel of the sock over the thumb. See how the puppet "talks" as the thumb and other fingers are pulled together and apart. Decide how to decorate the puppet making good use of the mouth of the sock puppet in the design. Begin sewing or gluing on scraps and other materials to give the puppet eyes, nose, hair, and personality. When done, help the puppet talk by opening and closing the puppet's mouth with a hand inside the sock.

More ideas: Stuff the toe of a sock with a ball of cotton stuffing or tissue paper. Tie a piece of string around the neck (not too tight). The rest of the sock is the puppets body. Glue or sew on decorations as desired. Insert fingers in the head of the puppet.

As with all puppets, make up an original story or act out a favorite book or fairy tale. Puppets can sing along with a favorite recording.

Stick Puppets (fine & performing arts)

Materials: thing wooden sticks such as dowels, long bamboo skewers, or wooden gardener's stakes, pencil, file cards, scissors, glue, crayons or markers, paper clips, tape.

Draw and color puppets on file cards. Cut them out. Trace the puppets on a second file card and color these for the backs of puppets. Glue each front and back of the puppet to a stick. Be sure the stick comes out of the puppet's head upward. Hold until the glue sticks. Tape an opened paper clip to the top of the stick to work as a hook and a handle. You can hang the puppets when they are not moving but must remain on stage, on the scenery hooks in the puppet theatre. You can also attach small toys or other items such as toy cars, animals, dinosaurs, or doll furniture on the sticks to use as puppets or props.

Topical signs to be learned: puppet, hand, box, glue, crayon, pencil, scissors, paint, decorate, audience, perform, face, eye, nose, smile, person, animal, elephant, sock, stick, soap, wash, dry, light.

Presto! Magic Wand (fine & performing arts)

Materials: sturdy stick or dowel about 1 foot long, fabric glue, ten 6-inch strips of colored ribbon or fabric and another that's 2 inches long, sequins, pom-poms, feathers, or other decorations.

Use the stick or dowel as the handle for the wand. One end will be for holding, and the other end will be decorated with ribbons. Make sure you have 10 strips of ribbon or fabric, about 6 inches long and about an inch wide. Lay the wand down on newspaper or a work surface that glue won't ruin. Smear a small amount of glue on one end of the ribbon, and attach the glue side of the ribbon to the top of the wand. Continue gluing all the pieces of the ribbon around the top of the wand. Make sure you place the ribbon at the same point on the stick, all the way around, so that you have an even edge. Let the wand sit for about 20 minutes, or until it's dry. Turn the wand upside down, so that the streamers are hanging away from the stick. Smear glue all over the 2-inch piece of ribbon or fabric and wrap it around the top of the wand. This creates a border on top of where the other ribbons are glued. Let the wand dry for 20 minutes. Turn the wand back upright and the ribbons will fall back over the wand like a waterfall. Glue decorations onto the ribbon or fabric that will glitter or move when you turn the wand. Make a wish!

Topical signs to be learned: glue, ribbon, dry, make, wish, decorations.

Indicators: A.1.b, A.1.c, A.1.d, A.2.a, A.2.b, A.2.c, B.1.c, B.2.a, C.2.b, F.1.b, F.2.b, F.2.d, F.2.e, F.2.h, F.3.c, F.4.a, G.1.a, .G.1.b, G.2.a, H.1.a, H.1.b, H.1.c, H.1.d.

Recorder (fine & performing arts)

Materials: Paper towel tube, cone shaped drinking cup, aluminum foil, tape, circle shapes (either stickers or cut out circles), scissors.

Have the children cover the tubes with foil. Then create a mouthpiece out of foil, being sure to leave an opening on both ends of the mouthpiece. Insert one end of the tube, being sure it is snug and then glue or tape it into position. Cut off the pointed end of the cone shaped cup, then cover the cone with foil. Insert it into the opposite end of the tube and affix with tape or glue. Arrange and affix five colored stickers in a row. After the recorder is complete, let the glue dry if necessary, then have the children pretend to play by blowing and pressing on the keys. Now we are ready to play. Compare the sounds each of the different recorder makes. Play the recorder to one of your classes favorite songs having half the class play the recorder, while the other half sign. Then switch and lay the song again or play another class favorite.

Topical signs to be learned: music, song, horn, paper, drinking cup, circle, glue, scissors, colors, hear, share, please, thank you.

Indicators: A.1.b, A.1.c, A.1.d, A.2.a, A.2.b, A.2.c, B.1.c, B.2.a, C.2.b, E.1.a, F.1.b, F.2.b, F.2.d, F.2.e, F.2.h, F.3.c, F.4.a, G.1.a, .G.1.b, G.2.a, H.1.a, H.1.b, H.1.c, H.1.d.

Scrolling Story Box (fine & performing arts, stories)

Materials: cardboard box, strong and medium sized; tape, scissors (or sharp knife for adult only), crayons, markers, long roll of butcher paper (or sheets of paper taped together to make a long roll), 2 wooden dowels about 12" long (or an old broomstick or paper towel tubes).

Cut a rectangular piece from the smooth side of a cardboard box for the viewing screen. Next cut two slits on the side ends of the box a little bigger than the paper width, about 12" x 2". Spread the roll of paper out on a table or smooth floor surface with the beginning edge at the right, and any extra paper to the left. Think of a story, book, fairy tale, song, or movie to draw. Draw the story on the roll of paper in a sequence of events, from the first thing that happens to the last thing that happens. When finished drawing the story, re-roll the paper onto a dowel or paper towel tube with the right edge (where the first pictures is) free. To prepare the drawings for a show, feed the paper from the left slit and across the viewing rectangle to the right slit. Pull it through and tape it to the second dowel or paper towel tube. Now the drawings are ready to scroll. Slowly roll the drawings from the left to the right onto the dowel. Tell the story out loud, or simply enjoy viewing the drawings. When finished, roll the drawings back onto the left dowel or paper towel tube. Add music or a story tape to enhance the show. The first "page" in the viewing window could be a title, design box, or sign.

Topical signs to be learned: box, scissors, paper, story, book, song, movie, draw, event, first, last, happen, finished, roll, tell, title.

Indicators: A.1.b, A.1.c, A.1.d, A.2.a, A.2.b, A.2.c, B.1.c, B.2.a, B.4.a, C.2.b, E.1.a, F.1.b, F.2.b, F.2.d, F.2.e, F.2.h, F.3.c, F.4.a, G.1.a, .G.1.b, G.2.a, H.1.a, H.1.b, H.1.c, H.1.d.

Secondary Colors (colors, art)

Have children paint using the three primary colors. Demonstrate how colors are formed, then allow them to experiment.

Materials: tag board, red, yellow and blue paint, and smocks.

Indicators: A.1.a, A.1.b, A.1.c, A.1.d, A.2.a, A.2.b, A.2.c, F.2.b, F.4.a., G.1.a, and G.2.a

Splatter Painting (art)

Materials: 6-inch square of wire screen, old toothbrush, thin paint, manila tag or cardboard, simple shapes to be used as a stencil, straight pins (optional).

Lay or pin stencil on paper. Hold screen two to three inches above paper. Dip toothbrush into paint and brush across the screen to produce spatters on the paper below.

Variations:

Fold paper in half. Unfold and place on work surface. Lay a stencil on the right-hand fold of the paper. Spatter paint the paper. Carefully lift off the stencil to reveal the design. Refold paper to form greeting card.

Fold paper in half. Unfold again and lay flat. Lay cutout letter of child's name on the right-hand fold of the paper. Spatter paint. Remove the stencil letters to reveal personalized stationary. Refold paper into greeting card form.

Fold paper in half. Unfold again and lay flat. Use pressed leaves, ferns, or flowers as stencils, and lay them on the right-hand fold of the paper. Spatter paint. Remove leaf, fern, or flower stencils to reveal botanical prints. Refold paper into greeting card form.

Topical signs to be learned: paper, paint, shape signs, color signs.

Indicators: A.1.b, A.1.c, A.1.d, A.2.a, A.2.b, A.2.c, B.1.c, B.2.a, C.2.b, F.1.b, F.2.b, F.2.d, F.2.e, F.2.h, F.3.c, F.4.a, G.1.a, .G.1.b, G.2.a, H.1.a, H.1.b, H.1.c, H.1.d.

Textured Collage (basic vocabulary, fine & performing arts)

Materials: colored construction paper, glue, water, plastic cup, paint, brush, and tissue paper.

Have children bring in items that have different textures. Glue items to a piece of cardboard or display board and have children sign back to you what textures are.

Topical signs to be learned: texture, glue, paper, water, paint, brush, paper.

Indicators: A.1.b, A.1.c, A.1.d, A.2.a, A.2.b, A.2.c, B.1.c, B.2.a, C.2.b, F.1.b, F.2.b, F.2.d, F.2.e, F.2.h, F.3.c, F.4.a, G.1.a, .G.1.b, G.2.a, H.1.a, H.1.b, H.1.c, H.1.d.

Textured Crayon Pictures (fine & performing arts)

Materials: crayons, paper, glue, decorating materials such as fabric, sponges, cotton, ribbon or string, felt, sticks, paper, beans or seeds, glitter, beads, etc.

Draw a picture with crayons, and when finished use as many materials as possible to give texture to it. Clothes can be real fabrics glued on, but avoid porous materials such as linen, which shows the glue. Trees or bushes could be covered with tiny bits of green craft paper, glued over another like shingles. String or yarn can be used for a kite's tale and string. The possibilities for ingenuity are almost unlimited.

Topical signs to be learned: texture, crayon, draw, glue, paper, string, ribbon, decorate, clothes, tree, string, kite.

Indicators: A.1.b, A.1.c, A.1.d, A.2.a, A.2.b, A.2.c, B.1.c, B.2.a, C.2.b, F.1.b, F.2.b, F.2.d, F.2.e, F.2.h, F.3.c, F.4.a, G.1.a, .G.1.b, G.2.a, H.1.a, H.1.b, H.1.c, H.1.d.

Textured Painting (fine & performing arts)

Materials: sawdust, poster paint, cardboard, pencil, paste or glue, paint or crayons (optional), coffee ground or sand (optional).

Dye the sawdust (any except redwood or cedar) the color desired by covering with poster paint. When the color has soaked in, drain sawdust on newspaper and dry. Draw the outlines of a picture on a cardboard back. Then spread paste or glue on all the areas that are to be a certain color. When dry, paste over the areas of another color, and repeat until the textured area has been covered color by color. For better contrast cover only part of the picture with sawdust; perhaps just the figure, in front of a painted or crayon-colored background. In this case, do the textured part last. Experiment by adding dried coffee grounds or sand, plus a little glue, to small quantities of poster paints, if desired.

Topical signs to be learned: texture, paint, pencil, glue, paint, crayon, draw, color signs, dry.

Indicators: A.1.b, A.1.c, A.1.d, A.2.a, A.2.b, A.2.c, B.1.c, B.2.a, C.2.b, F.1.b, F.2.b, F.2.d, F.2.e, F.2.h, F.3.c, F.4.a, G.1.a, .G.1.b, G.2.a, H.1.a, H.1.b, H.1.c, H.1.d.

Three Sculpting Dough Recipes (fine & performing arts)

Basic Breadcraft (excellent flour and salt dough)

Materials: 4 cups flour, 1 cup salt, 1 cup water (plus more), mixing bowl, tempera paint or food color (optional), foil or waxed paper, paint and brushes (optional).

Combine 4 cups flour and 1 cup salt in a bowl. Make a well in the center and pour in 1 cup water. Mix with hands. Add up to ½ cup more water and continue mixing by hand. Dough should form a ball but not be crumbly or sticky. Knead five minutes on a floured board until smooth. If desired, knead in tempera paint or food coloring for color. Work with small portions of dough on foil or wax paper. Bake for one hour at 325 degrees F until hard. Then cool. Can be painted when cool.

Funclay (smooth white dough, dries in several hours)

Materials: 2 cups salt, 1 cup water, 1 cup cornstarch, pan, bowl, mixing spoon, waxed paper, tempera paint or food color (optional), paint and brushes (optional).

Mix 2 cups salt and 2/3 cup water in a pan. Bring to a boil. Mix 1 cup cornstarch and 1/3 cup cold water in a bowl. Mix cornstarch mixture into the salt mixture. Cool. Knead on waxed paper until dough-like. Knead in tempera paint or food coloring, if desired. Now sculpt and model with the clay. Remember to pull out clay to make arms, heads, and legs rather than sticking separate pieces on. Dries in several hours. Can be painted when dry.

Basic Play Clay (white and hard, dries quickly)

Materials: 1 cup baking soda, ½ cup cornstarch, 2/3 cup water, pan, food coloring or paint (optional), nail polish or clear hobby coating.

Mix baking soda and cornstarch in pan. Add about 2/3 cup water and stir until smooth. Cook over medium heat. Boil until like mashed potatoes. Pour on a board to cool. Then knead. Add color to the dough with drops of food coloring or paint, if desired. Sculpt and model clay. Let dry for an hour or so. Paint, if desired. For a protective coating, paint with nail polish or any clear hobby coating.

Topical signs to be learned: salt, water, cup, measure, bowl, paint, food color, paint, pour, ball, bake, cold, dry.

Indicators: A.1.b, A.1.c, A.1.d, A.2.a, A.2.b, A.2.c, B.1.c, B.2.a, C.2.b, F.1.b, F.2.b, F.2.d, F.2.e, F.2.h, F.3.c, F.4.a, G.1.a, .G.1.b, G.2.a, H.1.a, H.1.b, H.1.c, H.1.d.

Waxed Garfield (fine & performing arts)

Materials: comic strips (preferably through not essentially in color), waxed paper, spoon.

Place a piece of waxed paper over a picture from the comic pages (or a comic book). Using the edge (not the rounded base) of a spoon, rub over the picture. Be sure to rub all of the picture. Don't rub over anything you don't want to capture on the waxed paper or you'll have inadvertently included a tree, half a person, or the edge of the next panel. Rub firmly, though be careful not to tear the paper. Remember that whatever you pick up will come out reversed. With a little practice, you'll eventually be ready to make composite strips. You can create quite a menagerie of comic strip canines and felines...or a playground full of comic strip kids, or any other sort of composite you want.

Topical signs to be learned: paper, picture, spoon.

Indicators: A.1.b, A.1.c, A.1.d, A.2.a, A.2.b, A.2.c, B.1.c, B.2.a, C.2.b, F.1.b, F.2.b, F.2.d, F.2.e, F.2.h, F.3.c, F.4.a, G.1.a, .G.1.b, G.2.a, H.1.a, H.1.b, H.1.c, H.1.d.

Water Bells (fine & performing arts)

Materials: 8 clear 6" high water glasses, water, 2 metal spoons, numbered cards from 1-8.

Line up the 8 glasses in a row, close together, but not touching. Place the numbers in front of the glasses in order from 1-8. Add water to the glasses as follows:

½ inch in glass 1	3 ½ inches in glass 5
1 ¼ inches in glass 2	4 ¼ inches in glass 6
2 inches in glass 3	5 inches in glass 7
2 ¾ inches in glass 4	5 ¾ inches in glass 8

Now we are ready to play. Compare the sounds each of the different glass bell makes. Play the glass bells to one of your classes favorite songs having half the class play some of their other instrument creations, while the other half sign (all sing). Then switch instruments and take turns playing the glass bells to other familiar favorites

Topical signs to be learned: Music, song, water, glass, measurement, hear, share, please, thank you.

Indicators: A.1.b, A.1.c, A.1.d, A.2.a, A.2.b, A.2.c, B.1.c, B.2.a, C.2.b, E.1.a, F.1.b, F.2.b, F.2.d, F.2.e, F.2.h, F.3.c, F.4.a, G.1.a, .G.1.b, G.2.a, H.1.a, H.1.b, H.1.c, H.1.d.

Math, Colors & Shapes
Songs, Stories, Games & Activities

Counting

Time to Sign Curriculum: Signs can be found in the Math, Science and Nature Module; Music Module for all music and Preschool Activity Guide for hands on activities.

Learn: Counting – as specified in the weekly planning guide

Song: 3 Little Monkeys

Song: Six Little Ducks

Song: Ten Little Amigos or Ten Little Indians (use instrumental "10 Little Indians")

Song: The Ants Go Marching

Activity: Counting dice (role dice and count the dots. The number of dots you roll tells how many small blocks that child can play with.

Activity: complete "Adding Numbers in Sign Language" activity in activity guide

Song: Hands Can Count

Art Activity: Fruit Loops Fun! (Add fruit loops to a string to tie around the wrist. The children can count how many fruit loops they can fit on the string.)

Activity: Waddle-a-way

Activity: Duck Relay

Activity: Counting Clothes

Story: <u>Five Little Monkeys Sitting in a Tree</u> by Eileen Christelow (math, animals)

Story: <u>Fish Eyes</u> by Lois Ehlert (math, animals)

Story: <u>Five Little Ducks</u> by Pamela Palarone (animals, counting, family)

Story: <u>Counting on the Woods</u> by George Ella Lyon (count, math, nature)

Activity: Complete letter of the week and number activities in the activity guide

Activity: Complete letter of the week and "Find the Missing Number" activities in the activity guide

Props: Sign Language Number Cards and Placemat Numbers Signs

Colors

Time to Sign Curriculum: Signs can be found in the Language Arts Module; Music Module for all music and Preschool Activity Guide for hands on activities.

Learn: Color signs - red, green, blue, yellow

Learn: Color signs - Black, blue, brown, colors, gold, gray, green, orange, pink, purple, rainbow, red, silver, white, yellow

Song: Colors (Use instrumental-Farmer in the Dell)

Activity: I Spy

Song/Activity: Color Exercise Activity (in the activity guide)

Activity: Sounds of Rainbow

Activity: Circle Call Game - Endangered Species with Colors

Song: Make New Friends

Activity: Complete color match in activity guide

Story: <u>Little Blue & Little Yellow</u> by Leo Lioni (colors, family)

Story: <u>White Rabbit's Color Book</u> by Alan Baker (colors)

Time to Sign Props: Colors and Shapes Poster

Shapes

Time to Sign Curriculum: Signs can be found in the Math, Science and Nature Module; Music Module for all music and Preschool Activity Guide for hands on activities.

Learn: car, airplane, book, toilet, bath, bed, play

Learn: Shapes signs - Circle, heart, square, and triangle

Learn: Shapes signs - Circle, diamond, heart, oval, rectangle, shape, square, and triangle

Activity: Body Shapes

Song: Shape Song

Play: I Spy (with shapes and colors)

Story: <u>Brown Rabbit's Shape Book</u> by Alan Baker (colors, shapes)

Time to Sign Props: Colors and Shapes Posters

Math Stories

<u>Colorful Tiger</u> Time to Sign Book by Elisabeth Nichols, Illustrated by Brian Miller (shapes)
Topical signs to be learned: colors, tiger, far, away,

Indicators: A.1.a, A.1.b, A.1.c, A.1.d, A.2.a, A.2.b, A.2.c, B.1.a, B.1.e, B.2.a, B.2.b, B.2.c, B.2.c, B.3.a, B.4.a, H.1.a, and H.1.b

<u>Brown Rabbit's Shape Book</u> by Alan Baker (colors, shapes)

Topical signs to be learned: Brown, rabbit, red, triangle, shape, rectangle, square, box, underneath, inside, circle, five, flat, balloons, different, colors, big, round, orange, oval, egg, away, flew, green, long, purple, smaller, pear, long, curly.

Indicators: A.1.a, A.1.b, A.1.c, A.1.d, A.2.a, A.2.b, A.2.c, B.1.a, B.1.e, B.2.a, B.2.b, B.2.c, B.2.c, B.3.a, B.4.a, H.1.a, and H.1.b

Counting on the Woods by George Ella Lyon (math, nature)

Topical signs to be learned: numbers 1-10, path, bird, bug, worm, earth, new (or baby), rest, who, come, stone/rock, flower, dirt, shower (rain), vine, sky, climb, tree, many, leaves, clean.

Indicators: A.1.a, A.1.b, A.1.c, A.1.d, A.2.a, A.2.b, A.2.c, B.1.a, B.1.b, B.1.c, B.1.d, B.2.a, B.2.b, B.2.c, B.3.a, B.3.b, B.4.a, C.1.a, C.1.b, C.1.d, C.2.b, D.2.c, D.2.d, F.1.b, F.2.d, F.2.e, F.2.h, G.1.a, G.1.b, G.2.a, H.1.a, H.1.b

Fish Eyes by Lois Ehlert (math, animals)

Topical signs to be learned: get dressed, eyes, wish, change, beautiful, fish, river, sea, swim, far, catch, me, see, numbers 1-10, green, plus, equal, jump, smile, skinny/thin, shiny, look.

Indicators: A.1.a, A.1.b, A.1.c, A.1.d, A.2.a, A.2.b, A.2.c, B.1.a, B.1.b, B.1.c, B.1.d, B.2.a, B.2.b, B.3.a, B.3.b, B.4.a, C.1.a, C.1.b, C.1.d, C.2.b, F.1.b, F.2.d, F.2.e, F.2.h, G.1.a, G.1.b, G.2.a, H.1.a, H.1.b.

Five Little Ducks by Pamela Paparone (animals, counting, family)

Topical signs to be learned: five, little, ducks, went, play, over, hill, far, away, Mother, said, Quack, four, came, back, three, two, one, no, Daddy, all.

Indicators: A.1.a, A.1.b, A.1.c, A.1.d, A.2.a, A.2.b, A.2.c, B.1.a, B.1.b, B.1.c, B.1.d, B.2.a, B.2.b, B.2.c, B.3.a, B.3.b, B.4.a, C.1.a, C.1.b, C.1.d, C.2.b, F.1.b, F.2.d, F.2.e, F.2.h, F.5.a, G.1.a, G.1.b, G.2.a, H.1.a, H.1.b

Five Little Monkeys Sitting in a Tree by Eileen Christelow (math, animals)

Topical signs to be learned: numbers 1-5, monkey, mama, walk, river, picnic, sleep, climb, tree, crocodile/alligator, tease, can't, catch, me, where, no, look, hug, eat.

Indicators: A.1.a, A.1.b, A.1.c, A.1.d, A.2.a, A.2.b, A.2.c, B.1.a, B.2.a, B.2.b, B.2.c, B.3.a, B.3.b, B.4.a, C.1.a, C.1.b, C.1.d, C.2.b, F.1.b, F.2.d, F.2.e, F.2.h, G.1.a, G.1.b, G.2.a, H.1.a, H.1.b.

Gray Rabbit's 1, 2, 3 by Alan Baker (numbers, animals)

Topical signs to be learned: one, day, Gray, Rabbit, find, clay, worm, one, two, three, bird (toucan), bear, four, dog, five, frog, six, snakes, seven, snails, eight, elephants, nine, bugs, ten, mice (mouse), sleep.

Indicators: A.1.a, A.1.b, A.1.c, A.1.d, A.2.a, A.2.b, A.2.c, B.1.a, B.1.b, B.1.c, B.1.d, B.2.a, B.2.b, B.3.a, B.3.b, B.4.a, C.1.a, C.1.b, C.1.d, C.2.b, F.1.b, F.2.d, F.2.e, F.2.h, G.1.a, G.1.b, G.2.a, H.1.a, H.1.b.

The Grouchy Ladybug by Eric Carle (insects, math, available in Spanish)

Topical signs to be learned: night, firefly, dance, moon, 1-12 o'clock, sun, ladybug, leaf, bug, eat, breakfast, grouchy, fly, good morning, go away/away), want, share, mine, fight, not, big, enough, bird, lobster, snake, gorilla, rhinoceros, elephant, whale, answer, start, hungry, dinner, thank you, tired, sleep.

Indicators: A.1.a, A.1.b, A.1.c, A.1.d, A.2.a, A.2.b, A.2.c, B.1.a, B.1.b, B.1.c, B.1.d, B.2.a, B.2.b, B.3.a, B.3.b, B.4.a, C.2.b, D.1.c, D.2.b, F.1.b, F.2.d, F.2.e, F.2.h, G.1.a, G.1.b, G.2.a, H.1.a, H.1.b

Just a Minute: A Trickster Tale and Counting Book by Yuyi Morales (math)

Topical signs to be learned: grandma, door, wait, come on, minute, numbers 1-10, house, tea, corn, hat, fruit, more, time, salad, cheese, hurry, food, candy, plate, count, beautiful, come, sit, table, grandma, where, number, birthday, cake, blow, candles, party, finish, kiss, ready, fun, miss.

Indicators: A.1.a, A.1.b, A.1.c, A.1.d, A.2.a, A.2.b, A.2.c, B.1.a, B.1.b, B.1.c, B.1.d, B.2.a, B.2.b, B.3.a, B.3.b, B.4.a, C.1.a, C.1.b, C.1.d, C.2.b, F.1.b, F.2.d, F.2.e, F.2.h, G.1.a, G.1.b, G.2.a, H.1.a, H.1.b

Little Blue & Little Yellow by Leo Lioni (colors, family)

Topical signs to be learned: little, blue, yellow, papa, mama, many, friends, best, play, hide and seek, "Ring around the Rosie", sit, rows, school, run, jump, looked, here, there, everywhere, hugged, green, ran, chased, orange, climbed, mountain, tired, cried.

Indicators: A.1.a, A.1.b, A.1.c, A.1.d, A.2.a, A.2.b, A.2.c, B.1.a, B.1.e, B.2.a, B.2.b, B.2.c, B.2.c, B.3.a, B.4.a, H.1.a, and H.1.b

White Rabbit's Color Book by Alan Baker (colors)

Topical signs to be learned: white, rabbit, three, tubs, paint, red, yellow, blue, sunshine, lovely, bright, sun, white, orange, look, together, make, time, wash, hot, cool, purple, important, princess, shower, icy, cold, warm, no more, water, brown, just, right, for, me.

Indicators: A.1.a, A.1.b, A.1.c, A.1.d, A.2.a, A.2.b, A.2.c, B.1.a, B.1.e, B.2.a, B.2.b, B.2.c, B.2.c, B.3.a, B.4.a, H.1.a, and H.1.b

White Rabbit's Color Book by Alan Baker (colors)

Topical signs to be learned: white, rabbit, three, tubs, paint, red, yellow, blue, sunshine, lovely, bright, sun, white, orange, look, together, make, time, wash, hot, cool, purple, important, princess, shower, icy, cold, warm, no more, water, brown, just, right, for, me.

Indicators: A.1.a, A.1.b, A.1.c, A.1.d, A.2.a, A.2.b, A.2.c, B.1.a, B.1.e, B.2.a, B.2.b, B.2.c, B.2.c, B.3.a, B.4.a, H.1.a, and H.1.b

Math Songs

Ant Go Marching In (numerals and sets)

Indicators: A.1.a, A.1.b, A.1.c, A.1.d, A.2.a, A.2.b, A.2.c, B.1.a, B.1.c, B.1.d, B.2.a, B.2.b, B.3.a, B.4.a, C.1.a, C.1.b, C.1.d, C.2.b, E.1.a, E.2.a, F.1.b, F.2.e, F.2.h, F.3.c, G.1.a, G.1.b, H.1.a, H.1.b, H.1.d

Shape Song (shape)

Indicators: A.1.a, A.1.b, A.1.c, A.1.d, A.2.a, A.2.b, A.2.c, B.1.a, B.1.c, B.1.d, B.2.a, B.2.b, B.3.a, B.4.a, C.2.a, C.2.b, E.1.a, E.2.a, F.1.b, F.2.e, F.2.h, F.3.c, G.1.a, G.1.b, H.1.a, H.1.b, H.1.d

Six Little Ducks (numerals)

Indicators: A.1.a, A.1.b, A.1.c, A.1.d, A.2.a, A.2.b, A.2.c, B.1.a, B.1.c, B.1.d, B.2.a, B.2.b, B.3.a, B.4.a, C.1.a, C.1.b, C.1.d, C.2.b, E.1.a, E.2.a, F.1.b, F.2.e, F.2.h, F.3.c, G.1.a, G.1.b, H.1.a, H.1.b, H.1.d

Square Song (shape)

Indicators: A.1.a, A.1.b, A.1.c, A.1.d, A.2.a, A.2.b, A.2.c, B.1.a, B.1.c, B.1.d, B.2.a, B.2.b, B.3.a, B.4.a, C.2.a, C.2.b, E.1.a, E.2.a, F.1.b, F.2.e, F.2.h, F.3.c, G.1.a, G.1.b, H.1.a, H.1.b, H.1.d

Ten Little Indians (numerals and sets)

Indicators: A.1.a, A.1.b, A.1.c, A.1.d, A.2.a, A.2.b, A.2.c, B.1.a, B.1.c, B.1.d, B.2.a, B.2.b, B.3.a, B.4.a, C.1.a, C.1.b, C.1.d, C.2.b, E.1.a, E.2.a, F.1.b, F.2.e, F.2.h, F.3.c, G.1.a, G.1.b, H.1.a, H.1.b, H.1.d

Triangle Song (shapes)

Indicators: A.1.a, A.1.b, A.1.c, A.1.d, A.2.a, A.2.b, A.2.c, B.1.a, B.1.c, B.1.d, B.2.a, B.2.b, B.3.a, B.4.a, C.2.a, C.2.b, E.1.a, E.2.a, F.1.b, F.2.e, F.2.h, F.3.c, G.1.a, G.1.b, H.1.a, H.1.b, H.1.d

What Shape is This? (shapes)

Indicators: A.1.a, A.1.b, A.1.c, A.1.d, A.2.a, A.2.b, A.2.c, B.1.a, B.1.c, B.1.d, B.2.a, B.2.b, B.3.a, B.4.a, C.2.a, C.2.b, E.1.a, E.2.a, F.1.b, F.2.e, F.2.h, F.3.c, G.1.a, G.1.b, H.1.a, H.1.b, H.1.d

Math Games & Activities

Beans in a Jar (math)

Materials: clear glass jar, beans.

Place a random number of beans, between one and ten, in the jar. Ask the child(ren) to look at the beans and guess how many are in the jar. After the child(ren) guesses, empty the beans and count the beans. The number of beans can be increased slowly.

Topical signs to be learned: guess, numbers 1-10, count.

Indicators: A.1.a, A.1.b, A.1.c, A.1.d, A.2.a, A.2.b, A.2.c, B.1.a, B.1.c, B.2.a, B.3.a, C.1.a, C.1.b, C.1.c, C.1.d, C.2.b, F.1.b, F.2.b, F.2.d, F.2.e, F.2.h, F.3.c, F.4.a, G.1.a, G.1.b, G.2.a, G.3.a, H.1.a H.1.b

Colors

Circle game. Use the color cards to help teach the children the signs for colors. Have the children take turns telling you the color then show them the sign. The color signs can be reused again and again to reinforce the learning of colors and their signs.

Indicators: A.1.c, A.1.d, A.2.a, A.2.b, A.2.c, G.1.a, G.2.a, H.1.a, and H.1.b

Color Games I

Have the children sit with you in a circle. Teach/review the color signs that make up your rainbow. Have the children repeat all the signs to the leader as they are demonstrated. Children each select, or are assigned, a color. The children take turns going around the circle clockwise demonstrating the sign for their chosen color. The leader begins the game by signing their color then that of another person. The person they have 'called', signs their sign then that of another in the circle. In about 5 minutes they should have learned all the color signs. Assist anyone who needs help with the signs, especially the last to go to insure they succeed. Praise the children for their success.

Indicators: A.1.c, A.1.d, A.2.a, A.2.b, A.2.c, G.1.a, G.2.a, H.1.a, and H.1.b

Color Games II

Have the children sit with you in a circle. Teach/review the color signs for the various items to be picked up off the floor, as well as please and thank you. Have the children repeat all the signs to the leader as they are demonstrated. Go around the circle having each child take a turn picking an item out of the center of the circle. They sign the color of the item and then place it in the box/bag. (The teacher signs 'thank you' each time a child places an item in the bag/box.) In the first round, have all the children sign the appropriate color sign for every item put away. In the second round, have only the child whose turn it is sign the color. Assist anyone who needs help with the signs to insure success. End the game by having everyone do the rainbow sign together. Additional rounds: add the name of the item as well as the color. Assist anyone who needs help with the signs, especially the last to go to insure they succeed. Praise the children for their success.

Indicators: A.1.c, A.1.d, A.2.a, A.2.b, A.2.c, G.1.a, G.2.a, H.1.a, and H.1.b

Color Games III

Have the children sit with you in a circle. Show the children the colors and rainbow sign cards to teach/review the color signs that make up your rainbow. Have the children repeat all the signs to the leader as they are demonstrated. The children take turns going around the circle clockwise selecting a sign card and showing it to the other children. They display the sign shown on the chosen card. The children take turns going around the circle until all the cards have been used up. (If there are more children than colors, then the cards are placed back in the pile in the middle of the circle for reuse.) End the game by having all the children go through the color signs once again and finish with the rainbow sign. In about 5 minutes they should have learned all the color signs. Assist anyone who needs help with the signs, especially the last to go to insure they succeed. Praise the children for their success.

Indicators: A.1.c, A.1.d, A.2.a, A.2.b, A.2.c, G.1.a, G.2.a, H.1.a, and H.1.b

Color Games IV

Have the children sit with you in a circle. Show the children the colors and rainbow sign cards to teach/review the color signs that make up your rainbow. Have the children repeat all the signs to the leader as they are demonstrated. The children take turns going around the circle clockwise selecting a sign card and showing it to the other children. They create the sign they just picked and the sign(s) of the other children who have already gone. For example, the first person selects red, so she makes the red sign. The second person selects blue. So they do the red and blue signs. And so on. (If there are more children than colors, then the cards are placed back in the pile in the middle of the circle for reuse.) End the game by having all the children go through the color signs once again as they were selected and finish with the rainbow sign. In about 5 minutes they should have learned all the color signs. Assist anyone who needs help with the signs, especially the last to go to insure they succeed. Praise the children for their success.

Indicators: A.1.c, A.1.d, A.2.a, A.2.b, A.2.c, G.1.a, G.2.a, H.1.a, and H.1.b

Color Games V

Either you have an even amount of children or the leader has to play so that everyone has a partner. Start by playing any of the Games 1-4 Rainbow Color Games. When done, have the children pick a color card slip. They have to be quite during this phase of the game. When the leader says go, they will have to make their selected color's sign. Without talking they have to find the others who have the same color. The game ends when they get together with all their same color sign partners and make the rainbow sign. Assist anyone who needs help with the signs or finding their group to insure success. Praise the children for their signing.

Indicators: A.1.c, A.1.d, A.2.a, A.2.b, A.2.c, G.1.a, G.2.a, H.1.a, and H.1.b

Colors, Let's Look At Colors

Play "Find me the color..." and sign the color you want the children to find.

Indicators: A.1.c, A.1.d, A.2.a, A.2.b, A.2.c, G.1.a, G.2.a, H.1.a, and H.1.b

Color Vote

Review color signs they previously learned and have them "vote" for their favorite color. To vote, they need to sign their favorite color sign. When everyone has voted, graph results and help the children determine a winner! Materials: color pictures and signs, and graph of colors.

Indicators: A.1.c, A.1.d, A.2.a, A.2.b, A.2.c, G.1.a, G.2.a, H.1.a, and H.1.b

Counting Game (math)

Materials: goldfish crackers.

Have children pretend that their hand is a whale. Give each child five goldfish crackers. Recite the following rhyme. To make each 'fish' disappear, have the children eat a cracker.

> 5 little fishes in the deep blue sea,
>
> swimming along happily,
>
> along comes a whale, quiet as can be
>
> and snatches a fishy right out of that sea.
>
> Repeat for 4, 3, 2, 1...
>
> (tune of Three Little Monkeys or Teasing Mr. Alligator)

Topical signs to be learned: numbers 1-5, sea, happy, come, whale, quiet, fish.

Indicators: A.1.c, A.1.d, A.2.a, A.2.b, A.2.c, B.1.a, B.1.c, B.2.a, B.2.b, C.1.a, C.1.b, C.1.d, C.2.b, E.1.a, F.1.b, F.2.e, F.2.h, F.3.c, F.4.a, G.1.a, G.1.b, G.2.a, G.3.a, H.1.a, H.1.b

Full and Empty (math)

Materials: several different size containers, rice.

Put varying amounts of rice in each container. Some should be almost empty, some almost full, some half full, and some a quarter full of rice.

Have the children arrange the containers from the least amount to the most. After arranging the containers pour all of the rice out and have the children refill the containers from smallest amount to greatest amount. Identify "half-full" and "quarter-full."

Topical signs to be learned: full, empty, one-half, sort, less, more.

Indicators: A.1.a, A.1.b, A.1.c, A.1.d, A.2.a, A.2.b, A.2.c, B.1.c, B.2.a, C.2.b, D.1.a, D.1.b, D.2.d, F.1.b, F.2.e, F.2.h, F.3.c, F.4.a, G.1.a, G.1.b, H.1.a, H.1.b, H.1.d.

I Feel Heavy (math)

Materials: paper, pen/pencil, scale.

Have the children put on all their winter clothing and write down their names and what they weigh. Once all the children have done this weigh them again without their winter clothing on. Tell them what the differences were. Tell them what the average difference was by adding up all the weights and dividing by the number of children. Talk to them about how they feel when they are wearing all the winter clothes. Heavy, uncoordinated, stiff, etc.

Topical signs to be learned: winter, clothes, clothing signs, write, name, weigh, feel.

Indicators: A.1.a, A.1.b, A.1.c, A.1.d, A.2.a, A.2.b, A.2.c, B.1.c, B.2.a, B.2.b, B.2.c, C.1.a, C.1.b, C.1.c, C.2.b, D.1.a, D.1.b, D.2.c, F.1.b, F.2.b, F.2.d, F.2.e, F.2.g, F.2.h, F.3.a, F.3.c, F.4.a, G.1.a, G.1.b, G.2.a, G.3.a, G.1.a, G.2.a, H.1.d, H.2.a.

Matching Bead Patterns (math, patterns)

Materials: different shaped beads, 12 3"x5" cards with a bead pattern drawn on each, several lengths of string, yarn, or shoelaces.

Have children choose a card and reproduce the pattern on the card by stringing the beads in the correct order.

Topical signs to be learned: color signs, shape signs, same, string.

Indicators: A.1.a, A.1.b, A.1.c, A.1.d, A.2.a, A.2.b, A.2.c, B.1.c, B.2.a, C.1.d, C.2.a, C.2.b, F.1.b, F.2.b, F.2.e, F.2.h, F.3.a, F.3.c, G.1.a, G.1.b, G.2.a, G.3.a, H.1.a, H.1.b, H.1.d.

Matching Color/Shape Cards (colors, math)

Materials: white poster board, scissors, plastic bags, tape, felt pen, crayons.

Cut the poster board into card-shaped sizes, 10 for each child. Place sets of 10 in plastic bags and write names of child on each bag.

Give each child a set to make a game. Have them color two cards the same color until they have colored all their cards. To play, children lay cards face down on table or floor and turn over two cards at a time until they have found all the matching cards. Children can play alone or in pairs.

Shape cards: draw shapes for the children to color on the cards or have them cut out and paste on shapes of different colored construction paper.

Can also play go fish with the cards.

Topical signs to be learned: color and/or shape signs, same, pick/find.

Indicators: A.1.a, A.1.b, A.1.c, A.1.d, A.2.a, A.2.b, A.2.c, B.1.c, B.2.a, C.1.d, C.2.a, C.2.b, , F.1.b, F.2.b, F.2.e, F.2.h, F.3.a, F.3.c, G.1.a, G.1.b, G.2.a, G.3.a, H.1.a, H.1.b, H.1.d.

Number Sequencing (math, numbers)

Materials: coat hanger, poster board, marker, green construction paper, clothespins, glue.

Cut out five pieces of poster board and number them 1-5. Cut out a small circle from the green construction paper. Hang the coat hanger on a doorknob or other place. Glue the green dot on the left side of the coat hanger. Glue the poster board numbers in sequence from one to five beginning to the right of the green dot. Have the children pin the correct number of clothespins to the correct number card.

Topical signs to be learned: numbers 1-5, count.

Indicators: A.1.c, A.1.d, A.2.a, A.2.b, A.2.c, B.1.c, B.2.a, B.3.a, C.1.a, C.1.b, C.1.d, C.2.b, F.1.b, F.2.b, F.2.e, F.2.h, F.3.c, G.1.a, G.2.a, H.1.a, H.1.b, H.1.d.

Number Worm (numbers & counting, sequencing)

Materials: heavy cardboard/poster board, markers, scissors.

Construct a number worm by drawing a worm and dividing it into sections with a number from 1-10 written on each section. Cut the numbers so they will only fit when arranged in consecutive order (like a puzzle). Children will discover sequence of numbers as they fit together the number worm.

Topical signs to be learned: numbers 1-10, worm, count, puzzle.

Indicators: A.1.c, A.1.d, A.2.a, A.2.b, A.2.c, B.3.a, C.1.a, C.1.b, C.1.d, C.2.b, F.1.b, F.2.b, F.2.e, F.2.h, F.3.c, G.1.a, G.2.a, G.3.a, H.1.a, H.1.b, H.1.d.

Ordinal Numbers (math)

Materials: paper cups, shelled peanuts.

Place four cups with the numbers 1-4 on them on the table. Have child cover their eyes while a peanut is hidden under one of the cups. Have the child open their eyes and guess which cup the peanut is under. The child must say "the peanut is under the (first, second, third, fourth) cup." and not simply point or say "that' one." Label and add more cups as the child learns more ordinal numbers.

Topical signs to be learned: number signs, hide, which, pick.

Indicators: A.1.c, A.1.d, A.2.a, A.2.b, A.2.c, B.3.a, C.1.a, C.1.b, C.1.d, C.2.b, F.1.b, F.2.b, F.2.e, F.2.h, F.3.c, F.4.a, G.1.a, G.2.a, G.3.a, H.1.a, H.1.b, H.1.d.

Ordinal Number Bones (numbers, animals)

Materials: heavy paper, marker.

Cut out a dog and nine bones from heavy paper. Write an ordinal number on each bone ("1st" through "9th"). Tell a story about how much a dog loves bones. After he collects bones, he likes to eat the first one he found first and the second one he found second, etc. The dog has gotten his bones all mixed up. Ask the children if they can help the dog by lining up his bones in the correct order.

Topical signs to be learned: numbers 1-9, dog, find, eat.

Indicators: A.1.c, A.1.d, A.2.a, A.2.b, A.2.c, B.3.a, C.1.a, C.1.b, C.1.d, C.2.b, F.1.b, F.2.b, F.2.e, F.2.h, F.3.c, G.1.a, G.2.a, G.3.a, H.1.a, H.1.b, H.1.d.

Playing with Shapes (math, shapes)

Materials: colored construction paper, scissors, felt pen, paper, crayons or markers.

Draw a variety of different shapes in different sizes on the construction paper and cut them out. Give the children the shapes and have them sit together on the rug to discuss the different sizes and shapes. Give each child a large sheet of paper and have them use the shapes to create different designs on the paper. Have the children trace around the shapes using a crayon. When they take away the shapes, they will have a picture. Or have the children glue the shapes onto their paper to create a picture.

Topical signs to be learned: shape signs, picture, draw, size signs.

Indicators: A.1.c, A.1.d, A.2.a, A.2.b, A.2.c, C.2.a, C.2.b, F.1.b, F.2.b, F.2.e, F.2.h, F.3.c, G.1.a, G.2.a, G.3.a, H.1.a, H.1.b, H.1.d.

Shape Walk (math, shapes)

Materials: paper, crayons or markers, pieces of cardboard.

Give each child a piece of paper, a crayon or marker and a flat piece of cardboard. Then take the children on a shape walk. Have the children sign and draw the shapes they see outdoors or in the classroom. When finished, you can have a discussion of what shapes they saw and what types of objects had those shapes. Have children use shape signs or draw the shape with their index finger if unusual.

Topical signs to be learned: shape signs, draw, paper, walk, see.

Indicators: A.1.c, A.1.d, A.2.a, A.2.b, A.2.c, B.1.c, C.2.a, C.2.b, D.1.b, F.1.b, F.2.b, F.2.e, F.2.h, F.3.c, F.4.a, G.1.a, G.2.a, H.1.a, H.1.b, H.1.c, H.1.d.

Walking Through Numerals (math)

Materials: colored construction paper, markers, clear contact paper.

Trace a foot on different colored pieces of construction paper. Number the footsteps 1-10. Cover with contact paper. Have children (individual or small group) align the footsteps in the correct order 1-10. Then have the children step on the footsteps and call out and/or sign the color and number of each.

Topical signs to be learned: numbers 1-10, color signs, walk, sign, name.

Indicators: A.1.a, A.1.b, A.1.c, A.1.d, A.2.a, A.2.b, A.2.c, B.1.a, B.1.c, B.2.a, B.2.b, B.3.a, B.4.a, C.1.a, C.1.b, C.1.d, C.2.b, F.1.b, F.2.b, F.2.e, F.2.h, F.3.c, G.1.a, G.1.b, G.2.a, H.1.a, H.1.b

What's Missing? (math)

Have children sit in a circle. Place a variety of different color hearts in the center. Have children hide their eyes. Remove one heart from the center. Have the children open their eyes and see if they can guess which one is missing. As they get better at this skill, add other shapes to center to help reinforce shape recognition. Be sure to reinforce color signs as the children tell you which item is missing. Have them sign back the color after you. Materials: different colored construction paper hearts, and various shapes in different colors.

Indicators: A.1.a, A.1.b, A.1.c, A.1.d, A.2.a, A.2.b, A.2.c, B.1.c, B.2.a, B.2.b, C.2.a, C.2.b, D.1.b, D.2.a, D.2.c, D.2.d, F.1.b, F.2.b, F.2.e, F.2.h, F.3.c, F.4.a, G.1.a, G.1.b, H.1.a, H.1.b, H.1.d

Math Crafts

Beaded Bracelets and Wristbands (math)

Materials: assorted pony beads, assorted colored pipe cleaners.

Trim the pipe cleaners if necessary, and bend down the ends so they are not sharp and pointy. Show children how to string beads onto the pipe cleaners and curve the ends to make bracelets. You can have children count out how many beads it takes to complete each bracelet or create patterns with the beads.

Topical signs to be learned: color signs, number signs.

Indicators: A.1.c, A.1.d, A.2.a, A.2.b, A.2.c, B.1.c, B.2.a, C.1.a, C.1.b, C.1.d, C.2.b, F.1.b, F.2.b, F.2.d, F.2.e, F.2.h, F.3.c, F.4.a., G.1.a, G.2.a, H.1.a, H.1.b, H.1.d.

Building Shapes (math, shapes)

Materials: craft sticks or Popsicle sticks.

Have children use the sticks to make shapes or make shapes and have the children copy what you make. You can count how many sticks were used for the shapes

The children may glue their shapes on construction paper to take home, if desired.

Topical signs to be learned: shape signs, count, number signs.

Indicators: A.1.c, A.1.d, A.2.a, A.2.b, A.2.c, B.1.c, B.2.a, C.1.a, C.1.b, C.1.d, C.2.a, C.2.b, F.1.b, F.2.b, F.2.d, F.2.e, F.2.h, F.3.c, F.4.a., G.1.a, G.2.a, H.1.a, H.1.b, H.1.d.

Circle Shape Puppet (math)

Materials: 1 large construction paper circle and 4 small circles, two 6-in. strips of paper and two 4-in. strips, markers, Popsicle stick, glue, pair of scissors.

Fold strips like an accordion and glue on for arms and legs. Glue on small circles for arms and feet, draw on a face and glue on a stick for a handle.
(Try triangles, hearts and squares)
Circle Puppet, circle puppet, jump up high.
Circle Puppet, circle puppet, fly, fly, fly.
.....bend down low, there you go./.....twirl around, touch the ground.....hop, hop, hop, now you stop.

Topical signs to be learned: shape signs, glue, puppet, jump, fly, spin, stop.

Indicators: A.1.a, A.1.b, A.1.c, A.1.d, A.2.a, A.2.b, A.2.c, B.1.a, B.1.c, B.2.a, C.2.a, C.2.b, F.1.b, F.2.b, F.2.d, F.2.e, F.2.h, F.3.c, F.4.a., G.1.a, G.2.a.

Clip the Tubes (math)

Materials: cardboard tubes, clothespins, paint, sequins, glue, construction paper.

Cut cardboard tubes into 2" lengths. Set out the tubes and a box of clothespins. Have the children use the clothespins to clip the tubes together anyway they wish. Or encourage them to try making simple shapes such as worms or flowers. Decorate with paints, sequins, etc.

Topical signs to be learned: shapes, together, paint, decorate.

Indicators: A.1.c, A.1.d, A.2.a, A.2.b, A.2.c, B.1.c, B.2.a, C.1.a, C.1.b, C.1.c, C.1.d, C.2.b, F.1.b, F.2.b, F.2.d, F.2.e, F.2.h, F.3.c, F.4.a., G.1.a, G.2.a, H.1.a, H.1.b, H.1.d. Edible Finger Paint (math)

Materials: light corn syrup, food coloring (liquid works best), paper plates for mixing newsprint or other paper for painting.

For each portion, pour 1 tablespoon (15 ml) corn syrup onto paper plate. Squirt food coloring into the puddle. Mix and paint with fingers. (Can also use pudding)

Topical signs to be learned: plate, color signs, paint.

Indicators: A.1.a, A.1.b, A.1.c, A.1.d, A.2.a, A.2.b, A.2.c, B.1.c, B.2.a, C.2.b, F.1.b, F.2.b, F.2.d, F.2.e, F.2.h, F.3.c, F.4.a., G.1.a, G.2.a.

Marble Painting (math)

Materials: coffee Can (any size), marbles, golf balls, ping pong balls (any kind of round rolling objects), construction paper (cut to fit inside of can), paint (tempera slightly thinned), eye droppers, scissors.

Cut paper to fit around inside of can. Using eye droppers, drip in small amounts of paint. Limit number of colors to 1 or 2. Drop in marbles or gold balls, etc. Replace lid. Roll on the floor or in hands in a circular motion to distribute paint. Remove finished painting to dry.

Topical signs to be learned: paint, color signs, ball, circle, dry.

Indicators: A.1.a, A.1.b, A.1.c, A.1.d, A.2.a, A.2.b, A.2.c, B.1.c. B.2.a, C.2.b, F.1.b, F.2.b, F.2.d, F.2.e, F.2.h, F.3.c, F.4.a., G.1.a, G.2.a, H.1.a, H.1.b.

Shape Clown (shapes)

Materials: construction paper, glue, scissors, scrap paper, and scrap supplies.

Make clown faces on construction paper by using cut out circles and triangles. Let the children add various supplies to it.

Topical signs to be learned: shape signs, paper, scissors.

Indicators: A.1.c, A.1.d, A.2.a, A.2.b, A.2.c, B.1.c, B.2.a, C.2.a, C.2.b, F.1.b, F.2.b, F.2.d, F.2.e, F.2.h, F.3.c, F.4.a., G.1.a, G.2.a, H.1.a, H.1.b, H.1.c, H.1.d.

Shaping Up (shapes, math)

Materials: white paper, markers, tape, crayons, stencils.

Draw a different shape on separate sheets of white paper. Draw the shape as large as the paper. Tape these shapes on a wall low enough for a child to touch.

Place crayons, markers and stencils on a table. Point to the shapes on the wall. Have the children look close at the shapes and identify them. Each child selects a shape, pulls it off the wall and brings it to the table. Have the children add color and designs to their shapes with the crayons, markers and stencils. When the children are finished, sit in a circle and have the children show their beautiful shapes and identify them.

Topical signs to be learned: shape signs, color signs, crayon, paper, draw.

Indicators: A.1.c, A.1.d, A.2.a, A.2.b, A.2.c, B.1.c, B.2.a, C.2.a, C.2.b, F.1.b, F.2.b, F.2.d, F.2.e, F.2.h, F.3.c, F.4.a., G.1.a, G.2.a, H.1.a, H.1.b, H.1.c, H.1.d.

Seasons
Songs, Stories, Games & Activities

Seasons Stories

<u>The Berenstain Bears Four Seasons</u> by Stan & Jan Berenstain (seasons)

Topical signs to be learned: look (see), out, window, what, green, buds (leaves), grow, home tree, crosuses (flowers), bear, snow, Spring, April, showers, May, Summer, warm, June, hot, mother, hose (water), father, cool, pool, share, thunder, clouds, storm, Fall, September, colors, red, yellow, gold, cold, leaves, wind, brother, sister, under, Winter, ice, river, snow, big, bear, hill, adventure, outside, see.

Indicators: A.1.a, A.1.b, A.1.c, A.1.d, A.2.a, A.2.b, A.2.c, B.1.a, B.1.b, B.1.c, B.1.d, B.2.a, B.2.b, B.2.c, B.3.a, B.3.b, B.4.a, C.2.b, D.2.b, D.2.c, D.2.d, F.1.b, F.2.d, F.2.e, F.2.h, G.1.a, G.1.b, G.2.a, H.1.a, H.1.b

<u>Five Little Snowmen</u> (Felt Board Fingerplays by Liz and Dick Wilmes) (weather)

Topical signs to be learned: five, little, snowmen, standing, row, each, has, hat, big, red, bow, out, came, sun, shown, all, day, one, melted, away, four, three, two

Indicators: A.1.a, A.1.b, A.1.c, A.1.d, A.2.a, A.2.b, A.2.c, B.1.a, B.1.b, B.1.c, B.1.d, B.2.a, B.2.b, B.3.a, B.3.b, B.4.a, C.1.a, C.1.b, C.1.d, C.2.b, F.1.b, F.2.d, F.2.e, F.2.h, G.1.a, G.1.b, G.2.a, H.1.a, H.1.b

<u>The Mitten</u> by Jan Brett (seasons, weather)

Topical signs to be learned: boy, new, mitten, white, snow, grandmother, find, make, home, safe, see, dropped, mole, inside, warm, rabbit, stop, hedgehog, owl, badger, fox, bear, mouse, sky, sneeze, animals, lost,

Indicators: A.1.a, A.1.b, A.1.c, A.1.d, A.2.a, A.2.b, A.2.c, B.1.a, B.1.b, B.1.c, B.1.d, B.2.a, B.2.b, B.3.a, B.3.b, B.4.a, C.2.b, D.1.b, D.2.b, D.2.c, D.2.d, F.1.b, F.2.d, F.2.e, F.2.h, G.1.a, G.1.b, G.2.a, H.1.a, H.1.b

Seasons Games & Activities

Seasons/Weather Matching and Categorizing (seasons, weather)

Materials: pictures of weather and seasonal pictures, boxes for categorizing (if desired).

Use various pictures of different forms of weather and different things you would find throughout the seasons. Have children match and categorize pictures into appropriate groups.

Topical signs to be learned: weather signs, season signs, separate/sort.

Indicators: A.1.c, A.1.d, A.2.a, A.2.b, A.2.c, B.1.c, C.2.b, D.1.a, D.1.b, D.1.c, D.2.a, D.2.c, D.2.b, D.2.d, F.1.b, F.2.b, F.2.e, F.2.h, F.3.c, G.1.a, G.2.a, H.1.a, H.1.b

Seasons Crafts

Sequencing Seasons (science & nature, weather)

Materials: four small boxes, adhesive shelf paper or construction paper (white, pink, yellow, red), scissors, glue, magazines or catalogs.

Cover the boxes with shelf paper or construction paper. Make the winter box white, the spring box pink, the summer box yellow, and the fall box red. Paste a seasonal picture on each box, and label the box with its season. Cut out seasonal pictures (ice, rain, sun, leaves, evergreens, flowers, ice skating, holidays, seasonal clothing, etc.)

Have the children look at all the pictures and name them. Show the children the seasonal boxes and have them name the seasons and put the boxes in sequential order. Have the children match the pictures and place them with their appropriate seasonal box (Some may be placed in more than one box).

Topical signs to be learned: season signs, picture, white, yellow, red, pink, seasonal signs from pictures.

Indicators: A.1.c, A.1.d, A.2.a, A.2.b, A.2.c, B.1.c, C.2.b, D.1.a, D.1.b, D.1.c, D.2.a, D.2.c, D.2.b, D.2.d, F.1.b, F.2.b, F.2.e, F.2.h, F.3.c, G.1.a, G.2.a, H.1.a, H.1.b

Sports & Recreation
Songs, Stories, Games & Activities

Sports

Time to Sign Curriculum: Signs can be found in the Sports, Recreation and Arts Module; Music Module for all music; and Preschool Activity Guide for hands on activities.

Learn: Sports signs – Ball, throw, play, outside

Learn: Sports signs - Ball, basketball, catch, dodge ball, football, golf, throw, gymnastics, ice skating, soccer, swimming, throw, volleyball

Activity: Be the Bouncing Ball

Activity: Basketball (Nerf)

Activity: Dodge Ball (Nerf)

Activity: Football (Nerf)

Activity: Golf (putting)

Activity: Be the Bouncing Ball

Activity: Gymnastics (tumbling)

Activity: Ice Skating (in socks)

Activity: Soccer (kick, Nerf)

Activity: Swimming (strokes in air, swim on floor)

Activity: Volleyball (balloon or beach ball volleyball)

Song: It's Summer Time Again

Story: Froggy Plays T-Ball by Jonathan London (sports, baseball)

Story: Franklin Plays the Game by Paulette Bourgeois (sports)

Sports & Recreation Stories

Franklin Plays the Game by Paulette Bourgeois and Brenda Clark (sports & recreation)

Topical signs to be learned: shoes, can, walk, can't, kick/soccer, problem, want, best, team, love, running, clothes, purple, yellow, shirt, sleep, ball, dream, game, practice, mad, win, lose, coach, wrong, father, never, cheer, friend, work, together, share, sad, think, everyday, rain, what, do, final/last, head, happy, proud, all, help, tired, dirty.

Indicators: A.1.a, A.1.b, A.1.c, A.1.d, A.2.a, A.2.b, A.2.c, B.1.a, B.1.b, B.1.c, B.1.d, B.2.a, B.2.b, B.2.c, B.3.a, B.3.b, B.4.a, C.2.b, F.1.b, F.2.d, F.2.e, F.2.h, F.5.a, G.1.a, G.1.b, G.2.a, H.1.a, H.1.b.

<u>Franklin Rides a Bike</u> by Paulette Bourgeois and Brenda Clark (sports & recreation)

Topical signs to be learned: swim, climb, swing, problem, bicycle, wheels, friend, practice, look, but, picnic, come on, hungry, home, eat, mother, help, fall, can't, lonely, Saturday, fun, best, try, hard, baseball, again, can.

Indicators: A.1.a, A.1.b, A.1.c, A.1.d, A.2.a, A.2.b, A.2.c, B.1.a, B.1.b, B.1.c, B.1.d, B.2.a, B.2.b, B.2.c, B.3.a, B.3.b, B.4.a, C.2.b, F.1.b, F.2.d, F.2.e, F.2.h, F.5.a, G.1.a, G.1.b, G.2.a, H.1.a, H.1.b.

<u>Froggy Learns to Swim</u> by Jonathan London (sports & recreation)

Topical signs to be learned: hot, wonderful, swim, mother, father, where, come on, no, know, swing, help, frogs, not, can't, show, want, again, cold, out, wait, what, all, night.

Indicators: A.1.a, A.1.b, A.1.c, A.1.d, A.2.a, A.2.b, A.2.c, B.1.a, B.1.b, B.1.c, B.1.d, B.2.a, B.2.b, B.2.c, B.3.a, B.3.b, B.4.a, C.2.b, F.1.b, F.2.d, F.2.e, F.2.h, F.5.a, G.1.a, G.1.b, G.2.a, H.1.a, H.1.b.

<u>Froggy Plays T-Ball</u> by Jonathan London (sports & recreation)

Topical signs to be learned: ball, shout, bed, go, dad, day, know, coach, eat, run, baseball, field, sing, team, play, mom, try, long, throw, not, your, home, more, red, green, wonderful, hot dog.

Indicators: A.1.a, A.1.b, A.1.c, A.1.d, A.2.a, A.2.b, A.2.c, B.1.a, B.1.b, B.1.c, B.1.d, B.2.a, B.2.b, B.2.c, B.3.a, B.3.b, B.4.a, C.2.b, F.1.b, F.2.d, F.2.e, F.2.h, F.5.a, G.1.a, G.1.b, G.2.a, H.1.a, H.1.b.

<u>Get Set! Swim!</u> By Jeannine Atkins (sports & recreation, family)

Topical signs to be learned: swim, team, race, together, house, ocean, sky, blue, win, mother, learn, never, dream, scared, "I love you", coach, equal, water, pay attention, dive, breathe, teach, ready, go, proud, lose, cheer, hug, friends, last, fast, look, thank you.

Indicators: A.1.a, A.1.b, A.1.c, A.1.d, A.2.a, A.2.b, A.2.c, B.1.a, B.1.b, B.1.c, B.1.d, B.2.a, B.2.b, B.2.c, B.3.a, B.3.b, B.4.a, C.2.b, F.1.b, F.2.d, F.2.e, F.2.h, F.5.a, G.1.a, G.1.b, G.2.a, H.1.a, H.1.b.

<u>Sophie Skates</u> by Rachel Isadora (sports & recreation)

Topical signs to be learned: start, skating, age/old, three, house, now, eight, become, ice, skater (skating + agent), work, like, shows (act), cheer/applause, lesson, afternoon, week, morning, friends, hello, coach, dress, warm, cold, clothes, easy, move, close, new, hurt, walk, house, long, time, right/correct, again, fall, way, stop, practice, help, circle, shape, school, jump, spin, dance, flexible, competition, favorite, choose, purple, excited, green, happy, music, smile, fun, nice, home, asleep.

Indicators: A.1.a, A.1.b, A.1.c, A.1.d, A.2.a, A.2.b, A.2.c, B.1.a, B.1.b, B.1.c, B.1.d, B.2.a, B.2.b, B.2.c, B.3.a, B.3.b, B.4.a, C.2.b, F.1.b, F.2.d, F.2.e, F.2.h, F.5.a, G.1.a, G.1.b, G.2.a, H.1.a, H.1.b.

Sports & Recreation Songs

The Camping Song

Indicators: : A.1.a, A.1.b, A.1.c, A.1.d, A.2.a, A.2.b, A.2.c, B.1.a, B.1.b, B.1.c, B.1.d, B.2.a, B.2.b, B.2.c, B.3.a, B.3.b, B.4.a, C.2.a, E.1.a, E.2.a, F.1.b, F.2.b, F.2.e, F.2.h, F.3.c, G.1.a, G.1.b, H.1.a, H.1.b, H.1.d

Did You Ever Go A Camping

Indicators: : A.1.a, A.1.b, A.1.c, A.1.d, A.2.a, A.2.b, A.2.c, B.1.a, B.1.b, B.1.c, B.1.d, B.2.a, B.2.b, B.3.a, B.4.a, C.2.b, E.1.a, E.2.a, F.1.b, F.2.b, F.2.e, F.2.h, F.3.c, G.1.a, G.1.b, H.1.a, H.1.b, H.1.d

Sports & Recreation Activities

Baseball	Fishing	Skateboarding
Basketball	Football	Soccer
Bicycling	Golf	Swimming
Boating	Gymnastics	Tennis
Camping	Horseback Riding	Track & Field
Cheering	Ice Skating	Volleyball
Climbing	Olympics	

Sports & Recreation Games and Activities

Airplane Scale (sports & recreation)

This balance skill is performed on one foot. The student raises one leg behind them and leans forward. Their arms should be spread out to the sides. This position will resemble an airplane. Hold this balance for ten seconds. You will be surprised how difficult it is to hold this position without moving and losing balance.

Topical signs to be learned: airplane, skill, look, like, numbers 1-10, don't move.

Indicators: A.1.a, A.1.b, A.1.c, A.1.d, A.2.a, A.2.b, A.2.c, B.1.a, B.1.b, B.1.c, B.1.d, B.2.a, B.2.b, B.2.c, B.3.a, B.3.b, B.4.a, C.2.b, F.1.b, F.2.d, F.2.e, F.2.h, F.5.a, G.1.a, G.1.b, G.2.a, H.1.a, H.1.b, H.2.a.

Back Roll (sports & recreation)

Equipment: mats

Here's how to perform a back roll. From a standing start, sit down and tuck the body into a tight ball. Roll backwards with the hands placed on either side of the head. When the hands come in contact with the mats, push downwards. The hands will continue to be pushed downward as the feet are swung around to contact the floor. Watch out for your students trying to "throw" their backs backwards. This will cause them to land with a hard "thump" on the mat. The back needs to remain in a tight tuck as the student rolls backwards to his hands.

Topical signs to be learned: tight, roll, stand, sit, ball, hands.

Indicators: A.1.a, A.1.b, A.1.c, A.1.d, A.2.a, A.2.b, A.2.c, B.1.c, B.2.a, B.2.b, B.2.c, C.2.b, F.1.b, F.2.d, F.2.e, F.2.h, F.3.a, F.3.c, F.4..b, G.1.a, G.1.b, G.2.a, G.3.a, H.1.b, H.2.a.

Balloon Volleyball (sports & recreation)

Equipment: rope or clothesline, balloons.

Clear a playing court, and the area around it. Place a length of rope or clothesline across the floor in the middle of the room to indicate sides. Blow up a balloon to use as a volleyball. Then divide into two teams and swat the balloon back and forth across the line. A team gets a point if the balloon hits the floor on the opponent's side or if an opponent fails to hit it back over the string to the opposite side in three tries. For a livelier game, inflate two balloons of different colors and play with both at once. One team gets a point each time the first balloon hits the floor on the opponent's side; the other team scores with the other balloon.

Topical signs to be learned: balloon, volleyball, team, across, line, touch, try, three.

Indicators: A.1.a, A.1.b, A.1.c, A.1.d, A.2.a, A.2.b, A.2.c, B.1.c, B.2.a, B.2.b, B.2.c, C.2.b, F.1.b, F.2.b, F.2.e, F.2.h, F.3.a, F.3.b, F.3.c, F.4.b, G.1.a, G.1.b, G.2.a, G.3.a, H.1.b, H.1.d, H.2.a.

Blob (sports & recreation)

This game can have 10-50+ players. The name of this game was derived from the movie "The Blob." In playing the game, we can pretend that a UFO has landed in our town and, just like in the movie, some kind of gooey alien has started catching people and turning them into blobs. And, also like in the movie, when a blob gets to be a certain size, it splits into two blobs. In this game, however, the human race loses as everyone becomes a blob. Oh, well.

What actually happens in the game is that, after defining the play area, we somehow find someone to be our initial blob. Then that person must, within the defined boundaries, catch another person by tagging. They then link by holding hands and can catch someone only while being linked. When they catch someone, the third person links with them as well. Only the outside hand on either end of the blob can tag players. However, when a fourth person is caught, something special happens: mitosis! For non-biologists, it means the blob divides in two. Now two blobs stalk humans. Each time there are four in a blob, they can divide again. After a while, there is nowhere a poor human can go to escape. What fun! Reminds players to be aware of each other to avoid crashing into on another.

Topical signs to be learned: game, divide/separate, catch.

Indicators: A.1.a, A.1.b, A.1.c, A.1.d, A.2.a, A.2.b, A.2.c, B.1.c, B.2.a, B.2.b, B.2.c, C.2.b, F.1.b, F.2.b, F.2.e, F.2.h, F.3.a, F.3.c, F.4.b, G.1.a, G.1.b, G.2.a, G.3.a, H.1.b, H.1.d, H.2.a.

Body Sculptures (sports & recreation)

Players construct body sculptures of victory, defeat, excitement, suspense, and disappointment or any emotion desired. Any number of players can contribute to each sculpture.

Topical signs to be learned: body, sculpture (statue), win, lose, excited, other sports signs.

Indicators: A.1.a, A.1.b, A.1.c, A.1.d, A.2.a, A.2.b, A.2.c, B.1.c, B.2.a, B.2.b, B.2.c, C.2.b, E.3.a, F.1.b, F.2.a, F.2.b, F.2.e, F.2.h, F.3.a, F.3.c, F.4.b, G.1.a, G.1.b, G.2.a, G.3.a, H.1.b, H.1.d, H.2.a.

Concentration Activity: I'm Going to the Game (sports & recreation)

Players build a list by naming items they would take to a game. Each player must name all the things the previous players have said and then add an item.

Example: Leader: I'm going to the game and I'm going to take binoculars.

Player 1: I'm going to the game and I'm going to take binoculars and a seat cushion.

You can play this for any type of activity or outing such as going on vacation, or going to the park etc.

Topical signs to be learned: name, game, all, things, before, add, I, go, bring.

Indicators: A.1.a, A.1.b, A.1.c, A.1.d, A.2.a, A.2.b, A.2.c, B.1.c, B.2.a, B.2.b, B.2.c, C.2.b, F.1.b, F.2.b, F.2.e, F.2.h, F.3.a, F.3.c, F.4.b, G.1.a, G.1.b, G.2.a, G.3.a, H.1.b, H.1.d.

G-man (sports & recreation)

For each game use 7-10 players, you may have more than one game going at once. The leader selects a G-Man who turns their back and cover their eyes while players are lined up behind them. When the leader says, "Look," the G-Man is given one minute to look at the players, after which the G-Man turns around again and cover their eyes. The leader then motions one player to leave the line and keep out of sight. The line is then rearranged, and the G-Man turns around and is asked to name or describe the missing player. Whether the G-Man has succeeded or failed, the player who left the line becomes the G-Man for the next game.

Topical signs to be learned: line-up, look, minute, leave, name, describe/explain, missing/guess.

Indicators: A.1.a, A.1.b, A.1.c, A.1.d, A.2.a, A.2.b, A.2.c, B.1.c, B.2.a, B.2.b, B.2.c, C.2.b, F.1.b, F.2.a, F.2.b, F.2.e, F.2.h, F.3.a, F.3.c, F.4.b, G.1.a, G.1.b, G.2.a, G.3.a, H.1.b, H.1.d.

Hidden People (sports & recreation)

Divide into 2 or more groups (3 or 4 groups is best). Each group picks a person to hide and makes this person known to the other teams. Each team may communicate with their hidden person in any way before they leave, so that they know where they will be. At the signal, the "hidden people" hide within specified boundaries. All other players must remain in a group for five minutes. At the next signal, the search for all opposing "hidden people" begins. When found, each must return home to base without a struggle. The team of the last hidden person to be brought back is the winner.

Topical signs to be learned: person, hide, teams, other, where, search/look for, find, last, win.

Indicators: A.1.a, A.1.b, A.1.c, A.1.d, A.2.a, A.2.b, A.2.c, B.1.c, B.2.a, B.2.b, B.2.c, C.2.b, F.1.b, F.2.a, F.2.b, F.2.e, F.2.h, F.3.a, F.3.c, F.4.b, G.1.a, G.1.b, G.2.a, G.3.a, H.1.b, H.1.d.

Imaginary Ball Toss (sports & recreation)

Players begin the game by tossing an imaginary ball that has no unusual characteristics. Once they have established successful reception and release patterns, new properties are assigned to the ball such as those below. The ball is now...the shape of a football, the size of a tennis ball, made of popcorn, the weight of a ping-pong ball, sticky, made of rubber, made of yarn, the shape of a basketball, the weight of a bowling ball etc.

Topical signs to be learned: ball, throw/toss, shape, size, weight, made, change, sports signs.

Indicators: A.1.a, A.1.b, A.1.c, A.1.d, A.2.a, A.2.b, A.2.c, B.1.c, B.2.a, B.2.b, B.2.c, C.2.b, F.1.b, F.2.b, F.2.e, F.2.h, F.3.a, F.3.c, F.4.b, G.1.a, G.1.b, G.2.a, G.3.a, H.1.b, H.1.d.

Jump Rope Rhymes (sports & recreation)

Equipment: jump rope or suitable rope (for either an individual or a group).

Johnny Over the Ocean

Johnny over the ocean, Johnny over the sea,

Johnny broke a milk bottle and blamed it on me.

I told Ma, Ma told Pa,

Johnny got a lickin', so Ha, Ha, Ha.

How many lickings did he get?

(Count until jumper misses)

Mama, Mama, I Feels Sick

Mama, Mama I feel sick:

Send for the doctor,

Quick, Quick, Quick.

How many pills will he give me?

(Count until jumper misses.)

Worms in the Jelly Bowl

Worms in the jelly bowl, Wiggle, Waggle, Wiggle

Worms in the jelly bowl, Wiggle, Waggle, Wiggle

I'm Mae West, I try to do my best

Worms in the jelly bowl, Wiggle, Waggle, Wiggle

Peal an Orange

Peal an orange, round and round (jumper turns in circle)

See if you can touch the ground; (jumper tries to touch the ground)

If you jump to twenty-two

Another turn will be given to you!

(If jumper jumps to twenty-two they are given another turn)

My Mother, Your Mother

My mother, your mother, live across the street,

Eighteen, Nineteen, Chestnut Street.

Every night they have a fight and this is what they say:

Acka backa soda cracker, Acka backa boo.

In comes (next child's name) and out goes you! (jumper runs out and new one jumps in)

Charlie Chaplin

Charlie Chaplin went to France

To teach the ladies how to dance,

First the heel and then the toe,

Around and around and around you go.

Topical signs to be learned: jump, rope, over, sea/ocean, break, milk, bottle, mother, father, tell, feel sick, send, doctor, quick, how, many, medicine, give, worm, bowl, try, do, my, best, orange, round, see, you, can, touch, ground, if, another (other), give, live, across, street, every, night, fight, what, say, in, out, come, go, teach, lady, dance, first.

Indicators: A.1.a, A.1.b, A.1.c, A.1.d, A.2.a, A.2.b, A.2.c, B.1.c, B.2.a, B.2.b, B.2.c, C.2.b, E.1.a, F.1.b, F.2.b, F.2.e, F.2.h, F.3.a, F.3.c, F.4.b, G.1.a, G.1.b, G.2.a, G.3.a, H.1.b, H.1.d, H.2.a.

Miniature Golf (sports & recreation)

Materials: kids' golf clubs or a new sponge and a yard stick, masking tape, doormat, felt-tipped marker, ball (golf or small rubber ball), oatmeal container, shoe box, cardboard, coffee can. If you have a set of kids' golf clubs, use them. If you don't, you can make your own by attaching a stiff new sponge to the end of a yardstick with masking tape. Use a regular golf ball or a smaller rubber ball and a doormat for the tee. Make eight or ten obstacles for the course. Here are some ideas to help you get going. For a tunnel, cut out the bottom of an empty oatmeal box and place the box on its side. For a house, turn a shoe box upside down and cut out an entrance from one end of the box and an exit from the other end. Fold a piece of cardboard in half and set it up like a tent for the ball to go through. For a ramp, take a large piece of cardboard and score it in two places to divide it in thirds. To score, run one point of a pair of scissors along the cardboard. Ask an adult assistant to help you. Bend the cardboard slightly at the score marks and place the center portion on a book. Angle the two ends to form slopping ramps. Place two or three Frisbees on the floor to form a curved fairway for the ball to go through. For a straight fairway, make two parallel rows of building blocks. Use a hula hoop to make a sand trap that you want to avoid. Put a chair or stool in the center of the room for the ball to go under. Use an empty, clean coffee can placed on its side as the end cup. Set up obstacles around the room and use masking tape to secure them to the floor. Write numbers on the masking tape to indicate hole numbers for the course. Start at the beginning and see how many strokes it takes to get your ball through the course and into the coffee can at the end. Don't forget you're indoors, so use more finesse than force when you tee up.

Topical signs to be learned: golf, ball, bridge/ramp, tape, scissors, write, numbers, careful, how many.

Indicators: A.1.a, A.1.b, A.1.c, A.1.d, A.2.a, A.2.b, A.2.c, B.1.c, B.2.a, B.2.b, B.2.c, C.2.b, F.1.b, F.2.b, F.2.e, F.2.h, F.3.a, F.3.c, F.4.b, G.1.a, G.1.b, G.2.a, G.3.a, H.1.b, H.1.d, H.2.a.

Parachute Games (sports & recreation)

Materials: parachute (large blanket or sheet works well), foam balls,

Merry-Go-Round

The children circle the parachute. Grab hold with their right hand and begin to go round. Then turn around and its off in the other direction.

Odd Man Out

Have the children sit around the parachute. Have them count off in numbers from 1-4. Have them lift the parachute as high as they can and as their numbers are called they get to enter the parachute. They want to go and fill in another of their numbers slots around the parachute before the trap closes.

Popcorn

Place all different size foam balls on the parachute. Have the children grab the ends and shake the chute. Watch as the popcorn pops. Have the children retrieve any balls that go astray.

Parachute Ball

Use just one ball as the children try to get the ball to go as high as they can. Then you can add another ball or 2.

The Dome

Have the children lift the parachute as high as they can. Then get inside and seal the dome by sitting on the edge.

Topical signs to be learned: parachute, circle, sit, count, shake, popcorn, ball.

Indicators: A.1.a, A.1.b, A.1.c, A.1.d, A.2.a, A.2.b, A.2.c, B.1.c, B.2.a, B.2.b, B.2.c, C.2.b, F.1.b, F.2.b, F.2.e, F.2h, F.3.a, F.3.c, F.4.b, G.1.a, G.1.b, G.2.a, G.3.a, H.1.b, H.1.d, H.2.a.

Relays (sports & recreation)

"B" Team Relay

Divide your group up into 2 teams. Mark off a starting and turn around point. Assign a different injury to each of the different pairs of racers as follows:

Bad knee - hop on one leg

Hurt heel - tip toe

Injured ankle - must keep a hand on ankle while racing, Etc.

Topical signs to be learned: move, start, end, two, together, race, hurt.

Indicators: A.1.a, A.1.b, A.1.c, A.1.d, A.2.a, A.2.b, A.2.c, B.1.c, B.2.a, B.2.b, B.2.c, C.2.b, E.3.a, F.1.b, F.2.b, F.2.e, F.2.h, F.3.a, F.3.c, F.4.b, G.1.a, .G.1.b, G.2.a, G.3.a, H.1.b, H.1.d, H.2.a.

Chariot Relay

Two players hold their inside hands together. The third player stands behind the two and grabs hold of their outside hands. This forms one chariot. Divide the group into two or more teams and have a chariot race/relay.

Topical signs to be learned: move, start, end, two, together, race, hurt.

Indicators: A.1.a, A.1.b, A.1.c, A.1.d, A.2.a, A.2.b, A.2.c, B.1.c, B.2.a, B.2.b, B.2.c, C.2.b, E.3.a, F.1.b, F.2.b, F.2.e, F.2.h, F.3.a, F.3.c, F.4.b, G.1.a, .G.1.b, G.2.a, G.3.a, H.1.b, H.1.d, H.2.a.

Fingerspell Name Relay

Divide your group up into 2 teams. Mark off a starting and turn around point. They have to get to the turn-around point and fingerspell their names. Then run back and tag the next person to go.

Topical signs to be learned: team, start, fingerspell, name, alphabet signs, run, touch.

Indicators: A.1.a, A.1.b, A.1.c, A.1.d, A.2.a, A.2.b, A.2.c, B.1.c, B.2.a, B.2.b, B.2.c, B.4.a, B.5.a, B.5.b, B.5.c, C.2.b, E.3.a, F.1.b, F.2.b, F.2.d, F.2.e. F.2.h, F.3.a, F.3.c, F.4.b, G.1.a, .G.1.b, G.2.a, G.3.a, H.1.b, H.1.d.

Flag Relay

Each team of 4-8 players should have a flag of a different color. Half of the team stands directly opposite the other half, which is 30 feet distant. The runners stand in file formation, one direction behind the other. There should be a space of 4-5 feet between each file. The first runner for each team is given a flag, one flag to a team. All players start from one side. On the word "Go!" the players with the flags race to the players opposite and hand the flag to the first runner in the line. This second runner must not step forward to take the flag. When a player hands over the flag he should go immediately to the end of the line to avoid interfering with the next player. The second runner races to the next player, etc., until every runner has carried their team's flag. The running distance may vary, depending on the age of the runners and the size of the available playing area.

Topical signs to be learned: flag, race, run, give, go, line-up, next, team, finish.

Indicators: A.1.a, A.1.b, A.1.c, A.1.d, A.2.a, A.2.b, A.2.c, B.1.c, B.2.a, B.2.b, B.2.c, C.2.b, E.3.a, F.1.b, F.2.b, F.2.e, F.2.h, F.3.a, F.3.c, F.4.b, G.1.a, .G.1.b, G.2.a, G.3.a, H.1.b, H.1.d, H.2.a.

Iceberg Relay

Equipment: construction paper "icebergs" and scissors

Divide the group into two separate groups. The students must use the icebergs to get across the raging sea to a turning point and back to their group. The first players have a set of two icebergs. By placing the first iceberg on the ground, the player can step on it and place the second iceberg further on toward the turning point. Each player must step only on the icebergs as they tries to get from the starting line and back again. The activity continues until all the students have had a chance to participate.

Topical signs to be learned: group, ice, across, sea, two, start, finish.

Indicators: A.1.a, A.1.b, A.1.c, A.1.d, A.2.a, A.2.b, A.2.c, B.1.c, B.2.a, B.2.b, B.2.c, C.2.b, E.3.a, F.1.b, F.2.b, F.2.e, F.2.h, F.3.a, F.3.c, F.4.b, G.1.a, .G.1.b, G.2.a, G.3.a, H.1.b, H.1.d, H.2.a.

Over/Under Relay

Equipment: one ball per team

Divide your class into two or more teams. Have each team line up in a single file with the students' legs apart. On a signal, the first player takes the ball and lifts it up and over his head with his two hands. The player behind him takes the ball and brings it under his legs. The next player grabs the ball and lifts the ball up and over his head. The ball continues to go over and under all the players until it reaches the last player. The last player then runs with the ball to the front of the line and passes the ball over their head to the next player. When the original leader gets to the front of the group again, the team quickly sits down.

Topical signs to be learned: team, line-up, ball, over, under, next, sit. Indicators: A.1.a, A.1.b, A.1.c, A.1.d, A.2.a, A.2.b, A.2.c, B.1.c, B.2.a, B.2.b, B.2.c, C.2.b, E.3.a, F.1.b, F.2.b, F.2.e, F.2.h, F.3.a, F.3.c, F.4.b, G.1.a, .G.1.b, G.2.a, G.3.a, H.1.b, H.1.d, H.2.a.

Partner-Pair Relay

In this relay have your students hold hands in pairs. Certain loco motor movements have to be performed. First, have the pairs run to a certain point. Skipping, hopping, leaping movements can also be used in this relay. Divide your class into smaller groups and have a partner pair relay race.

Topical signs to be learned: run, jump, go, group, together, two.

Indicators: A.1.a, A.1.b, A.1.c, A.1.d, A.2.a, A.2.b, A.2.c, B.1.c, B.2.a, B.2.b, B.2.c, C.2.b, F.1.b, F.2.b, F.2.e, F.2.h, F.3.a, F.3.c, F.4.b, G.1.a, .G.1.b, G.2.a, G.3.a, H.1.b, H.1.d, H.2.a.

Picket Fence Relay

Equipment: one traffic cone per group

Divide your class into two groups. Each team lines up. The first player runs around the marker and places his arm to the wall. The next player runs as soon as the leader touches the wall. They go under the arm of the first player and hold up their hand. That will signal the next player to run. This continues until every player has had a turn to run.

Topical signs to be learned: group, line-up, touch, wall, go, under, finish.

Indicators: A.1.a, A.1.b, A.1.c, A.1.d, A.2.a, A.2.b, A.2.c, B.1.c, B.2.a, B.2.b, B.2.c, C.2.b, F.1.b, F.2.b, F.2.e, F.2.h, F.3.a, F.3.c, F.4.b, G.1.a, .G.1.b, G.2.a, G.3.a, H.1.b, H.1.d, H.2.a.

Potato Relay

Divide players into teams. The first player is given a large tablespoon and a potato. He must carry the potato in the spoon to a goal line 10-15 feet distant and back, then hand the spoon with the potato in it to the second player who repeats the action. If a potato is dropped, the team must start over from the beginning. The first team to finish wins.

Topical signs to be learned: spoon, potato, line-up, carry/bring, give, person, next, drop, start/begin, finish.

Indicators: A.1.a, A.1.b, A.1.c, A.1.d, A.2.a, A.2.b, A.2.c, B.1.c, B.2.a, B.2.b, B.2.c, C.2.b, E.3.a, F.1.b, F.2.b, F.2.e, F.2.h, F.3.a, F.3.c, F.4.b, G.1.a, .G.1.b, G.2.a, G.3.a, H.1.b, H.1.d, H.2.a.

Sack-Race Relay

Equipment: one burlap sack per team

Divide the class into two or more teams. Each team lines up in a single file behind a starting line. The first player is given the sack and steps into it. On a signal, the first player has to hop to the turning point and back to their team. They then give the sack to the next player. The game continues with each player stepping into the sack and hopping around the turning point and back.

Topical signs to be learned: team, line-up, bag, jump, go, come, finish.

Indicators: A.1.a, A.1.b, A.1.c, A.1.d, A.2.a, A.2.b, A.2.c, B.1.c, B.2.a, B.2.b, B.2.c, C.2.b, F.1.b, F.2.b, F.2.e, F.2.h, F.3.a, F.3.c, F.4.b, G.1.a, .G.1.b, G.2.a, G.3.a, H.1.b, H.1.d, H.2.a.

Three-Legged Relay

Equipment: one burlap bag per team

Divide your class into two teams. Each team is broken down into pairs. On a signal, the first pair places their inside legs in the burlap sack. They then have to walk around a designated turning point and back to their team. They walk by holding the back with their inside hands and stepping together first with their inside feet and then with their outside feet.

Topical signs to be learned: team, line-up, walk, together, bag, go, come, finish.

Indicators: A.1.a, A.1.b, A.1.c, A.1.d, A.2.a, A.2.b, A.2.c, B.1.c, B.2.a, B.2.b, B.2.c, C.2.b, F.1.b, F.2.b, F.2.e, F.2.h, F.3.a, F.3.c, F.4.b, G.1.a, .G.1.b, G.2.a, G.3.a, H.1.b, H.1.d, H.2.a.

Tunnel Relay

Equipment: 20 foot strip of plastic or durable material (may be purchased in large rolls at building supply stores, hardware stores, or garden centers)

Staple or sew the sides of the plastic together to make a tunnel about three feet in diameter.

Select two teams. Each team puts half of its members at either end of the tube. Two opponents start crawling through the tunnel from opposite ends and must inevitably pass each other in the middle. When passing, they should not interfere with each other. When they reach the other end, they tag a teammate who starts back through. The first team finished wins but the most fun is watching the wiggling tunnel from the outside.

Topical signs to be learned: team, through, go, finish, pass, don't touch.

Indicators: A.1.a, A.1.b, A.1.c, A.1.d, A.2.a, A.2.b, A.2.c, B.1.c, B.2.a, B.2.b, B.2.c, C.2.b, F.1.b, F.2.b, F.2.e, F.2.h, F.3.a, F.3.c, F.4.b, G.1.a, .G.1.b, G.2.a, G.3.a, H.1.b, H.1.d, H.2.a.

Tunnel-Ball Relay

Equipment: one ball per team

Have each team line up with their legs spread apart in the straddle position. The first player passes the ball under their legs to the last player in the line. The last player gets the ball and runs to the front of the group. They then straddle their legs and roll the ball under all the legs of the group to the last player. When the first player to roll the ball is in the front of the group again, all the team members sit down.

Topical signs to be learned: team, ball, pass, through, run, finish, sit.

Indicators: A.1.a, A.1.b, A.1.c, A.1.d, A.2.a, A.2.b, A.2.c, B.1.c, B.2.a, B.2.b, B.2.c, C.2.b, F.1.b, F.2.b, F.2.e, F.2.h, F.3.a, F.3.c, F.4.b, G.1.a, .G.1.b, G.2.a, G.3.a, H.1.b, H.1.d, H.2.a.

Zig-Zag Relay

Equipment: twelve traffic cones (or other similar objects)

In this relay the players have to run through a zigzag maze to a turning line and back again. Arrange the cones so that each team has its own zigzag course in front of it. On a signal, the first player runs the course and tags the hand of the next player. The first team to finish has to wait for the rest of the class to run the course.

Topical signs to be learned: team, line-up, run, touch, finish, wait.

Indicators: A.1.a, A.1.b, A.1.c, A.1.d, A.2.a, A.2.b, A.2.c, B.1.c, B.2.a, B.2.b, B.2.c, C.2.b, F.1.b, F.2.b, F.2.e, F.2.h, F.3.a, F.3.c, F.4.b, G.1.a, .G.1.b, G.2.a, G.3.a, H.1.b, H.1.d, H.2.a.

The Queen's Headache (sports & recreation)

One student is selected to be queen. She sits in the middle of the room on a chair. The rest of the group is lined up on one side of the room. The object of the game is to quietly get from one side of the room to the other without having the Queen moan. The Queen has such a bad headache that any sound makes her moan. One by one, the students walk across the room. If the Queen hears the student and moans, that student must sit down at the spot where he was when the Queen moaned. The Queen should have her face covered so as to not be accused by the players of showing royal favoritism. After all the students have had a turn, choose another King or Queen to start the game again. This is a game that can be used from time to time whenever you need that added reassurance that your group can be quiet.

Give one of the following suggestions to the students in your group who find it easy to be quiet walkers. Walk with a book balanced on their head, walk with their shoes tied together, or walk holding one foot with the opposite hand.

Topical signs to be learned: queen, king, headache, chair, quiet, walk, sit, line, room, sound, face, cover, book, on, head, shoes.

Indicators: A.1.a, A.1.b, A.1.c, A.1.d, A.2.a, A.2.b, A.2.c, B.1.c, B.2.a, B.2.b, B.2.c, C.2.b, F.1.b, F.2.b, F.2.e, F.2.h, F.3.a, F.3.c, F.4.b, G.1.a, .G.1.b, G.2.a, G.3.a, H.1.b, H.1.d, H.2.a.

Steal the Bacon (sports & recreation)

Divide players evenly into two teams. Line them up in two rows facing each other about 20 feet apart, the bacon in the middle. Each person in line receives a number from one to whatever the number of players on the team. The ones of each team or on opposite sides of the lines (The last player from one team, say number twelve, would be facing the person who is number one on the opposite team). Any object can be the bacon such as a block of wood or rolled up newspaper. The leader calls numbers and decides points in disputes.

When the game starts, the leader calls a number, e.g. "two," where upon #2 from each side makes a run for the bacon. The person who secures the bacon makes a point for their side. The game should continue at least until each person has had a chance to steal the bacon or until one team has reached a determined amount of points.

Topical signs to be learned: team, line, bacon, number signs, run.

Indicators: A.1.a, A.1.b, A.1.c, A.1.d, A.2.a, A.2.b, A.2.c, B.1.c, B.2.a, B.2.b, B.2.c, C.1.a, C.1.b, C.1.d, C.2.b, F.1.b, F.2.b, F.2.e, F.2.h, F.3.a, F.3.c, F.4.b, G.1.a, .G.1.b, G.2.a, G.3.a, H.1.b, H.1.d, H.2.a.

Tag Games (sports & recreation)

Equipment: nerf ball, bean bag or other soft ball or object; colored paper squares, four basketballs, flashlight

Ball Tag

Use a nerf ball (soft foam), bean bag, or other soft ball or object. "It" has the ball which he throws (gently) at any other player. The other player may attempt to dodge. If they are hit, they become "it."

Chain Tag

The players are scattered around a designated area with boundaries. Two captains are chosen. At the starting signal, the two captains try to tag as many players as possible. The first person tagged links hands with the captain, and they run together, As each person is tagged, he joins the line. The line may encircle a player, but only the captain may tag him. The longest line wins and the last player to escape being tagged wins. If the lines are fairly even, they may be used to form lines for another game.

Chinese Tag

The tagged player is "it" and must hold the part of the body where he was tagged.

Color Tag

This game is played the same as plain tag but there are colored square scattered around—colored paper will do. Players are safe when standing on a colored square but a player may stand on each color only once. For example, if he takes refuge from "it" on a red square, he must not use a red square again, but must next run to another color.

Cross Tag

"It" chases another. Some other player may run in between "it" and the one being chased. This crossing goes on indefinitely and "It" must always chase the last person who ran between him and the one he was chasing. Anyone who is tagged becomes "it."

Dribble Tag (sports & recreation)

This game is played on a basketball court. Select four players to be It. These four players will have the basketballs. It is up to them to dribble the ball and try to tag as many players as possible. The players who are tagged must sit down. While it may not seem fair that the taggers must dribble the basketball, the four players can easily "track down" certain players by cooperating together. You can also play another variation of this game by having eight players be IT. These eight players can then dribble and pass the basketball in attempts to tag the other player. Once again, the taggers must be dribbling the ball when tagging the other students. Once all the students have been tagged, start the game over by selecting new players to be IT.

Flashlight Tag

This game must be played in deep shade or darkness. "It" has only to zap a wanderer in the dark with a beam of light from a flashlight to tag them and thus convert the wanderer to "it." Those being chased must keep on the move to avoid being zapped. It's best to set boundaries and provide adult supervision to keep younger children from getting lost or scared. Check the terrain out in daylight to make sure there are no holes, water or other dangers.

Hug Tag

Game can have 10-50+ players. The game is played by choosing an It. The It carries a ball or other object so that everyone knows who It is. It tries to catch and touch another player, making them It. When the It tags someone, the ball or object is passed on to the new It. Other players who are not It can avoid being tagged by either running away or hugging another player. Hugs can last for only three seconds, however, and the It can count to three to make sure.

To make the game more interesting, more than one person can be It at the same time, thereby increasing the action. After a while, another challenge is to require more than two people in a hug—try three, four, or more? Last, for the truly daring, players can be tagged in a hug if the It can touch the abdomen of any person in a hug. The result is closer hugs. This last measure is not for all groups, but if players are open to the idea, it can add a lot of fun. Any way you play this game, people seem to get closer.

Remind players to look out for other players. Modifications can be made for players who are a bit shy or reluctant to hug, such as putting hands on one another's shoulders, holding hands, or maybe even touching elbows. In extreme circumstances where players do not want to touch at all, having them hold on to a piece of clothing (like a sleeve) of another player might work.

Link Tag

Designate a base. Two players link hands and try to tag the other players. These two players are the only ones who can tag others throughout the game. All those tagged take their places between the first two players, all linking hands. The chain grows longer with each new addition. The players being chased may try to break the chain by forcing clasped hands apart while avoiding the two players at either end of the chain. If the chain is broken, it must be joined again before the tagging can continue. Players dropping out to rest must return to base and remain there until they re-enter the game. Players may not return to base to escape being tagged.

Shadow Tag

Requires a sunny day. To tag a person, "it" must step on that person's shadow.

Swat Tag

"It" tags others with a swatter (rolled up newspaper etc.) then drops it. The new "it" must pick up the swatter and continue. Remind the students to be gentle when swatting each other.

Topical signs to be learned: catch, touch, ball, cooperate, line, hug, color signs, join, runaway.

Indicators: A.1.a, A.1.b, A.1.c, A.1.d, A.2.a, A.2.b, A.2.c, B.1.c, B.2.a, B.2.b, B.2.c, C.2.b, F.1.b, F.2.b, F.2.e, F.2.h, F.3.a, F.3.c, F.4.b, G.1.a, .G.1.b, G.2.a, G.3.a, H.1.b, H.1.d, H.2.a.

Talking Ball (fine & performing arts)

Materials: ball

Sit in a circle (or across from each other if there are two people playing). One person holds the ball and, while they hold the ball, they are the storyteller. The storyteller begins telling a story about anything. After a few sentences, the storyteller tosses the ball to someone else. Now they are the new storyteller. The new storyteller continues the story where the old storyteller left off. The second person must build off the story that was started by the first person. After a few sentences, the ball is passed again and the story continues with a new storyteller. Keep tossing the ball until the story comes to an end. You can only talk if you are holding the talking ball. You can toss the ball at the end of a sentence or in the middle. If the ball toss is in the middle, the new storyteller continues the story exactly from where the first person stopped. Listen closely to the story, so when it's your turn to be the storyteller, everything makes sense.

Topical signs to be learned: ball, sit in circle, pass (give), story, tell, storyteller (narrator), sentence, few, end, listen, throw.

Indicators: A.1.a, A.1.b, A.1.c, A.1.d, A.2.a, A.2.b, A.2.c, B.1.c, B.2.a, B.2.b, B.2.c, B.4.a, C.2.b, F.1.b, F.2.b, F.2.e, F.2.h, F.3.a, F.3.c, F.4.b, G.1.a, .G.1.b, G.2.a, G.3.a, H.1.b, H.1.d, H.2.a.

Tin Can Bowling (sports & recreation)

Equipment: softball, 10 tin cans, backdrop (for behind pins).

You will need a level stretch of ground for this activity. Set up the "pins" with a backdrop behind them. Experiment with the terrain to judge how long the alley should be. It will also depend on the age of the bowlers. Have someone who sets up the pins.

Topical signs to be learned: ball, ground, long, should, age.

Indicators: A.1.a, A.1.b, A.1.c, A.1.d, A.2.a, A.2.b, A.2.c, B.1.c, B.2.a, B.2.b, B.2.c, C.2.b, F.1.b, F.2.b, F.2.e, F.2.h, F.3.a, F.3.c, F.4.b, G.1.a, .G.1.b, G.2.a, G.3.a, H.1.b, H.1.d, H.2.a.

Tug-of-War (sports & recreation)

Equipment: rope.

Several volunteers can serve as broadcasters who provide the "play-by-play" in response to team actions for a tug-of-war that is being shown on television. Other players form the competing teams.

Topical signs to be learned: team, volunteer, action.

Indicators: A.1.a, A.1.b, A.1.c, A.1.d, A.2.a, A.2.b, A.2.c, B.1.c, B.2.a, B.2.b, B.2.c, C.2.b, F.1.b, F.2.b, F.2.e, F.2.h, F.3.a, F.3.c, F.4.b, G.1.a, .G.1.b, G.2.a, G.3.a, H.1.b, H.1.d, H.2.a.

Ball Player's Game (sports & recreation)

Equipment: balls, drum, music.

Using a variety of balls, players may bounce them to the beat of a drum, to chants or poems, or to recorded music. It is suggested to approach practice with larger balls (e.g. volleyball size) at a moderate temp. Older players with well-developed skills may be invited to select smaller balls and use faster tempos.

Topical signs to be learned: ball, bounce, drum, music, slow, fast.

Indicators: A.1.a, A.1.b, A.1.c, A.1.d, A.2.a, A.2.b, A.2.c, B.1.c, B.2.a, B.2.b, B.2.c, C.2.b, F.1.b, F.2.b, F.2.e, F.2.h, F.3.a, F.3.c, F.4.b, G.1.a, .G.1.b, G.2.a, G.3.a, H.1.b, H.1.d, H.2.a.

Un-volleyball (sports & recreation)

Materials: volley ball and net.

This game is played like regular volleyball with one exception. If the person hits the ball over the net then they have to cross over and join the opposing team.

Topical signs to be learned: volleyball, join, other, team.

Indicators: A.1.a, A.1.b, A.1.c, A.1.d, A.2.a, A.2.b, A.2.c, B.1.c, B.2.a, B.2.b, B.2.c, C.2.b, F.1.b, F.2.b, F.2.e, F.2.h, F.3.a, F.3.c, F.4.b, G.1.a, .G.1.b, G.2.a, G.3.a, H.1.b, H.1.d, H.2.a.

Sports & Recreation Crafts

Stilts (sports & recreation)

Materials: 2 pieces of 6-8' long 2"x2" lumber, 2"x4" pieces of wood, screws; OR medium sized tin cans (such as soup cans), sharp object to punch holes, small rope or stout cord.

For wooden stilts, screw the 2"x4" pieces of wood into the larger pieces of wood. Place the "platforms" lower for beginning stilt walkers. Walking on stilts is simply fun and is reward enough. Racing is too hazardous.

For tin can stilts, punch two holes in the bottom rim of each can, large enough to admit the stout cord or small rope. The cards are grasped tightly in each hand to hold the cans against the feet. Thus one can walk fairly rapidly but precariously.

Topical signs to be learned: big, little, walk, fun, careful.

Indicators: A.1.b, A.1.c, A.1.d, A.2.a, A.2.b, A.2.c, B.1.c, B.2.a, C.2.b, F.1.b, F.2.b, F.2.d, F.2.e, F.2.h, F.3.c, F.4.a, G.1.a, .G.1.b, G.2.a, H.1.a, H.1.b, H.2.a.

Weather
Songs, Stories, Games & Activities

Using Guide with Time to Sign Curriculum: *Signs can be found in the Math, Science and Nature Module; Music Module for all music; and Preschool Activity Guide for hands on activities. Stories were found in the local public library.*

Learn: Weather signs – Cold, hot, sun, rain, wind, snow

Learn: Weather signs (cold, clouds, hot, lightning, rain, rainbow, snow, storm, sun, thunder, warm, weather, wind)

Activity: Clouds in the Breeze

Activity: Storm Winds

Activity: Mighty Wind

Activity: Boat Adventure

Song: What will the Weather be?

Song: Rain, Rain Go Away (use Instrumental CD-"Row, Row, Row your Boat-Slow)

Song: Itsy bitsy Spider

Song: The Weather Song (to the tune of "Clementine"-no music provided)

Song: You Are My Sunshine

Song: What Will the Weather Be?

Song: Mr. Sun

Story: Little Cloud by Eric Carle (weather)

Story: The Mitten by Jan Brett (seasons, weather)

Time to Sign Props: Weather Poster

Winter

Learn: Winter signs - Cold, winter, blanket, outside

Learn: Winter signs - Cold, sled/sleigh, snow, white, winter

Activity: Snow Ball Starter

Activity: Melt Down

Activity: Color letter of the week page in the activity guide

Activity: Complete letter of the week activities in the activity guide

Song: She'll Be Coming Around the Mountain

Song: Over the River and Through the Woods

Story: <u>The Snowy Day</u> by Ezra Jack Keats (weather)

**Time to Sign Props: Weather Poster*

Weather Stories

<u>It Looked Like Spilt Milk</u> by Charles G. Shaw (nature, weather)

Topical signs to be learned: sometimes?, look (see), like (similar), milk, not, rabbit, bird, tree, ice cream, flower, pig, birthday, cake, sheep, owl, squirrel?, angel (wings?), cloud, sky.

Indicators: A.1.a, A.1.b, A.1.c, A.1.d, A.2.a, A.2.b, A.2.c, B.1.a, B.1.b, B.1.c, B.1.d, B.1.e, B.2.a, B.2.b, B.3.a, B.3.b, B.4.a, C.2.b, D.1.b, D.2.c, D.2.d, F.1.b, F.2.d, F.2.e, F.2.h, G.1.a, G.1.b, G.2.a, H.1.a, H.1.b

<u>Little Cloud</u> by Eric Carle (nature, weather)

Topical signs to be learned: cloud, little, sky, behind, up, down, change, big, sheep, airplane, shark, two, tree, rabbit, hat, clown (silly), come, one, rain.

Indicators: A.1.a, A.1.b, A.1.c, A.1.d, A.2.a, A.2.b, A.2.c, B.1.a, B.1.b, B.1.c, B.1.d, B.2.a, B.2.b, B.3.a, B.3.b, B.4.a, C.2.b, D.1.a, D.1.b, D.2.c, D.2.d, F.1.b, F.2.d, F.2.e, F.2.h, G.1.a, G.1.b, G.2.a, H.1.a, H.1.b

<u>The Mitten</u> by Jan Brett (seasons, weather)

Topical signs to be learned: boy, new, mitten, white, snow, grandmother, find, make, home, safe, see, dropped, mole, inside, warm, rabbit, stop, hedgehog, owl, badger, fox, bear, mouse, sky, sneeze, animals, lost,

Indicators: A.1.a, A.1.b, A.1.c, A.1.d, A.2.a, A.2.b, A.2.c, B.1.a, B.1.b, B.1.c, B.1.d, B.2.a, B.2.b, B.3.a, B.3.b, B.4.a, C.2.b, D.1.b, D.2.b, D.2.c, D.2.d, F.1.b, F.2.d, F.2.e, F.2.h, G.1.a, G.1.b, G.2.a, H.1.a, H.1.b

<u>Planting a Rainbow</u> by Lois Ehlert (nature, weather, colors, available in Spanish)

Topical signs to be learned: seeds, wait, all, winter, spring, soil/dirt, time, go, garden, store, pick, plants, watch, rainbow, grow, color signs, flower, summer, home, next, year.

Indicators: A.1.a, A.1.b, A.1.c, A.1.d, A.2.a, A.2.b, A.2.c, B.1.a, B.1.b, B.1.c, B.1.d, B.2.a, B.2.b, B.3.a, B.3.b, B.4.a, C.2.b, D.1.a, D.1.b, D.2.a, D.2.d, F.1.b, F.2.d, F.2.e, F.2.h, G.1.a, G.1.b, G.2.a, H.1.a, H.1.b

The Snowy Day by Ezra Jack Keats (weather , available in Spanish)

Topical signs to be learned: winter, morning, look, snow, cover, breakfast, outside, street, walk, slow, find, down, fun, smile, snowman (SNOW + MAN), mountain, climb, house, mother, socks, think, bed, empty, sad, dream, sun, melt (dissolve), new, friend.

Indicators: A.1.a, A.1.b, A.1.c, A.1.d, A.2.a, A.2.b, A.2.c, B.1.a, B.1.b, B.1.c, B.1.d, B.2.a, B.2.b, B.3.a, B.3.b, B.4.a, C.2.b, D.1.a, D.1.b, D.2.a, D.2.c, D.2.d, .1.b, F.2.d, F.2.e, F.2.h, G.1.a, G.1.b, G.2.a, H.1.a, H.1.b

Weather Songs

Over the River and through the Woods (weather)

Indicators: A.1.a, A.1.b, A.1.c, A.1.d, A.2.a, A.2.b, A.2.c, B.1.a, B.1.c, B.1.d, B.2.a, B.2.b, B.3.a, B.4.a, C.2.b, D.1.c, D.2.a, D.2.b, D.2.c, D.2.d, E.1.a, E.2.a, F.1.b, F.2.e, F.2.h, F.3.c, G.1.a, G.1.b, H.1.a, H.1.b, H.1.d

What Will the Weather Be? (weather)

Indicators: A.1.a, A.1.b, A.1.c, A.1.d, A.2.a, A.2.b, A.2.c, B.1.a, B.1.c, B.1.d, B.2.a, B.2.b, B.3.a, B.4.a, C.2.b, D.1.c, D.2.a, D.2.b, D.2.c, D.2.d, E.1.a, E.2.a, F.1.b, F.2.e, F.2.h, F.3.c, G.1.a, G.1.b, H.1.a, H.1.b, H.1.d

Weather Games & Activities

Backyard Weather Station (weather)

Materials: thermometer, empty tin can, ruler.

Help the children keep track of how hot or cold it is, the amount of rain that falls, or the amount of snow. Mount the thermometer on a post or tree out of the sun. Mount the can close-by where the rain can fill the can. Help the children read the thermometer and record the readings on a daily basis. When it rains, help the children measure the amount of rain that falls each month. Talk about relationships between temperatures and rain or snow and differences between snow and rain.

Topical signs to be learned: temperature, hot, cold, rain, snow, sun, read, measure, different, same.

Indicators: A.1.a, A.1.b, A.1.c, A.1.d, A.2.a, A.2.b, A.2.c, B.1.b, B.1.c, B.1.d, B.2.a, C.2.b, D.1.a, D.1.b, D.2.a, D.2.b, D.2.c, D.2.d, F.1.b, F.2.e, F.2.h, F.3.c, F.4.a, G.1.a, G.1.b, G.2.a, G.3.a, H.1.a, H.1.b, H.1.d, H.2.a

Cloud Gazing (weather)

Go outside and lie on your backs and look at the clouds. Take turns finding clouds with shapes that look like something familiar. You can also teach the different types of clouds and have the children tell what types of clouds they see.

Topical signs to be learned: outside, lie down, look, cloud, find, shape, like, type.

Indicators: A.1.a, A.1.b, A.1.c, A.1.d, A.2.a, A.2.b, A.2.c, B.1.c, B.2.a, C.2.b, D.1.a, D.1.b, D.2.a, D.2.c, D.2.d, F.1.b, F.2.e, F.2.h, F.3.c, F.4.a, G.1.a, G.1.b, G.2.a, G.3.a, H.1.a H.1.b.

Detective Snow (weather)

Materials: white paper, scissors, felt pen, small classroom items, small box, cotton batting.

Cut white paper in half. Make a half sheet for each child. On each sheet draw a picture or glue a picture of a small object in the classroom, such as a block, a small toy, a box of crayons, a pot in the kitchen area, a small stuffed animal, etc. Fold each sheet in half twice. Place them in a small box.

Explain that each child will become Detective Snow! Walk slowly around the classroom. Notice the many things in the classroom, where the objects are located and their size. Talk about what you are seeing. Now have the children close their eyes. The teacher places cotton batting (snow) over objects in the classroom that are pictured on the folded papers. The children open their eyes. Objects have changed shape! Do they look different? Choose a child to be Detective Snow. The child chooses a paper square from the box and identifies the picture. Detective Snow tries to remember where he or she saw the object. They search the classroom and uncover the object. The teacher replaces the snow (cotton batting) over the object. Now choose another child to be Detective Snow!

Topical signs to be learned: snow, see, find, cover.

Indicators: A.1.a, A.1.b, A.1.c, A.1.d, A.2.a, A.2.b, A.2.c, B.1.c, B.2.a, B.2.b, B.2.c, C.2.b, D.1.a, D.1.b, D.2.a, D.2.c, D.2.d, F.1.b, F.2.e, F.2.h, F.3.c, F.4.a, G.1.a, G.1.b, G.2.a, G.3.a, H.1.a, H.1.b, H.1.d, H.2.a

Five Little Snowmen Fingerplay

Materials: 5 white felt snowmen, 5 red felt bows, 5 black felt hats, and 1 yellow felt sun.

Teach children this poem about snowmen, signing the key words as you go. Make the appropriate felt pieces and place them on the board as you read.

Five Little Snowman Fingerplay

Five little Snowman standing in a row,
Each had a hat and a big red bow.
Out came the sun and it shone all day,
One Little snowman melted away.

Four Little Snowman standing in a row,
Each had a hat and a big red bow.
Out Came the sun and it shone all day,
One Little snowman melted away.
Etc....

Topical signs to be learned: numbers 1-5, snow, man, little, each, hat, red, out, sun, day.

Indicators: A.1.c, A.1.d, A.2.a, A.2.b, A.2.c, B.1.a, B.1.c, B.1.d, B.2.a, B.4.a, C.1.a, C.1.b, C.1.d, C.2.b, D.1.b, D.2.a, D.2.b, D.2.c, E.1.a, F.1.b, F.2.e, F.2.h, F.3.c, F.4.a, G.1.a, G.2.a, H.1.a, H.1.b.

Floating Icebergs (science & nature)

Materials: food coloring, various shaped bowls and containers, wading or swimming pool, large freezer.

Fill the containers with water. Add food coloring. Place in the freezer and allow to freeze completely. Take the frozen container out, remove the ice, and place the icebergs in the pool. Notice how much of the ice is under water. Have the children place their hands near the iceberg and move them away. How far does the cold water extend from the ice? Watch the shape of the iceberg as it melts. Does the shape change? How long does the iceberg take to melt? Does the color and size make a difference?

Freeze objects inside your iceberg to see how long it takes for them to melt free. Do other liquids float when frozen? Try indoors in water table with toy boats.

Topical signs to be learned: ice, freeze, water, melt (fade) food, color, under, cold, shape, change, size.

Indicators: A.1.a, A.1.b, A.1.c, A.1.d, A.2.a, A.2.b, A.2.c, B.1.c, B.2.a, C.2.b, D.1.a, D.1.b, D.2.a, D.2.b, D.2.c, D.2.d, F.1.b, F.2.e, F.2.h, F.3.c, F.4.a, G.1.a, G.1.b, H.1.a, H.1.b, H.1.d.

Hot Chocolate to Go (winter, foods)

Pour powdered milk and chocolate drink mix into a large bowl or bag and mix well. Pour into large plastic bag and seal it. Fill a cup ¾ full with hot water. Add 2 heaping tablespoons of chocolate mix and stir.

Topical signs to be learned: banana, knife, bake, raisins, dried fruit, nut, pretzel, seeds, milk, chocolate, hot, cup, spoon, bowl.

Indicators: A.1.c, A.1.d, A.2.a, A.2.b, A.2.c, B.1.c, B.2.a, C.2.b, F.1.b, F.2.b, F.2.d, F.2.e, F.2.h, F.3.c, F.4.a., G.1.a, G.2.a, H.1.a, H.1.b, H.1.c, H.1.d.

Ice Melting Contest (science)

Materials: block of ice for each team.

Divide the group into equal teams and give each team a block of ice. At a signal, each team tries to melt the ice without scraping or breaking it. Usual methods are rubbing it, blowing on it, putting it in the sun, etc. After a certain amount of time (this depends on the original size of the block), the team with the smallest block wins. A bathroom scale comes in handy to determine this.

Topical signs to be learned: ice, melt (dissolve), time, team, blow, sun, weigh.

Indicators: A.1.a, A.1.b, A.1.c, A.1.d, A.2.a, A.2.b, A.2.c, B.1.c, B.2.a, B.2.b, B.2.c, C.2.b, D.1.a, D.1.b, D.1.c, D.2.a, D.2.b, D.2.c, D.2.d, F.1.b, F.2.d, F.2.e, F.2.g, F.2.h, , F.3.a, F.3.c, F.4.a, G.1.a, G.1.b, G.2.a, G.3.a, H.1.a, H.1.b, H.1.d.

Icy Icicles (weather)

Materials: large plastic soda bottles, food coloring, instrument with a sharp point, string.

Take the children outside to a place where they can examine icicles without the danger of being hit by a falling icicle. Encourage them to look for several areas where icicles can be found. Back in the classroom have the children discuss their discoveries with the whole group. List the locations and any other information on the chalkboard or chart paper. Divide children into groups to make icicles (optional). Give each group or child a soda bottle. Have them fill the bottles with water and a small amount of food coloring. Using an instrument with a sharp point, make a very small hole in the side of each bottle near the bottom. Hang the bottles outside in trees or other areas. As the water drips slowly from the bottles it will freeze to form icicles. Take the children outside periodically to observe their icicles. Have them compare the size of their icicles to other objects

Topical signs to be learned: ice/free, water, cold, find, talk, group, color signs, outside, slow, look at, compare, size signs, like/same.

Indicators: A.1.a, A.1.b, A.1.c, A.1.d, A.2.a, A.2.b, A.2.c, B.1.c, B.2.a, B.2.b, B.2.c, B.2.d, C.2.b, D.1.a, D.1.b, D.2.a,D.2.b, D.2.c, F.1.b, F.2.b, F.2.d, F.2.e, F.2.g, F.2.h, F.3.a, F.3.c, G.1.a, G.1.b, G.2.a, G.3.a, H.1.a, H.1.b, H.1.d.

It's Snowing (weather)

Materials: different sizes of white paper, markers, scissors.

Draw long skinny triangles on a sheet of white paper. These are icicles! Make an icicle sheet for each child. Fold small sheets of white paper in half and in half again. Make at least two folded sheets for each child.

Demonstrate how to make snowflakes! Cut out designs on the folded edge of a folded piece of paper. Round off the corners and also make cuts on this side. Open the paper and you have a snowflake! (The older children can make more folds to make more intricate designs.) A snowflake is a tiny drop of snow. Each snowflake has a beautiful and unique design!

Show an icicle sheet. Explain that icicles form in cold weather. Water drips from an object such as a tree branch. The water drop freezes and forms an icicle! Place the folded papers and icicle sheets on the table. The children cut out snowflake designs and a sheet of icicles! Print the children's names on the backs of their snowflakes and icicles.

Topical signs to be learned: snow, water, weather, cold, winter, freeze, paper, scissors.

Indicators: A.1.a, A.1.b, A.1.c, A.1.d, A.2.a, A.2.b, A.2.c, B.1.c, B.2.a, C.2.b, D.1.a, D.1.b, D.2.a,D.2.b, D.2.c, D.2.d, F.1.b, F.2.b, F.2.d, F.2.e, F.2.h, F.4.a., F.3.a, F.3.c, G.1.a, G.1.b, G.2.a, G.3.a, H.1.a, H.1.b, H.1.d.

Kite Making (weather)

Materials: pre-drawn kite pattern, watercolor paints, paintbrushes, water and smocks.

Use water colors to paint pre-cut kite shapes, glue or tape on string, glue on pre-cut bows to complete the tail.

Topical signs to be learned: paint, kite, water, string, fly, sky.

Indicators: A.1.a, A.1.b, A.1.c, A.1.d, A.2.a, A.2.b, A.2.c, B.1.c, B.2.a, C.2.b, F.1.b, F.2.b, F.2.d, F.2.e, F.2.h, F.3.c, F.4.a., G.1.a, G.2.a, H.1.a, H.1.b, H.1.c, H.1.d.

Magnifying Snowflakes (weather)

Materials: magnifying glass, black velvet, pie pan.

Keep a piece of black velvet in the refrigerator. When there is a fresh snowfall take out the piece of black velvet and place it on top of a pie pan and run outdoors with it. Catch a few small snowflakes. Then get your magnifying or reading glass and really LOOK at a snowflake up close! Count the sides. Can you find any two that are the same?

Topical signs to be learned: snow, outside, catch, look, count, same.

Indicators: A.1.a, A.1.b, A.1.c, A.1.d, A.2.a, A.2.b, A.2.c, B.1.c, B.2.a, C.2.b, D.1.a, D.1.b, D.2.a, D.2.b, D.2.c, D.2.d, F.1.b, F.2.b, F.2.e, F.2.h, F.3.a, F.3.c, F.4.a, G.1.a, G.1.b, G.2.a, G.3.a, H.1.a, H.1.b, H.1.d.

Recording Weather (weather)

Materials: poster board, construction paper, scissors, crayons, marker.

Prepare a chart in advance. Use a poster board and divide it into three sections. In the first section, place a piece of blue construction paper with a gray cloud drawn on it. In the second section, place a piece of blue construction paper with a white cloud drawn on it. In the third section, place a piece of blue construction paper without a cloud. For a period of at least two weeks, have the children record the cloud conditions in the sky each day. Place a tally mark on the chart to record the cloud status for each day. At the end of the recording period, count the results. Does anyone want to predict tomorrow's sky condition? You can add more detail to your chart by adding more categories for weather besides just cloud descriptions.

Topical signs to be learned: weather signs, look, days of the week, chart, draw, gray, blue, white, count.

Indicators: A.1.a, A.1.b, A.1.c, A.1.d, A.2.a, A.2.b, A.2.c, B.1.c, B.2.a, B.2.b, B.2.c, C.2.b, D.1.a, D.1.b, D.1.c, D.2.a, D.2.b, D.2.c, D.2.d, F.1.b, F.2.b, F.2.e, F.2.h, F.3.a, F.3.c, G.1.a, G.1.b, G.2.a, G.3.a, H.1.a, H.1.b, H.1.d.

Seasonal Workers (weather, community)

Materials: magazines or catalogs, scissors, glue, poster board or construction paper.

Cut out pictures of seasonal workers (lifeguards, ice cream truck drivers, baseball players, football players, hockey players, basketball players, snowplow operators, skiers, furnace service people, etc). Mount the pictures on poster board or construction paper. Show pictures of these workers and have the children identify the jobs they perform. Discuss how weather effects their jobs: How do their jobs change when weather and seasons change? Which workers are busy on snowy days? Sunny days? All seasons? Have the children decide which people are busy in the summer but not in the winter. Or you can have children find pictures and mount them then share with everyone about the seasonal worker and their job etc.

Topical signs to be learned: picture, work, occupations signs, show, weather signs, change, season signs.

Indicators: A.1.c, A.1.d, A.2.a, A.2.b, A.2.c, B.1.c, C.2.b, D.1.a, D.1.b, D.1.c, D.2.a, D.2.c, D.2.b, D.2.d, F.1.b, F.2.b, F.2.e, F.2.h, F.3.c, G.1.a, G.2.a, H.1.a, H.1.b

Seasons/Weather Matching and Categorizing (seasons, weather)

Materials: pictures of weather and seasonal pictures, boxes for categorizing (if desired).

Use various pictures of different forms of weather and different things you would find throughout the seasons. Have children match and categorize pictures into appropriate groups.

Topical signs to be learned: weather signs, season signs, separate/sort.

Indicators: A.1.c, A.1.d, A.2.a, A.2.b, A.2.c, B.1.c, C.2.b, D.1.a, D.1.b, D.1.c, D.2.a, D.2.c, D.2.b, D.2.d, F.1.b, F.2.b, F.2.e, F.2.h, F.3.c, G.1.a, G.2.a, H.1.a, H.1.b

Snowman, Snowman (weather, seasons)

Materials: 2 white felt snowman, 1 set of blue felt mittens, 1 green felt hat, 1 pair of red felt boots, 1 yellow felt scarf, and 1 orange felt carrot nose.

Based on the book "Brown Bear, Brown Bear, What Do You See?" White Snowman, White Snowman, What do you see? I see blue mittens (green hat, red boots, yellow scarf, orange carrot nose, another snowman) looking at me. Cut out felt pieces in the appropriate colors to place on the fleet board as you go through the story.

Topical signs to be learned: color signs, snow, man, what, see, look at, clothing signs, carrot.

Indicators: A.1.c, A.1.d, A.2.a, A.2.b, A.2.c, B.1.a, B.1.c, B.1.d, B.2.a, B.2.b, C.2.b, E.1.a, F.1.b, F.2.e, F.2.h, F.3.c, G.1.a, G.1.b, H.1.a, H.1.b, H.1.d.

Snow Walks (nature, weather)

Have the children pretend look out the window, and see snow falling softly to the ground. Ask them to create movements to show how they would move: How do you walk with boots and heavy coats on? How would you drive a car? How would you move on skates? How would you move on a sled quickly going down a hill? How would you move on a snowplow?

Topical signs to be learned: pretend, look, snow, move, how, walk, boots, coat, car, sled.

Indicators: A.1.a, A.1.b, A.1.c, A.1.d, A.2.a, A.2.b, A.2.c, B.1.c, B.2.a, B.2.b, B.2.c, C.2.b, D.1.a, D.1.b, D.2.a, D.2.c, E.2.a, .1.b, F.2.b, F.2.e, F.2.h, F.3.a, F.3.b, F.3.c, F.4.b, G.1.a, G.1.b, G.2.a, G.3.a, H.1.a, H.1.b, H.1.d, H.2.a.

Snowy Ideas (weather)

Materials: blue and white or silver balloons, music.

Inflate the balloons. Divide the children into two groups and have them take off their shoes. One group is the rain drops and gets blue balloons. The other group are ice crystals and get white or silver balloons. The children are going to act out the formation of snow. Tell them they are rain drops and ice crystals in a cloud, where snow falls from. Play music. The children dance around the room with their balloons. Stop the music. Have each rain drop find an ice crystal. Say and sign "It's snowing!" Now the pairs of children slowly fall to the ground. Each pair has turned into a snowflake. (When a water droplet and ice crystal attach and fall from a cloud, it turns to snow.) Play music again. Exchange the balloons. The water drops are now ice crystals and the ice crystals are water drops. Continue to become snowflakes.

Topical signs to be learned: water, ice, snow, cloud, dance, music, stop, become.

Indicators: A.1.a, A.1.b, A.1.c, A.1.d, A.2.a, A.2.b, A.2.c, B.1.c, B.2.a, B.2.b, B.2.c, C.2.b, D.1.a, D.1.b, D.2.a, D.2.c, E.1.a, E.2.a, F.1.b, F.2.b, F.2.e, F.2.h, F.3.a, F.3.b, F.4.a, F.4.b, F.3.c, G.1.a, G.1.b, H.1.a, H.1.b, H.1.d, H.2.a.

Thermometers (science, weather)

Materials: outdoor thermometer, ice cubs, small container, rubber bands.

Show the thermometer. Tell the children the red line (the mercury) in the thermometer becomes long or short depending on how warm it is. Put a rubber band around the temperature reading on the thermometer. Ask the children what they think will happen to the red line on the thermometer if it is put outside. Place the thermometer outside, and compare the difference in temperature after a while. Put another rubber band around the temperature reading. Is the red line higher inside or outside? Ask the children what they think will happen to the red line on the thermometer when it is placed in ice cubes. Fill the small container with ice cubes, and put the thermometer in it for a few seconds. Is the red line higher or lower after we put it in ice cubes?

You can make a chart and record the daily temperature also.

Topical signs to be learned: temperature, hot, cold, ice, outside, inside, chart, number signs.

Indicators: A.1.c, A.1.d, A.2.a, A.2.b, A.2.c, B.1.c, B.2.a, B.2.b, B.2.c, C.2.b, D.1.a, D.1.b, D.1.c, D.2.a, D.2.b, D.2.c, F.1.b, F.2.b, F.2.e, F.2.h, F.4.a, F.4.b, F.3.c, G.1.a, G.1.b, H.1.a, H.1.b, H.1.d, H.2.a.

Things in the Sky (nature, weather, math)

Materials: pictures of items found in the sky and items not found in the sky, two boxes.

Have the children sort the pictures into things that belong in the sky and things that do not belong in the sky. They can ask a friend to check their sorting or sort in groups.

Topical signs to be learned: separate/sort, sky, find, not, cloud, moon, sun, star, airplane, bird, other signs used for sorting.

Indicators: A.1.a, A.1.b, A.1.c, A.1.d, A.2.a, A.2.b, A.2.c, B.1.c, B.2.a, B.2.b, B.2.c, C.2.b, D.1.a, D.1.b, D.2.a, D.2.c, D.2.d, F.1.b, F.2.b, F.2.e, F.2.h, F.3.a, F.3.b, F.3.c, F.4.b, G.1.a, G.1.b, G.2.a, G.3.a, H.1.a, H.1.b, H.1.d

Weather Chart (science, weather)

Have pictures of different types of weather and additional pictures to correspond with each. Have children match pictures with appropriate weather. (Ex. Umbrellas, mittens, playing inside, sleigh riding, swinging, etc.)

Topical signs to be learned: weather signs, seasonal item signs.

Indicators: A.1.a, A.1.b, A.1.c, A.1.d, A.2.a, A.2.b, A.2.c, B.1.c, B.1.e, B.2.a, B.2.b, B.2.c, C.2.b, D.1.a, D.1.b, D.2.a, D.2.c, D.2.d, F.1.b, F.2.b, F.2.e, F.2.h, F.3.c, G.1.a, G.1.b, H.1.a, H.1.b, H.1.d, H.2.a

Weather Crafts

Cloud Differences (weather)

Materials: blue construction paper, white cotton balls, gray and white feathers, lint from clothes dryer, glue.

Go outside and observe the clouds, looking at their color and shapes. Explain how the different clouds look (cumulus are white and fluffy, cirrus are fast-moving and thin white clouds, stratus clouds are thin, grayish white clouds that cover the sky in streaks; nimbus clouds are dark gray rain clouds.) You can cloud watch over several days to see if you see different cloud types.

Glue cotton balls, feathers, or lint on blue construction paper in the shape of the clouds that were observed.

Topical signs to be learned: cloud, white, gray, long, thin, sky, look, glue, shape.

Indicators: A.1.c, A.1.d, A.2.a, A.2.b, A.2.c, B.1.c, B.2.aC.2.b, D.1.a, D.1.b, D.2.a, D.2.c, D.2.d, F.1.b, F.2.b, F.2.d, F.2.e, F.2.h, F.3.c, F.4.a., G.1.a, G.2.a, H.1.a, H.1.b, H.1.c, H.1.d.

Paper Doily Snowflakes (weather)

Materials: paper doilies in various sizes, scissors

Fold the doily in half and then half again. Snip out little pieces from each folded side and carefully cut out small shapes at the point. Then cut a piece down and out of the top of the folded-over doily. As each doily is unfolded a unique snowflake (tree or room ornament) appears!

Topical signs to be learned: scissors, half, shape, snow.

Indicators: A.1.c, A.1.d, A.2.a, A.2.b, A.2.c, B.1.c, B.2.a, C.2.b, D.1.a, D.2.d, F.1.b, F.2.b, F.2.d, F.2.e, F.2.h, F.3.c, F.4.a., G.1.a, G.2.a, H.1.a, H.1.b, H.1.c, H.1.d.

Rainbows Handprint (colors, weather)

Materials: paint in rainbow colors, paintbrushes or plates of paint for children to place their hands in, large piece of bulletin board paper or tag board (tag board works best) and smocks.

Have each child make handprints that are formed into a rainbow.

Topical signs to be learned: rainbow, rainbow color signs, paint, hands.

Indicators: A.1.a, A.1.b, A.1.c, A.1.d, A.2.a, A.2.b, A.2.c, B.1.c, B.2.a, C.2.b, D.2.d, F.1.b, F.2.b, F.2.d, F.2.e, F.2.h, F.3.c, F.4.a., G.1.a, G.2.a.

Snow Family (weather, family)

Materials: playdough, paper plats, felt pen

Give everyone a large lump of dough, this is a large snowball. Demonstrate how to make smaller snowballs to make a snow family. Tear off a piece of dough from the large ball. Roll it between your palms. To make a snowman place three snowballs on top of each other. Then roll tiny pieces of dough for eyes. Roll a skinny string for the mouth. When you have made a snowman, make a snow woman and a snow child. Make many snow people. Each child places their snow family on a paper plate with their name on it. You can also make a snow zoo and place them in a show box. Label each box "(Child's name)'s Snow Zoo!"

Topical signs to be learned: snow, family signs, ball, roll, eye, people, animal signs, zoo.

Indicators: A.1.c, A.1.d, A.2.a, A.2.b, A.2.c, B.1.c, B.2.a, C.2.b, D.2.d, F.1.b, F.2.b, F.2.d, F.2.e, F.2.h, F.3.c, F.4.a., F.5.a, G.1.a, G.2.a, H.1.b, H.1.d.

Snow and Ocean Scenes (weather, nature)

Materials: large washable table, shaving cream, small toy cars and trucks, toy animals and people, washable odds and ends, leaves, twigs, rocks, pinecones, blue food coloring, ocean and beach props.

Spray shaving cream on the table. Have the children create winter scenes. Provide props such as empty margarine containers, toy animals and people, pine tree twigs, sticks, toy cars and trucks, and cans. In the summer months, add blue food coloring and create an ocean of blue waves. Add props for a swim scenario.

Topical signs to be learned: winter, snow, summer, animal, people, tree, car, truck, ocean, swim.

Indicators: A.1.a, A.1.b, A.1.c, A.1.d, A.2.a, A.2.b, A.2.c, B.1.c, B.2.a, B.2.b, B.2.c, C.2.b, D.1.b, D.2.c, D.2.d, F.1.b, F.2.b, F.2.e, F.2.h, F.3.c, G.1.a, G.1.b, H.1.a, H.1.b, H.1.d.

Snow Jar (weather)

Materials: jar with screw-on lid, pinecone less tall than the jar is deep or other object smaller than jar, glue, baby oil, silver glitter, newspaper to work over.

Glue a pinecone or other small object to the middle of the lid of a jar and allow it to dry completely. Fill the jar almost completely with baby oil and add a handful of silver glitter. Screw the lid onto the jar very tightly. Turn the jar upside down and shake. Watch the "snow" fall on the "tree."

Topical signs to be learned: glue, silver, dry, shake, snow, tree.

Indicators: A.1.c, A.1.d, A.2.a, A.2.b, A.2.c, B.1.c, B.2.a, C.2.b, D.2.d, F.1.b, F.2.b, F.2.d, F.2.e, F.2.h, F.3.c, F.4.a., G.1.a, G.2.a, H.1.b.

Snow Pictures (weather)

Materials: white paper, crayons, white paint, cut up sponges.

Have each child draw a picture of something outside (a house, cars, a forest, etc.). After the pictures are finished, have children dip the sponges in white paint and then dab them on their pictures. The pictures will look like a recent snowfall has covered them.

Topical signs to be learned: draw, crayon, paint, paper, snow, cover.

Indicators: A.1.c, A.1.d, A.2.a, A.2.b, A.2.c, B.1.c, B.2.a, C.2.b, D.2.d, F.1.b, F.2.b, F.2.d, F.2.e, F.2.h, F.3.c, F.4.a., G.1.a, G.2.a, H.1.a, H.1.b, H.1.c, H.1.d.

Snowflakes (weather)

Materials: square sheets of lightweight paper (duplicating or mimeograph paper will do fine), scissors.

Although all real snowflakes have six points, paper "snowflakes" can have any number of points, for the fun of making "snowflakes" has nothing to do with reality. Fold paper in half and then in half again. Pieces are clipped out of the edges of the folded packet and then the paper is unfolded to reveal a decorative repeat design. Rather than folding the square as described above, try having the children fold their squares on the diagonal and then fold the two opposing corners so that they overlap each other.

Topical signs to be learned: paper, scissors, half, snow, shape.

Indicators: A.1.c, A.1.d, A.2.a, A.2.b, A.2.c, B.1.c, B.2.a, C.2.b, D.2.d, F.1.b, F.2.b, F.2.d, F.2.e, F.2.h, F.3.c, F.4.a., G.1.a, G.2.a, H.1.a, H.1.b.

Snowpeople (seasons, weather)

Materials: different size circles from white construction paper, various craft items for decorating, glue or glue sticks.

Set out different size precut circles and objects big enough to be used by age group to decorate the snowperson they will create by gluing three of the circles together. The objective for this project is to just provide them with the materials and let them create.

Topical signs to be learned: snow, circle, glue, white, people, face, eyes, nose, mouth, hat.

Indicators: A.1.a, A.1.b, A.1.c, A.1.d, A.2.a, A.2.b, A.2.c, B.1.c, B.2.a, C.2.b, F.1.b, F.2.b, F.2.d, F.2.e, F.2.h, F.3.c, F.4.a., G.1.a, G.2.a, H.1.d.

Made in the USA
Charleston, SC
23 September 2016